# CONTENTS

| | | |
|---|---|---|
| Introduction | | 7 |
| 1. | Pendulum swings: The reading debate | 15 |
| 2. | Historical perspectives: The origins of the alphabet, and the history of children's primers | 33 |
| 3. | Whole language and phonics: The debate | 81 |
| | Appendix: What is Phonics? (contributed by Doris Ferry) | 104 |
| 4. | The search for the best reading method | 127 |
| 5. | The reading process | 143 |
| 6. | Emergent literacy – what is it? | 159 |
| 7. | First steps in learning to read at school | 177 |
| 8. | Phonemic awareness and reading | 197 |
| 9. | Reading and spelling | 221 |
| 10. | Reading comprehension | 237 |
| 11. | Reading difficulties | 259 |

12.  Reading and motivation                        281

13.  Reading in the secondary school               299

14.  Conclusions: Putting it all together          313

Possible Assignment Questions                      331

Possible Quiz Questions for Tutorials              333

Index                                              343

The Author                                         347

# READING THE WRITING ON THE WALL

*Debates, Challenges and Opportunities
in the Teaching of Reading*

Best wishes,
Tom Nicholson

# READING THE WRITING ON THE WALL

*Debates, Challenges and Opportunities
in the Teaching of Reading*

## Tom Nicholson

d
P

Dunmore Press

©2000 Tom Nicholson
©2000 The Dunmore Press Ltd


First Published in 2000
by
Dunmore Press Ltd
P.O. Box 5115
Palmerston North
New Zealand

Australian Supplier:
Federation Press
P.O. Box 45
Annandale 2038 NSW
Australia
Ph: (02) 9552-2200
Fax: (02) 9552-1681


ISBN 0 86469 355 9

| | |
|---|---|
| Text: | Caslon 10.5-12.5 |
| Printer: | The Dunmore Printing Company Ltd |
| | Palmerston North |
| Cover design: | Stephanie Milne |

Copyright. No part of this book may be reproduced without written permission except in the case of brief quotations embodied in critical articles and reviews.

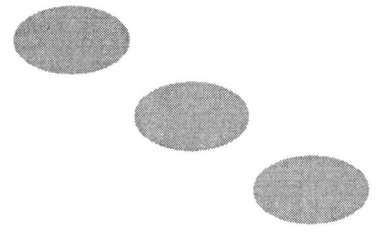

# INTRODUCTION

Who said reading is boring? It has everything. It has controversy, intrigue, amazing discoveries, public concern, media attention, political hype, optimism, and frustration. It has all the ingredients of an exciting topic to read about. In this book, we discuss some red-button issues: Have reading standards gone down? Does reading have to be political? Does reading have a future? What is the best way to teach reading? Can we achieve success for all? Here are the key points:

- When reading is debated in the media, many teachers squirm. They can feel the wrath of parents. But we forget that this debate has been going on for hundreds of years. We take a look at the "good old days" to find out which teaching methods have come and gone over the last several centuries.
- Many parents, and to some extent the media as well, think that traditional phonics is the tried and true way of teaching reading. Whole language is seen as modern and trendy, loose and without substance. But is there room for both approaches in the classroom?
- There are different theories of the reading process. How have they influenced our teaching of reading?
- How much can children learn without formal instruction? How much parental input is required? Is this enough for children to "crack the code"?

- In the last 30 years, new discoveries in speech research have shown us why it is hard for many children to become aware that words are made of phonemes. Lack of such awareness may be a major cause of reading and spelling difficulties.
- We look at several children who went to the top of the class in reading, and several who fell behind. What happened to them?
- Why do some children struggle with reading? What is dyslexia? How successful are interventions such as Reading Recovery?
- What happens to children's self-esteem as they become either good or poor readers? What do they think of themselves, and their teachers?
- What is reading comprehension? How do you teach it? We look at the research.
- We look at what can be done to improve the reading skills of teenagers.
- In the final chapter, we summarise the main points, the important issues, and the practical implications for teaching. We put all the pieces together.

Finding a better method of teaching reading – with whole language or phonics – is of interest not only to those who research reading, but also to the general public. Statistics on reading achievement in the United States, England, Australia and New Zealand all indicate that a sizeable number of children are not learning to read as well as they should. It could be the result of conservative politics, cuts in government spending, privatisation, social change, immigration, drugs – this is the 'social' explanation. But another explanation is that we have not delivered in our teaching of reading. These issues are at the heart of the reading debate.

The only difficulty with the 'social' explanation is that social stresses have always been with us. Specific stresses vary from one decade to the next, but stresses have always impacted on educators, complicating the work they do. On the other hand, the ways we have been teaching reading in recent years have changed. Traditional phonics has given way to 'whole language'. This change must have come about because teachers wanted the change. But why? What did phonics do wrong?

Chapter 1 looks at recent pendulum swings in public opinion about literacy, trying to understand whether reading standards have gone up or down. Public concerns about standards have always been with us, but now state governments actually legislate how to teach reading. This is an indication of how strong public and media concern was in the 1990s. The chapter also includes some 'letters to the author' illustrating some of the opinions of parents, retired teachers and others who have written to me about the reading debate. Finally, the chapter looks at reading and politics, and whether computers will soon replace books.

Chapter 2 is a short introduction to the story of the alphabet. It shows that English writing had its origins in an alphabetic system that was discovered many centuries ago.

This chapter also considers pendulum swings in the history of reading instruction. Every country has its own history of different classroom primers and methods of teaching reading, yet often the social and political messages of the primers are similar. The history of reading instruction also gives a perspective on the reading debate today, showing us that tensions about how best to teach reading are not new.

Chapter 3 examines phonics and whole language, two methods that are currently being closely scrutinised. What is the difference between them? In the last 30 years, phonics teaching seems to have become a lost art in some places. Does each method have its own strengths and its own weak points? The purpose of the chapter is to explain what each method tries to achieve and what the outcome is for individual pupils.

Chapter 4 reviews the research on which method is 'best', which seems to raise more questions than answers. The evidence favours phonics, but whole language has some good aspects as well. The chapter looks at the balance between the two, presenting research data on both whole language and phonics.

Chapter 5 looks at opposing theories about how we read and how children learn to read. Many researchers (and teachers) have nailed their allegiances to phonics or whole language on the basis of these theories. Since the 1970s, researchers have grappled with the implications of different theories. This is a review of the main theories and whether they have stood the test of time.

Chapter 6 is about emergent literacy. Emergent literacy refers to informal learning that begins at home, as children are exposed to literacy experiences such as being read to, and scribbling their ideas on paper. The vast majority of children do not learn to read until they go to school. Yet when they start school, many children are not 'blank slates' either. They may not be able to read or write properly, but they are not completely without knowledge. What do they know? What is still missing? Do phonics and whole-language teachers have different ways of building on these pre-reading skills.

Chapter 7 is about the first steps in learning to read. Children go through two stages. In the first stage, they 'pretend' to read. They learn words by focusing on special features of them (e.g. the 'tail' on dog). In this first stage they rely on memory for the text, on picture clues, anything but the letters on the page. In the second stage, they learn the alphabetic principle, which is the key to real reading. We discuss how children move from one stage to the next, and show how important it is to be able to recognise those 26 letters of the alphabet.

Chapter 8 is about the 'invisible phoneme'. Work on phonemic awareness has been described as the most significant breakthrough in reading in the last several decades. It may actually be our biggest breakthrough ever. Many children start school with no understanding that words rhyme or start with the same sound. Pre-school children can often spell their name, but look blankly at you if you ask them to tell you the first 'sound' in their name. This chapter explains why lack of phonemic awareness may cause reading difficulties. We look at case studies of some children who moved ahead, and some who fell behind. We explain how whole language and phonics teachers sometimes have different ways of developing this awareness.

Chapter 9 is on reading–spelling relationships. Reading and spelling have much in common. Good spelling skills reinforce good reading, and vice versa. We look at how best to teach spelling. We consider the difference between a traditional phonics-type approach to spelling, such as learning spelling rules and practising lists of words, and a whole-language approach, where children are encouraged to invent their own spellings. We consider what impact these different teaching approaches will have on children's spelling abilities. Are good spellers 'natural' spellers or are they brimful of 'rules' and over-learned spellings?

Chapter 10 is on reading comprehension. Comprehension is very important; paradoxically, it is difficult to improve. We can improve children's comprehension of specific text material, but improving their general level of comprehension is much more difficult. The teacher needs to have strategies for improving specific text comprehension. It is often necessary that specific material be well understood. For example, a class project on the lives of different kinds of birds, penguins or bears are all specific topics, and children can learn ways of breaking the material into easily understood chunks. General comprehension is much harder to improve. Making an impact on children's general comprehension requires a long-term commitment to the improvement of decoding, vocabulary and general knowledge. Whole language and phonics teachers sometimes have different ways of teaching comprehension.

Chapter 11 is about reading problems. For the vast majority of pupils who experience reading problems, the core of their difficulties is in the area of decoding. They have not learned successfully how to 'sound out' words. Language comprehension (vocabulary) and general knowledge are also important, but general language development is often hampered because there is no firm foundation in decoding. As a result, poor readers do not read much and lose many opportunities to learn new words and ideas. There are different ideas about how best to approach the task of turning a poor reader into a good one. Is whole language or phonics (or a combination) the best way for them to turn the corner?

Chapter 12 is on motivation and reading. Enjoying reading is a result of being good at it. Some people think that if you can make reading time a happy time and if you are enthusiastic about books, then children will enjoy reading as well. This may be true for the good reader, but it is often not the case for the poor reader. They will not be happy until they become good decoders. This is my short summary of what motivation research is saying about children's attitudes to reading. However, I also argue that being positive about reading and signalling your enthusiasm to children is a good thing to do as well. Sometimes children don't know how good they are. Whole language seems to excel at signalling to children that reading is 'fun', while phonics seems to excel at giving children the skills that accompany the fun of reading.

Chapter 13 is about reading in the secondary school. Research suggests that there are a number of things that teachers can do at secondary level to improve reading skills of all students, including those students who do not like to read and who are not good at it.

Chapter 14 is called 'Putting It All Together', where I tie the various strands of the book together. The message of the book is a very positive one. The reading debate has been tense at times, but we are getting some positive results. When we consider the big picture, the weight of evidence suggests there is a case for giving more emphasis to teaching word-level skills – decoding. This is the foundation stone of the reading process. Is whole language or phonics the best way to do it? My conclusion is that there should be a balance of phonics and whole language. Phonics can help children learn a core of rules, which will enable them to work out words for themselves. Whole language has one key message: children can become better readers by reading. Phonics teachers will agree with that. Reading interesting literature is a goal that both sides agree on. Children should be able to write their own stories, listen to stories, use the Internet – these are goals that phonics and whole language have in common.

**Finally ...**

The focus is on recent changes in the pendulum of reading instruction. We will show that there has always been public concern about whether children are reading as well as we want them to. And there has always been a search for better ways to teach reading and writing. We will look at the bigger picture of the many factors that affect learning to read. We will look at the mind of the reader, the classroom, the home, and at society in general. There have always been many stresses in the lives of young children, whether from rich homes or poor, and these stresses impact on learning to read. I am optimistic that children can do well, in spite of disadvantages. The children's story *Matilda,* by Roald Dahl, mirrors what sometimes happens in real life, where people can overcome huge obstacles and achieve success.

The story is about a little girl who grows up in a home where her parents don't pay attention to her. Her mum spends all her time at bingo parlours, and her dad is a crooked second-hand car dealer, obsessed with himself and with making money. There is a very funny point in *Matilda* where she asks her father, 'Daddy, do you think you could buy me a book?' 'A book?' he says. 'What d'you want a flaming book for?' 'To read, Daddy.' 'What's wrong with the telly, for heaven's sake? We've got a lovely telly with a 12-inch screen and now you come asking for a book! You're getting spoiled, my girl.' Yet those who have read the story know that Matilda was able to teach herself to read. She went on to become a very good reader and a happy person despite the fact that her parents were not very helpful. This is the kind of positive message I've tried to convey. Reading is for everyone. Every child can read.

# 1
# PENDULUM SWINGS:
# THE READING DEBATE

## The Situation in New Zealand

In New Zealand in the mid-1980s an analysis of survey data on reading and spelling achievement by Nuttall (1985) led him to believe that standards of spelling had consistently fallen since the 1930s. He came to this conclusion by piecing together various surveys. He was unable to come to any conclusions about reading because of the lack of national survey data. He made the point, 'It is easy for officials to dismiss complaints about the lowering of standards in schools as just another aspect of the way the older generation fails to understand and appreciate the young .... However, a modern public school system costs a lot of money ... and it should be the responsibility of the government to ensure that this money is well spent' (Nuttall, p. 1). A lack of longitudinal data on student achievement makes it very difficult to assess New Zealand's progress over the years. Even as late as 1994, the lack of assessment data was still a problem for commentators like Neil Reid of the New Zealand Council for Educational Research. 'New Zealand still has no system of national monitoring of student achievement. Even in such basic skill areas as reading, writing and mathematics, the evidence is fragmentary' (Reid, 1994, p. 5). Reid was able to cobble together evidence to suggest that standards probably hadn't changed much between 1968 and 1981, but after that time there was a void where no assessment had taken place.

New Zealand participated in IEA (International Evaluation of Achievement) reading surveys in both 1970 and 1990, but even here the picture is murky. The 1990 test had changed in content from that of 1970 and was marked with a different scoring system, and so was not comparable at all. In 1970 New Zealand had the highest average score of 15 countries at the 14-year-old level – higher than England, Scotland, the United States and Finland (Thorndike, 1973). The range of variation around the average was similar to that of other countries. There was no huge tail or huge top to the scores. In 1990 New Zealand was in fourth place (Elley, 1992), although of the 32 countries in the survey, only four were English-speaking (Canada, United States, Ireland and New Zealand). New Zealand also had the widest range of variation of any other country in the survey, indicating that it had more children at the bottom end of achievement and more at the top end.

England and Scotland were not in the 1990 survey. New Zealand was still ahead of the United States, but had fallen behind Finland. What did the results mean? It could be argued the results were positive. Elley (1992) and Smith (1996) have pointed to the large numbers of non-English speaking immigrants arriving in New Zealand over the last several decades and the effects of structural changes in the economy, which have put pressures on education. In spite of these changes, New Zealand was still near the top of the rankings. But it could also be argued that the results were negative, that other countries had gone ahead while New Zealand had gone backwards.

In 1970, New Zealand nine-year-olds had not been assessed. In 1990 they were assessed and placed sixth, behind Finland in first place and the United States in second. These were countries that New Zealand had surpassed in 1970. By the mid-1990s the New Zealand Government introduced a national monitoring system called NEMP (National Education Monitoring Project) (Crooks & Flockton, 1997). It used a 'light sampling' approach, in that only a small proportion of children in the country were assessed. The NEMP surveys covered various curriculum subjects, including reading. The survey measures of reading consisted of reading tasks that a panel of experts felt children should be able to cope with at certain age levels. The first set of survey results in 1997 showed that 20 per cent of eight- and 12-year-olds were reading below these benchmarks, and that ten per cent were reading very much below these levels (Crooks

& Flockton, 1997). These results paralleled surveys in Australia and America that showed a significant minority of children were unable to read successfully passages that expert panels had agreed were appropriate for children of that age.

This 20 per cent 'below expectation' figure is supported by data on the numbers of six-year-old children receiving special reading tuition in Reading Recovery programmes each year. For several years, the number has hovered around 20–25 per cent (Kerslake, 1998). Public concern about these figures may be the reason why in 1998 the New Zealand Government decided to introduce a 'Reading by 9' initiative, with funding for new programmes to help failing readers, and a task force of experts and laypeople to investigate the issues (Young, 1998).

The number of children struggling with reading vary from one socio-economic area to another. In very poor parts of the country, survey data indicate nine in ten high school 'new entrants' read below average. These are not just students from different cultural backgrounds or who speak another language other than English at home; the figures apply to European students as well (Nicholson & Gallienne, 1995).

At the end of 1998, the New Zealand Government set up a Literacy Task Force. The government's goal was that, 'by the year 2005 all nine-year-old children will be able to read and write for success'. The Literacy Task Force was asked to provide advice on how to meet the goal. The government had accepted statistics showing that at least 20 per cent of children were not doing well in reading and writing. Twenty million dollars was set aside to be spent on an advertising campaign and to provide special funds to pay for new programmes to help children having difficulties with reading. The campaign to raise reading levels was to be spread across the years 1999–2005, beginning with a national television campaign aimed at parents – especially parents of children in the underachieving groups, those from low-income backgrounds and non-European cultural backgrounds, and homes where English was not spoken. The report of the Literacy Task Force recommended:

- a clear description for teachers of what it means to 'read and write for success' at nine years of age
- more information for teachers on how to provide effective reading instruction

- analysis of the extent to which teachers are being adequately prepared in their initial training
- development of a professional training package to assist practising teachers
- opportunities for school principals to upskill their knowledge of how children learn to read and write
- a stronger base of interventions to help children struggling to read and write
- externally referenced assessments of reading and writing progress
- more reading assistance funds allocated to schools located in low-income socio-economic areas.

(Ministry of Education, 1999)

## The Situation in the United States

Has there been a decline in reading standards in the United States? In 1982 a survey of reading trend data by Farr and Fay led them to conclude that 'today's children are better readers than children from any period in the past' (p. 135). They pointed out that when America was founded, only 15 per cent could read; in World War I, only 45 per cent could read; in 1975, 80 per cent could read. They suggested that this should be cause for a sense of achievement. A similar conclusion comes from Calfee and Patrick (1995). Their analysis of data over the last 20 years led them to conclude that 'trends in reading are flat' (p. 33). They argued this was a good result, given the social pressures that have taken place in the last two decades where only 50 per cent of families follow the traditional nuclear pattern. In addition, schools have to cope with drugs and violence. Their assessment of the situation in America was that schools were 'holding their own' (p. 51), but were not in good shape compared with what they needed to be.

However, in California in the early 1990s, reading standards did seem to go backwards. The results of national surveys of reading achievement indicated that California children had slipped. In a 1992 survey of 39 states, California was second to last (Louisiana was last) and by 1994 they scored equal last (Campbell, 1996). As a result of these statistics, the governor of California set up a committee of investigation that concluded that reading instruction practices had to become more 'balanced' with a stronger emphasis on phonics. The new California state curriculum includes whole language features such as introducing children's literature, but there is also a strong emphasis on phonics (Simmons & Kameenui, 1998).

The California move back to traditional phonics attracted huge public interest in the United States (e.g. Levine, 1994; Collins, 1997). Lobby groups in favour of phonics, such as the Right to Read Foundation, have been documenting legislative action in various states, reporting that 27 states (in 1998) had taken action to increase the teaching of phonics. An indication of public interest in reading has been an initiative by the *Los Angeles Times* ('Reading by 9', 1998). They have committed $5 million to a programme which aims to ensure that children in their region achieve grade-level skills in reading by the time they reach nine years of age. They are promoting book festivals, kids' reading sections in their newspaper, and regular features on the state of reading issues. Even their employees receive training so they can act as voluntary tutors to children.

In late 1998, the United States Congress passed the Reading Excellence Act. Its promoter, William Goodling (1997), in proposing the Act, mentioned national survey data showing that 40 per cent of children in fourth grade were reading below the basic level. He also noted that fewer than ten per cent of American teachers had an adequate understanding of how children learn to read or how to help struggling readers. The act had a number of provisions, but high on the list was the teaching of phonemic awareness and phonics. Another provision stated that any funding applications from states to improve the teaching of reading had to be based on 'reliable, replicable research'. States were being asked to be accountable.

### The Situation in Australia and England

In Australia, similarly to the United States, reading levels have remained unchanged for the last 20 years. Yet Australian survey data also indicate that 30 per cent of Australian teenagers have 'not attained mastery in the important area of reading' (Marks & Ainley, 1997: 17).

In England, questions about the effectiveness of whole-language teaching were raised as far back as 1990 when Martin Turner, an educational psychologist, reported reading data from a sample of 400,000 seven-year-olds which showed a decline in reading achievement levels (Lightfoot, 1997). During the early 1990s, Her Majesty's Inspectorate in England was also critical of the lack of structured teaching of reading. In 1998 the English government introduced a national 'literacy hour'. Teachers were to use this hour each day to provide direct instruction and whole-class teaching, and the instruction was meant to include phonics (Lightfoot, 1998). The English Government in 1998 also introduced a National Year of Reading which would overlap into 1999, aiming to lift reading achievement in schools. According to the Department for Employment and Education, 'around 40 per cent of English 11-year-olds fall short of the standard expected for their age group in English' (www.yearofreading.org.uk). Their goal is to bring 80 per cent of 11-year-olds up to the standard expected for their age by the year 2002. Family literacy courses will be available to parents to help teach their children to read. Free books will be given to schools. Summer literacy school will offer courses for children who are about to start secondary school, yet need reading help. A television advertising campaign called 'A little reading goes a long way' will encourage parents to read to their children. High-profile personalities will participate in television advertising (e.g. stars of 'East Enders', 'Coronation Street'). A free advisory booklet will be available to parents.

**Public Concern**

What is interesting about analyses of 'reading standards' is that there is public concern that they are not as high as they should be. In the United States, it is claimed that 40 per cent of children are not reading at their grade-level; in England the figure is again 40 per cent; in Australia the figure is 30 per cent; in New Zealand it is at least 20 per cent. Yet these figures are not the sole reason for public concern. There appears to be a perception among many parents that their children are not receiving a 'balance' of instruction. The balance has been seen as favouring whole language and excluding the traditional phonics approach. There is a feeling that phonics has become the 'skinny kid on the block', and as a result children have been denied another way of learning to read.

Is this perception correct? Perhaps not. In the United States, survey data show that the vast majority (90 per cent) of teachers perceive themselves to be 'eclectic', in that they use both whole language and phonics (Baumann *et al.*, 1998). On the other hand, it is not clear what teachers think 'phonics' is. The survey found that two out of three K-2 (kindergarten through second grade) teachers reported that they taught phonics by teaching letter–sound correspondences and 'word families' (e.g. cat, mat, hat, sat, fat). This is phonics teaching. But the same number also reported that they used whole-language techniques; for example, encouraging children to 'invent' spellings, reading to children, using Big Books (i.e. enlarged books read to the whole class), and providing children's literature for their pupils to read.

There is a concern in the United States that teachers may not fully understand the teaching of phonics. In California, teacher training institutions are being asked to ensure that trainee teachers learn how to teach phonics. Millions of dollars have also been allocated to teach practising teachers in California about phonics. A similar problem exists in regard to 'phonemic awareness' knowledge. Research is now quite clear that learning to read and spell requires awareness that words are built of 'sounds' (i.e. phonemes), and that methods of teaching reading need to ensure that this awareness happens (Adams *et al.*, 1998). Are teachers ready to implement phonemic awareness instruction? Rath (1995) surveyed 121 classroom teachers, specialist reading teachers and teacher trainees. She found that many had difficulty understanding what 'phonemes' were. Many of the teachers surveyed were unclear about the difference between phonemic awareness and 'phonics'. Similar findings have also been obtained by Moats (1995) and Nicholson (1999).

In summary, public concern in the 1990s about whether or not we should make changes in our teaching of reading resulted in action at government levels in the United States and England, with moves back toward more traditional teaching methods, especially phonics. Public concern might come down to a perception that it seems wrong to exclude a method of teaching (i.e. phonics) which had done nothing wrong except become unfashionable. In reality, whole-language teachers may be more eclectic than they appear to be; there are some survey data to support this point. However, there are also data to support the public concern. It seems hard to believe that school inspectors in England, who visit schools regularly, were wrong in their claim that formal methods of teaching, such as phonics, were not happening throughout the 1990s (Lightfoot, 1998). It seems hard to believe that *American Educator*, the professional journal of the American Federation of Teachers, would be putting its support behind more teaching of phonemic awareness and phonics if it was already happening (McPike, 1995). Looking back over the 1980s and 1990s, it appears that the pendulum had probably swung too far toward naturalistic ways of teaching, as favoured by whole language. By the end of the 1990s, in some countries there is evidence of a correction back towards more traditional, structured teaching such as phonics.

### 'Letters to the Author'

In New Zealand, there is very little information on how reading is taught in schools. Perhaps the teaching of reading is well balanced between phonemic awareness, phonics and whole language, but my impression is that historically New Zealand has shown a move away from phonics and toward whole language (Nicholson, 1997).

Some of the letters I have received have argued the case for more emphasis on the traditional method of teaching reading – phonics. One retired teacher wrote, 'Phonics gives children their own key to learning and saves them from the frustration and heartaches resulting from illiteracy.' Another retired teacher wrote, 'I was educated in a country school in the years 1928–1935. As I listened to you [on radio] I realised I was very lucky. From my first day at school I was taught to read by sounding the letters. The only thing that matches that for me today is doing a cryptic crossword. For instance, one of today's clues in *The Press* was: a biting ditch insect (nine letters). The answer was trenchant – just a matter of putting the parts together to make the whole, isn't it?'

Another ex-teacher of reading in secondary schools wrote of an experience in the 1970s when she was questioned about teaching phonics: 'My espousal of phonics brought me into contact with the establishment – too old-fashioned. Reading advisors were patronising – one, I recall, upbraided me for teaching the digraph "ph" as sounding "f" as in "phone". He reasoned that students would be confused when confronted with the word "cuphook". Have you used the word "cuphook" lately? I would teach it [cuphook] as a compound word.'

Some teachers have written to me about innovative ideas that they still feel are worth trying. One teacher wrote about the initial teaching alphabet (i.t.a.) used at Flanshaw Road primary school in the 1960s. This was a method where every phoneme had a unique symbol (e.g. a̲ represented 'ar', a̲u̲ represented 'or'). Children's writing was a little bit different from conventional spelling (e.g. 'ie doent like the katipoe spieder it biets yw if yw get tw cloes').

Another ex-teacher wrote to me with a theory that one reason for difficulty in learning to read is the distortion of the vowel sounds in New Zealand English. She had noticed that many words are not the 'Queen's English'. She wrote, 'We have progressed (?) from 'fush and chups' to an ever-present 'ut us' and 'usunt ut?', and now our own 'Ulumpucs'. Our young children now count one, toe, thray, four, five, sucks, suvun, eight, nine, tun …'.

The debate about how best to teach reading seems to have had a history of polarised views. One school principal wrote to me that her teaching using the phonics method was criticised by a school inspector who visited her class in 1981. The inspector said, 'You aren't using phonics, are you? Good heavens, that went out with the ark.'

Another teacher wrote to me about the way in which methods of teaching reading seem to go in and out of fashion. She wrote, 'The difficulty arises when teachers are confronted with statements that research and statistics show that changes need to be made because something is not working. Suddenly some teachers make a turnaround in their teaching style, instead of incorporating new ideas and techniques. I feel that my reading programmes have had to be somewhat furtive to incorporate techniques that have not at that particular time been "in vogue".'

I've received a number of calls and letters from parents who worry about their children's reading and writing. One parent wrote to me, 'Our house is filled with books. My children are read to on a regular basis and are eager to learn. Yet they struggle with the logistics of written language. I am concerned that my children are going to miss the boat and I try to back up their efforts at home. But I lack the practical material to do so.'

Parents everywhere want their children to learn to read and write. This is not a new phenomenon. Here is a letter to the editor that I still remember. The letter was signed 'Angry Māori Mother'. It was published in the *New Zealand Herald* quite a few years ago ('Poor teaching', 1980):

Sir: One thing Māori parents want is for their children to be able to get good jobs. And this means being able to read and write, which my children in Standards Two and Three [seven- and eight-year-olds] can hardly do. This is not because they have no brains or come from an unhappy home, or are underfed or unloved. It is not because of any other condition teachers usually blame. The children have just not had enough teaching. No wonder Māori children get bitter. What chance have they got? Every complaint made to the school brings such answers as 'Don't worry about it' or 'They'll probably come right all of a sudden'. But how can they if they do not get enough teaching and there is too much talking and fooling in the classroom?

This issue of 'not enough teaching' was mentioned in a letter from a teacher who felt that the real problem was the effects of economic constraints on schools. He wrote:

I believe that a major contributing cause [of declining reading standards] is the economic constraints placed on all schools. This has resulted in large classes and a lack of funding for ancillary help, in the form of either teacher or teacher-aide time. As a result, those children who are in the "remedial" category, rather than being "retarded", are not getting the assistance which, in quite a short time, may resolve their problems and advance their ability considerably.... What we need is more dollars.

### What Will Reading be Like in the New Millennium?

It seems clear to me that classrooms of the near future will still require reading (and writing) skills. But reading skills will be applied very much to new technology, such as the ability to use wordprocessing packages, navigate the Worldwide Web, and use electronic mail systems (see Roberts, 1995). Children of the future may spend much more time reading computer screens and using computer keyboards to write. There are already many electronic journals and books. Children will have access to CD-ROMs that contain thousands of children's books (see photo opposite).

Is this the end of the book as we know it? Over the centuries the nature of writing and print have changed dramatically, from clay

*The author investigating the future of reading (Sony Building, New York).*

tablets to writing on papyrus with reed pens, to printer's type, to typewriters, and now to computers. But I don't think this electronic age we live in is the end of the book. Books made of paper will always be around, but they will have competitors. Just as radio has survived television and the Internet, books made of paper will co-exist with CD-ROMs. There is still a niche for the paper book. Not everyone wants to plug into a computer. Taking a book to bed still seems more natural, and perhaps more practical, than taking a laptop.

Whatever happens with computer technology, it seems hard to rule out the need to read, to spell and to be able personally to compose text. These reading and writing skills, for the moment, are crucially necessary in order to read books and also to read computer screens. Talking books, CD-ROM videobooks, spellchecks and other smart software are now available to help us with literacy tasks. These are wonderful literacy accessories, but the skilled reader, speller and writer will still have a competitive advantage. I can listen to books now, but prefer not to. I can use a spellcheck, but it's nice not to have to rely on it.

Educators have been speculating on the new world of technological literacy for decades now, but the reality is that we still need to be able to read and write. Television programmes make use of writing, newspapers have to be read by the reader, school examinations have to be read and written, and our local mail and email delivery still consist of letters that have to be read. It even seems likely that levels of literacy in the next several decades will have to rise even further. As technology becomes more sophisticated, it requires more complex literacy skills as well. For example, can you remember when we used to turn a knob to set the time on an alarm clock? Now we have to consult a manual in order to do the same thing.

## Why Does Reading Seem So Political?

John Smith (1996) has argued that reading sometimes becomes part of the political process as a way to justify cuts in government spending and to control education in the name of 'accountability' (p. 156). What can happen in the name of accountability is that reading is reduced to a technical level, with teachers having to tick boxes to say that they have taught skill number 223, and so on. Thus, one perspective on the politics of reading is that politics is about creating an impression in the public mind that children are not learning to read, so that politicians can then say they will solve the problem. This is a strategy to win votes, not to help children. The politician who promises 'literacy for all' might be seen as capitalising on a socially felt need in order to gain votes.

*Reprinted with permission of David Fletcher, author of the cartoon series* Politician.

But is this being too suspicious? Perhaps it is true sometimes. Politicians only get elected if people vote for them. Yet another interpretation of why politicians get involved in literacy is that they actually react to public concern. Political survival depends on anticipating where the mood of the public is going and finding ways of dealing with their concerns. Whatever the reasons for politicians getting involved in literacy, it is difficult to ask them to keep out of literacy. Literacy skills are a socially felt need, as are health care and the availability of work. It is the job of a politician to be sensitive to these needs. People want their children to learn to read and write. In the end, one positive thing about debates about reading is that parents are able to consider all evidence. Hopefully they will sense when they are being manipulated.

Weaver (1994, see also Pressley, 1998) has a darker view. Like Smith, she worries that phonics teaching brings with it a view that children should 'work' and that reading is about filling in worksheets and learning 'skills' instead of enjoying literature. Phonics kills interest in reading and turns children away from school. It has been asserted that phonics keeps children busy, but stops them from reading and thinking for themselves. In this way phonics perpetuates the current social structure where the rich stay at the top and the poor stay at the bottom and learn to be docile workers. Is this true? There are many instances in history where ordinary people have been 'socially structured' by reading. An extreme example of this can be seen in children's primers from the days of Juan and Evita Peron in Argentina (Ministerio de Educacion, 1962). The first primer is an example of how political messages can be sent into the reading classroom; in the opening pages is a picture of Evita and under the picture is the word 'mama'.

While it may be nearly impossible to take politics out of literacy, there are several reasons why we should try to keep the intrusion of politics to a minimum. One reason is that it doesn't seem proper for students to be exposed to any particular political ideology as part of the way they are taught to read. I am of the idealistic view that children should have the opportunity to work out their own political views.

To say that phonics is a tool of right-wing conservative groups wanting to perpetuate social inequalities seems incredible; even Paulo Freire taught the oppressed people of Brazil with phonics. He saw it as a way of liberating them, of making information available to them (Chall, 1987; Roberts,

1994). On a positive note, perhaps what we should take from the arguments of whole-language supporters is that we should be aware of the possibility of reading being used to promote political ends.

A second reason for keeping political issues to a minimum in discussions of how to teach reading is that we can focus too much on political issues relating to literacy. Of course there are important issues, such as whether or not children's minds are being socially constructed to make them docile workers of the future. But these are not just reading issues. There are many ways in which our lives can also be 'socially constructed'; for example, through television and radio. If we focus too closely on the political aspects of literacy, we may come to think that the basics of learning to pronounce words on the page are just small technical problems. For example, Christie (1995) wrote that proponents of teaching phonics 'perpetuate myths about the particular role of "phonics", understood as having overweening significance in literacy, when in fact awareness of sound–letter relationship has a modest, if essential, role in literacy development' (p. 14). This is not the case at all. Knowing how to decode words is not a 'modest' part of literacy. It is a very important part of reading. This is the problem of giving too much importance to politics in reading. Essential skills such as learning to read words on the page are diminished in importance. The big political issues of 'social construction' and 'far right' politics are given all the limelight, even though many children in schools everywhere are struggling to read 'cat'.

What is the difference between these two ways of thinking about literacy? Gough (1995) refers to Literacy 1 and Literacy 2. Literacy 1 means the ability to read and write. Literacy 2 means being educated. Literacy 1 takes children years of tuition and study. These skills, when polished and automated, give a child the ability to decode (or pronounce) almost any word on any page, no matter what it says. The ability to decode can provide the opportunity to achieve Literacy 2, which is about becoming educated and thinking critically about the printed word. If a child is unable to decode, then Literacy 2 will not be a possibility.

Perhaps as many as 20 per cent of children struggle to achieve Literacy 1, the ability to decode (Kerslake, 1998). Another 20 per cent appear to have a basic grasp of decoding, but are slow and lack the ability to apply these skills with ease (see Pinnell *et al.*, 1995). They have trouble pronouncing words and read too slowly to understand what they read. Without these basic skills of decoding, they are denied access to all the interesting ideas and issues that arise from literacy, including political ones. Sometimes the politics of literacy seem more important than the basic skills of literacy. The basic skills of decoding are seen as low level, technical and uninteresting. They may be technical, but it seems almost unethical to have a child leave school without their having acquired a high level of such basic skills.

## Conclusion

The reading pendulum has been swinging for many years. Reading is likely to be a much-needed skill of the future, so pendulum swings will continue as educators realise that by swinging one way or the other they have lost something. The status quo will continue to be challenged because there will always be an impulse to produce more positive results. At the core of these pendulum swings is a tension between the benefits of gaining something new versus the cost of losing something in the process. There is also a tension between a) making the teaching of reading overly mechanistic and boring, full of skill and drill, and b) making reading overly 'natural', with the risk that some children are unable to teach themselves to read. There is also a concern that reading should not be a political football. The purpose of this book is to put some perspective on these swings by looking at the nature of our reading system and where we have come from.

## References

Adams, M. J., Foorman, B. R., Lundberg, I., & Beeler, T. (1998). 'The elusive phoneme. Why phonemic awareness is so important and how to help children develop it'. *American Educator*, 22, 18–29.

Baumann, J. F., Hoffman, J. V., Moon, J., & Duffyhester, A. M. (1998). 'Where are teachers' voices in the phonics/whole language debate? Results from a survey of US elementary classroom teachers'. *The Reading Teacher*, 51, 636–650.

Calfee, R. C., & Patrick, C. (1995). *Teach our children well*. Stanford, CA: Stanford University Alumni.

Campbell, J. *et al.* (1996). *NAEP 1994 reading report card for the nation and the states: Findings from the National Assessment of Educational Progress and trial state assessment.* Washington, DC: National Center for Education Statistics.

Chall, J.S. (1987). 'Reading development in adults'. *Annals of Dyslexia*, 37, p. 245.

Christie, F. (1995, August 31). 'Misreading myths about literacy' (Letter to the Editor). *The Age*, p. 14.

Collins, J. (1997, October 27). 'How Johnny should read'. *Time Magazine*, 150.

Crooks, T., & Flockton, L. (1997). *National education monitoring project forum newssheet.* Dunedin: Otago University Educational Assessment Research Unit.

Elley, W. B. (1992). *How in the world do students read?* Hamburg, Germany: International Association for the Evaluation of Educational Achievement.

Elley, W. B. (1996). 'The phonic debate'. *Set: Research information for teachers*, 1, Article 7.

Farr, R., & Fay, L. (1982). 'Reading trend data in the United States: A mandate for caveats and caution'. In G. R. Austin & H. Garber (eds.), *The rise and fall of national test scores*. New York: Academic Press, (pp. 83–141).

Goodling, W. F. (1997, October 7). *Reading excellence act.* 'Extension of remarks', Washington DC: House of Representatives.

Gough, P. B. (1995). 'The new literacy: Caveat emptor'. *Journal of Research in Reading*, 18, 79–86.

Hughes, C.U. (1999). 'Teachers' perceptions of methods and practices employed in the teaching of reading and the language arts. Unpublished Master's thesis, The University of Auckland.

Kerslake, J. (1998). 'Annual monitoring of Reading Recovery. The data for 1997'. *The Research Bulletin*, (pp. 43–48). Wellington: Ministry of Education.

Levine, A. (1994). 'The great debate revisited'. *The Atlantic Monthly.*

Lightfoot, L. (1997, September 15). 'Teachers to be re-trained over literacy'. *Daily Telegraph*, p. 7.

Lightfoot, L. (1998, March 20). 'Schools told how to teach reading'. *Daily Telegraph.*

Marks, G. N., & Ainley, J. (1997). *Reading comprehension and numeracy among junior secondary school students in Australia.* Melbourne: Australian

Council for Educational Research.

McPike, E. (1995). 'Learning to read: Schooling's first mission'. *American Educator*, pp. 3–6.

Ministerio de Educacion (1952). *Las hadas buenas.* Buenos Aires: Author.

Ministry of Education (1999). *Report of the literacy taskforce.* Wellington: Author.

Moats, L. (1995). 'The missing foundation in teacher education'. *American Educator, 19*, 9, 43–51.

Nicholson, T., & Gallienne, G. (1995). 'A survey of reading achievement levels among 13-year-old pupils in two contrasting socioeconomic areas'. *New Zealand Journal of Educational Studies*, 30, 115–123.

Nicholson, T. (1997). 'From ABCs to Ready to Read'. *Set special: Language and Literacy*, Article 2.

Nicholson, T. (1999). A replication survey of the linguistic knowledge of trainee teachers. Paper presented to New Zealand Linguistics Conference, Palmerston North.

Nuttall, G. (1985). 'Standards of achievement in schools'. *Economic Bulletin*, No. 702, 1–5.

Pinnell, G. S., Pikulsi, J. J., Wixson, K. K., Campbell, J. R., Gough, P. B., & Beatty, A. S. (1995). *Listening to children read aloud: Data from NAEP's Integrated Reading Performance Record (IRPR) at grade 4.* Washington, DC: National Center for Educational Statistics.

'Poor teaching.' (1980, February 13). Letter to the Editor. *The New Zealand Herald*.

Pressley, M. (1998). *Reading instruction that works. The case for balanced teaching.* New York: The Guilford Press.

Rath, L. K. (1995). *The phonemic awareness of reading teachers: Examining aspects of knowledge.* Unpublished Doctoral dissertation, Harvard University, Boston.

Reading by 9 fact sheet. (1998, October 18). *The Los Angeles Times* (Website: http//www.latimes.com)

Reid, N. (1994). 'How literate are Kiwis? Who knows (or cares)?'. *Reading Forum N.Z.*, 2, 3–24.

Roberts, P. (1994). 'Education, dialogue and intervention: Revisiting the Freirean project'. *Educational Studies*, 20, 307–327.

Roberts, P. (1995). 'Literacy studies: A review of the literature, with signposts for future research'. *New Zealand Journal of Educational Studies*, 30, 189–214.

Simmons, D. C., & Kameenui, E. J. (1998). *Draft reading/language arts curriculum framework K–12*. Sacramento, CA: California Department of Education.

Smith, J, (1996). 'Whole language and its critics: A New Zealand perspective'. *The Australian Journal of Language and Literacy, 20*, 156–162.

Thorndike, R. L. (1973). *Reading comprehension in fifteen countries*. New York: John Wiley.

Weaver, C. (1994). *Understanding whole language: From principles to practice* (2nd ed.). Portsmouth, NH: Heinemann.

Young, A. (1998, October 22). 'Back to basics an insurance against failure'. *The New Zealand Herald*, A1.

# 2

# HISTORIAL PERSPECTIVES: THE ORIGINS OF THE ALPHABET, AND THE HISTORY OF CHILDREN'S PRIMERS

It is very important to understand the history of the English writing system. The short summary is that it is an alphabetic system. Sometimes criticisms are made that too many words are spelled irregularly. It is true that there are many spellings that are unusual (e.g. the spelling of 'arf' in 'laugh). But the vast majority of words follow the alphabetic principle that the 26 letters of the alphabet systematically represent sounds. Think about it. We do not spell a word like 'fish' with a random set of letters, such as 'akjh'. In alphabetic writing, a word is spelled according to its sequence of sounds. Even a word like 'through', which has an unusual spelling for 'oo', also has some regular letter-sound spellings (i.e. 'thr-' is spelled 'th' and 'r'). In this chapter, we look at the way in which the English spelling system evolved, and why it is more systematic than it sometimes appears. Let's start with the history of writing.

### Born Talking

Writing is a system for recording human speech. Nearly all humans, as a result of evolution, can talk. Talking is the ability to communicate our thoughts and ideas phonologically and understand other people's thoughts and ideas. Talking seems simple, but why is it that only humans can do it? Although animals have the ability to communicate, they are quite limited when compared with human communication. There are special parts of the human brain that produce and understand spoken language, that animals do not have. Humans can generate, understand and reflect on a great range of sentences. Animals can seem intelligent. A parrot seems able to talk, but in fact it is imitating what you say. Dogs and cats can communicate, but not the way we do with speech. I once purchased a reading programme called 'Teach Your Dog to Read'. I was attracted by the advertisement which argued that many owners of dogs feel that their dogs understand them when they talk. The reading programme consisted of some pictures (e.g. a cat, a car) and the words 'cat' and 'car' on flashcards. The idea was to teach the dog to read 'cat' and 'car'. But this is a very limited (and perhaps silly) accomplishment. In contrast, nearly every sentence we read or hear is different, and we have the ability to combine a limited number of consonants and vowels in all sorts of ways to produce a vast number of words (Pinker, 1994). A system of grammatical rules enables us to produce and understand all kinds of ideas conveyed in sentences. Developed through evolution, speech is far from simple in the way it works, even though nearly all of us have no difficulty talking (Chomsky, 1957; Liberman, 1996). Speech is a gift of evolution, like walking and breathing.

When did we start talking? Estimates vary. Some claim that speech appeared 150,000 years ago when *Homo sapiens* appeared in Africa. However, if you believe that speech has evolved from gestures (like waving hands, pointing, etc.), you could argue that speech is perhaps two million years old – as old as the human species. Corballis (1999) believes that gestures are an old and sophisticated way of communicating thoughts. The sign language of the deaf is very similar to spoken language, involving the ability to represent with gestures (or signs) the sounds, words and sentences of spoken language. Why don't we use sign language? Corballis argues that communication through speech may have provided humans with an evolutionary advantage – it freed up the hands, allowing people to talk and work at the same time. Our hands became specialised for technology such as making tools, and our voices became specialised for conveying messages.

## Written Communication

How do you make a permanent record of speech? Archaeologists have found cave paintings that date back at least 50,000 years. Cave paintings are not writing, just as art is not writing; this is because writing is speech in a visible form. Daniels (1996) has defined writing as 'a system of more or less permanent marks used to represent an utterance in such a way that it can be recovered more or less exactly without the intervention of the utterer' (p. 3). Why was writing invented at all? Although it is tempting to think that writing was invented in order to send messages and write books, Daniels believes the real reason was probably much more mundane: to keep business records such as numbers of livestock, the names of workers and their job descriptions.

Writing as a form of visible speech dates back at least 4,000 years (Gelb, 1963). Cuneiform appears to be the earliest form of writing, originating in the Middle East, in countries now known as Iran and Iraq. Daniels states: 'The earliest scribes we know about wrote on shaped lumps of clay – the durability of which is the reason we know about them – indenting wedge-shaped marks with a square corner of a reed stylus' (p. 19). Cuneiform was a way of recording the Sumerian language, which is now extinct. The word 'cuneus' means 'wedge'. This wedge-shaped writing was made on clay tablets that were later dried or baked hard. The cuneiform writing system consisted of 800 symbols. Many were pictographic (e.g. a picture of a stalk of barley represented 'grain'). Other symbols were logographic, where a special symbol represented a specific word (e.g. a sheep was a cross within a circle). Most of the cuneiform signs represented whole words, but since the language itself was mostly monosyllabic, the signs could also be used as syllables, especially to write personal names and some grammatical forms (Akmajian *et al.*, 1984).

Why was there such a huge time gap between the development of speech and the invention of this very early writing system? As Liberman (1997, p. 5) says, 'Speech has been around for 200,000 years or more, although the idea that it could be rendered alphabetically was born no more than 4,000 years ago. Subtracting the latter number from the former, we conclude that it took our ancestors at least 196,000 years just to discover how to describe what it was they did when they spoke.' Liberman says that the reason it took so long is that speech itself gives very few clues that it is a phonological system. For someone to think of a system for representing phonemes ('phone' means 'sound' in Greek) with alphabetic symbols, it would mean understanding that spoken words are made up of phonemes. Yet the nature of speech makes such a discovery very difficult.

Liberman (1996, 1997) says that our phonological system is a module in the brain that works automatically and unconsciously. The speaker of a language does not have to be aware of the phonological system. When we process speech sounds, we don't actually hear a series of separate sounds – we hear 'a seamless stretch of sound' (Liberman, 1996, p. 442). For example, when we hear the word 'bag' we hear just one sound. This is a great advantage in speech because this process of overlapping of sounds (called 'parallel transmission') enables us to talk more quickly than we could if we had to pronounce every phoneme separately. The problem in inventing a writing system is that phonemes are not separate acoustic units in the speech stream – they are not transmitted separately in the syllables of speech, but are transmitted together. The large time gap between the evolution of speech and the discovery of writing indicates that the ability to speak is a product of human evolution, whereas the creation of a writing system was an invention just as radio, television and computers are inventions (Pinker, 1994).

**Egyptian Writing**

Egyptian writing appeared at close to the same time as cuneiform writing, and it is still debated which writing system came first (Michalowski, 1996). Egyptians wrote their language with ink on papyrus for three thousand years (Daniels, 1996). The discovery in the early nineteenth century that Egyptian hieroglyphs represented consonants, was due to the work of an English mathematician, Thomas Young (1773–1829), and a French linguist, Jean-Francois Champollion (1790–1832), who were able to link ancient Greek writing to ancient Egyptian writing (Coe, 1992; Daniels, 1996). This was only made possible by the accidental discovery in 1799 of the Rosetta stone. This stone had the same message written in three different languages, ancient Greek, Demotic (the popular way of writing in Egyptian times),

*An example of hieroglyphic writing.*

and hieroglyphic, the official writing form of Egypt in the period of the Pharaohs. The hieroglyphs represented Coptic, an ancient Egyptian language known to linguists (Rayner & Pollatsek, 1989). Why did it take so long to decipher Egyptian writing? The reason was that hiero-glyphics, for many cent-uries, were thought to be pictorial, and not a writing system that represented speech (see illustration).

### Other Early Writing Systems

Egyptian writing is import-ant in the history of the alphabetic writing system. However, it was not the only early writing system. There were other unique writing systems unrelated to Egyptian writing. A separate development in writing occurred in China. This writing system goes back 3,000 years (Boltz, 1996). In Mexico and Guatemala, researchers have only recently, since the 1970s, gained an understanding of the Mayan writing system, which originated 2,000 years ago and mysteriously died out 1,000 years ago. The discovery that the Maya code was syllabic was made by Russian linguists working in Moscow, who had only photographs to work from (Coe, 1992). Like Egyptian writing, the Maya system was at first thought to be pictorial, but the Russians made the breakthrough discovery that it was a syllabic writing system. The Mayan script appears to have been a writing system that developed independently of other systems. As Daniels (1996) points out, it is foolish to try to rank one writing system as 'better' than another, or even to rank one language over another according to whether or not it had a writing system. Every language system is a thing of beauty, whether it has a writing system or not.

## Pictography

One simple way of representing an idea visually is to draw it (e.g. a picture of an ox to represent an ox). This is called pictography. Pictographs stand for objects you can see (e.g. the sun). They are iconic. But Daniels (1996) and other scholars do not accept that this is writing in that there are a lot of meanings that can't be represented by pictures, not just abstract words, but also grammatical endings and proper names. Pictographs can be adapted to represent abstract ideas. When this happens they are called ideographs (e.g. a picture of the sun can be used not only to represent 'sun', but also words that share some of its features, such as stands for 'warmth' or 'light'). Ideographs are symbolic, rather than having a one-to-one correspondence. The important feature of an ideographic system is that each symbol is not necessarily tied to a specific meaning.

Pictographs and ideographs are not writing. There are too many problems facing this system. Pictures are unable, by themselves to represent speech, since they don't enable us to recover exactly what was said in spoken form. It is hard to draw pictures to represent the meaning of thoughts such as, 'I bought a beautiful pig today'. Not every word can be illustrated (e.g. 'I', 'a'). Also, pictures are hard to draw unambiguously (e.g. is that a picture of a sheep or a pig?) It is hard to find a way of using pictures to express everything you want to say.

## From Picture Writing to Syllable Writing

For a scribe to represent in writing what people actually said, it was necessary to represent the sounds of words. It seems that pictures came to represent the syllables of speech. For example, it is possible to write the two-syllable word 'Sunday' with a picture of the 'sun' along with another picture showing the sun peeping over the horizon to represent 'day' (Crowder, 1982). To represent the word 'sold' you might use a picture of an old person, perhaps a man with a long beard and a walking stick. That would be 'old'. Then you put a picture of a 'snake' in front of that person and hope that the reader will think of the /s/

sound in 'snake' and link it to 'old'. This was the sort of thing that happened as writing systems tried to get closer to a way of representing in written form the words they expressed in spoken form.

All writing systems represent meaning and sound but some are more sound-based while others are more meaning-based. English is a writing system that is toward the phonemic end of the writing spectrum (e.g. 'fish' is not written as 'bufkibber'). The writing system tries to capture the phonemes of the word (i.e. /f-i-sh/). The English writing system is not just phonemic, however. It also it has a morphemic aspect to it. Some words are spelled in ways that do not mirror the exact sounds of the word, but do reflect words with similar meaning. For example, the /b/ in 'debt' is not pronounced, but it is related to the /b/ in the related word 'debit'. Despite this system of representing sound and meaning in the spelling of English words, Daniels (1996) points out that learning to read English without taking advantage of its strong phonemic character is to ignore the strengths of the basic nature of the writing system. He points out that statements by some early researchers that English spellings are only 50 per cent regular are 'chaotic' (p. 654) statements to make. He notes that George Bernard Shaw's statement that 'fish' can be spelled 'ghoti' misrepresents the rule system, in that 'gh' only represents the /f/ sound when used at the end of a word, never at the beginning. Also, 'o' only represents the /I/ sound in the very irregular word 'women', and 'ti' is only the /sh/ sound when it is used in Latin-borrowed words like 'nation'. Daniels (1996) comments that the many irregular spellings in English have mostly been caused by the huge number of borrowed words in the language, which he actually thinks is a good argument for making English an international language.

Some writing systems are more at the meaning end of the writing spectrum, though all of them have some kind of phonological dimension. Mair (1996) described Modern Chinese writing as 'an enormously large but phonetically imprecise syllabary.' (p. 201). He also acknowledged that 'Chinese characters function differently from a purely phonetic script in that they have a powerful ability to carry semantic weight in and of themselves.' (p. 201). The semantic and phonetic components of each character stand apart from each other, even though they are both within the square frame that makes up the character. Mair (1996) notes that some characters stand separately with no phonetic component but 81 per cent of words in the popular New China Character Dictionary have a phonetic component. There are about 60,000 characters in the language but 90 per cent of words used in Chinese writing are represented by just 1,000 characters. For most readers of Chinese, about 2000–2,500 characters need to be learned. Mair (1996) described this as a 'formidable task' (p. 200). The ancient Chinese script emerged in North Central China and from there it spread to Korea and Japan.

Japanese has a writing system that is multiscriptal. In this writing system, meaning is represented with kanji, which are characters derived from Chinese. In addition to Kanji, there are two syllabaries, hiragana and katakana, which are used to represent sound. To the outsider, Japanese and Chinese seem complex writing systems, yet they work well for the people who use them. Smith (1996) noted about Japanese that, 'Throughout this century, no writing system has been written about so pejoratively as Japanese' (p. 214). She noted that these criticisms related to the fact that kana syllabaries are quite capable of expressing any Japanese word, yet kanji are still used, even though they are difficult to learn, and complex. As she put it, 'The Japanese writing system, however, is associated with a highly literate and successful society, with a rich written tradition that makes full use of its multi-scriptal potentialities for the creation of nuanced, graphically vital texts. The high degree of literacy in Japan and the high consumption of published material suggest that the writing system is fully functional' (p. 214).

## The Origins of the Alphabet

The syllable system is very close to representing single sounds. So it was a possible next step for written symbols to come to represent single phonemes. This would be an advantage for languages that, unlike Japanese, did not suit a syllable writing system. A writing system of symbols to represent sounds was used by the Phoenicians, who lived and traded in the middle east, around the Mediterranean about 5,000 years ago. They spoke a language similar in lineage to that of Hebrew, which is one of the Semitic languages (O'Connor, 1996). Their writing symbols represented consonant sounds. The Phoenicians used schematised drawings such as the drawing of an ox's head, which they called 'aleph' and used that symbol to represent one consonant sound. The symbol was pronounced as a consonant in their language.

Another symbol was called 'beth' which meant house (Balmuth, 1982). Imagine the aleph symbol A. If it was written upside down, it would look vaguely like an 'ox', with horns on its head (see Bennett, 1980). The Phoenicians pronounced 'aleph' like a short cough. They did not use symbols for vowel sounds and their symbols represented only consonant sounds.

The Greeks, about 2,700 years ago, borrowed the Phoenician symbols and applied them to the sounds of their own language (Swiggers, 1996). We know they did this because the names of the Greek letters are very similar to the names of the Sumerian letters, even though the Phoenician letter names have no meaning in Greek. For example, 'aleph' meant 'ox' in Sumerian, but meant nothing in Greek, yet the Greeks borrowed the name, altering it a little to form 'alpha'. Since there were symbols in the Phoenician writing system (like 'aleph') that were not consonant sounds used by the Greeks, the Greeks decided to use the extra consonant symbols to represent their vowels (Swiggers, 1996). This is how the letter name 'aleph' came to represent the vowel sound 'a' in Greek. The Greeks used the Phoenician letter name 'he' for their vowel, epsilon (e). The Phoenician 'ayin' was used for omikron (o), and the Phoenician 'yod' for 'iota' (i). We can see now that even the word 'alphabet' has Sumerian ancestry. The Phoenician 'aleph' became the Greek 'alpha', and the name 'beth' became the Greek 'beta' (b). This is the origin of the word 'alphabet'. Today, in English, we do not use all the Greek letters, but we use quite a few of them.

The use of letters to represent phonemes (vowels and consonants) was a great insight on the part of the Greeks, though a large part of the credit has to go to the Phoenicians. According to O'Connor (1996), the difference between the Greek and Phoenician scripts is a 'difference of degree' (p. 88), in that both were phonemic in design. This is not to say that the alphabet emerged in just one exchange at the seashore, between Greek and Phoenician sailors. There were several Greek alphabets co-existing for many decades. Sparta and Athens used different alphabets. A single Greek alphabet did not emerge until about 400BC.

The Greek alphabet spread to Italy, then to Europe and England. The Etruscans in Italy (an ancient region that is now called Tuscany) borrowed a form of the Greek alphabet used in Western Greece (Bonfante, 1996). The Etruscans did not have the B, D, G or O sounds, so eliminated 'beta', 'delta', 'gamma' and 'omega'. They replaced K ('kappa') with a C. They had a sound /f/ which they represented with the symbol F. The Romans borrowed the Greek-based script of the Etruscans, so it was not quite the same as the one currently used in Greece (Threatte, 1996). The Romans added six more letters to the Greek alphabet, and dropped some letters. They had the /g/ sound, which the Etruscans did not have, so the letter G was created, by altering the letter C slightly. The Romans also used the Greek X ('chi') to represent the sound /ks/. The Latin writing system did not use Z either, since Roman did not have that sound. But it was introduced later, to enable Roman scribes to write Greek words. Thus, the letter Z, which was in sixth place in the Greek alphabet, was later placed last in the Roman alphabet. These were some of the changes that occurred in the development of the Roman alphabet (see illustration below). Almost all the letters we use today are from the Roman alphabet. The three letters the Romans did not have, J, U and W, came much later (Balmuth, 1982). Another interesting development in those ancient times was the trend toward use of cursive writing. This seemed to have begun quite early, even in the Pharaonic period, made easier by the use of writing materials such as the reed pen, that enabled letters to be connected to each other. Lower-case letters also emerged gradually, as an attempt to simplify the uppercase letters for ease of writing (Balmuth, 1982). As Daniels (1996) points

*The author in search of the Roman Alphabet (The Forum, Rome).*

out, changes in writing systems over time should not be thought of as evolutionary. Writing systems didn't evolve like language. They were invented, and then 'improved' on by various scribes and scholars.

With the colonial imperialism of the last several centuries, the alphabet has spread to many countries. The Roman alphabet appears to have been introduced into England by missionaries (Daniels, 1996). The first writings in English were Anglo-Saxon glosses of church documents written in Latin, in the late seventh century. English spelling today reflects the history of the country, with its many invasions from outside. There were Scandinavian invaders, Greek and Latin-speaking missionaries, French soldiers in the Norman invasion of 1066, and so on. In addition, the English language has absorbed words from perhaps as many as 100 other languages.

To summarise, there are two important things to note about writing systems. First, they are inventions; they are not part of our evolutionary inheritance, like talking. Second, they map letters (or characters) onto speech. Spoken words and utterances became written words, sentences, and paragraphs.

## Reading Instruction – A Short History

When I went to school, we learned to read with 1950s reading materials such as *Janet and John*. Those were the days of 'look and say'. But I also remember phonics drills and learning to break words into syllables, such as 'Con-stan-tin-ople', and then spelling out the letters in each syllable. I got a real buzz out of being able to read (and spell) such a long word. What I didn't know at the time was that I was using phonics. Today, many children learn to read with whole language, and many succeed. Whole language emphasises prediction, guessing what the word must be, and using only some of its letters to work it out. But what if the words are not easily guessed from context clues, such as the words the Big Friendly Giant speaks in the children's book, *The BFG* (Dahl, 1982)? The giant has his own special vocabulary, including words like 'snozzcumber'and 'pilfflefizz'. How are children able to pronounce these words? What is the best method of teaching them to read? Let's now look at how the reading pendulum has swung over time between emphasising 'reading for meaning' and 'sounding it out'.

*Europe and the United States in the 1800s and early 1900s*

Until about a hundred years ago, most children learned to read an alphabetic writing system like English through the ABC method. Thompson (1997) estimates that the ABC method has been the standard way of learning for 3,000 years. There were occasional new ideas over the centuries, but the vast majority of children learned to read with the traditional alphabetic method. Even in Greek times, children started with the names of the alphabet. They learned the alphabet backwards and forwards until they knew all the letter names. Then they learned to read two-letter syllables such as ab, eb, ib, ob, ub by spelling their names. For Greek children, this probably meant spelling the letter names 'alpha, beta, ab', and so on. Learning the alphabet was not easy even for them, as there is a story that one Greek family purchased 24 slaves and named each of them with a letter of the Greek alphabet to help their children learn their ABCs (Huey, 1908). In the 1700s another innovative strategy was recommended – to make gingerbread cookies in the shapes of the letters of the alphabet. It was recommended that every school employ a baker (Huey, 1908). In Europe, the United States and New Zealand, at least until the mid-nineteenth century, reading and spelling were taught with the traditional ABC method. Learning to read two-letter words meant practising them many times: 'ay bee, ab, ee bee, eb, eye bee, ib', and so on (Price, 1997). After two-letter words came three-letter words. Thus, children worked their way through words of different sizes, from small to large.

The ABC method has dominated school instruction since Greek and Roman times. In many countries, including England and Scotland, instruction manuals for teachers followed a similar pattern. Children were first to learn the names of the letters of the alphabet. Then they learned the various sounds made by letters (e.g. the short and long vowel sounds). Children learned single-syllable words first, and then they might be given a reading passage consisting of one-syllable words. Then they moved to two-syllable lists of words and so on. The instructional pattern was very linear, building up slowly from short words to long.

In England from 1450 on, the only reading materials available to many children were 'hornbooks'. A hornbook was made of wood, shaped in the form of a paddle. A page of reading material was tacked onto the wood under a sheet of horn, which was like a plastic covering. The reading material consisted of first the letters of the alphabet, then a list of two-letter words, and then a religious passage, such as the Lord's Prayer. There were no illustrations. The Puritans also brought hornbooks with them to the United States. Many children also used 'samplers', where similar written material had been sewn onto cloth (Huey, 1908).

In 1690, the *New England Primer* began to take hold in American schools. This primer dominated the education market for the next hundred years. It followed the traditional teaching pattern of learning the alphabet, followed by two-letter words, followed by lists of words of one syllable, two syllables, and so on. It included a number of religious passages and rhymes, as well as illustrations. For example, the letters of the alphabet each had a rhyme and an illustration (Huey, 1908). The rhyme for the letter X was 'Xerxes did die, and so must I'. Venezky (1995) noted that 'In the Calvinistic society of New England, religious training began as early as the child was able to hold a book.'

At the turn of the nineteenth century, the *New England Primer* gave way to *Webster's Spelling Book*, which was used throughout that century for teaching both reading and spelling. *Webster's Spelling Book* followed the traditional pattern of long lists of words, from short to long, and used the ABC method of teaching. This spelling book sold over 100 million copies (Balmuth, 1982). Why was it so popular? It appears that Webster was very adept at marketing his spelling book, making sales tours across the United States on a regular basis. It was direct marketing; he often rode on horseback from village to village selling directly to customers (Balmuth, 1982).

As the United States moved away from its religious early beginnings and became more of a frontier society, reading materials changed. Books were written more for the child's world than for issues that preoccupied the world of adults. The trend of reading education was toward the use of reading materials graded in difficulty level. With *McGuffey's Readers*, for example, children started with a primer consisting of simple, regularly spelled words and then moved through a set of six readers and anthologies graded in difficulty (Venezky, 1995). The McGuffey series, first published in 1850, was a best-seller.

By 1850 in the United States, the ABC method was receiving considerable criticism, especially from then secretary of the Board of Education in Massachusetts, Horace Mann. He was very critical of the meaningless reading exercises used in the ABC method. He attacked the system of first learning the alphabet letters, arguing that the 26 letters of the alphabet had 'as little variety as twenty-six grains of sand' (Balmuth, 1982, p. 190). Mann advocated the whole-word approach to teaching reading that he had seen used in Germany. He wanted children to read for meaning and recommended that they read regularly spelled, real words in their primers. After children had learned to read whole words, then they could learn to analyse words according to their component sounds, which he referred to as phonics. Mann's ideas were not accepted overnight; many teachers still defended the ABC method and regarded the idea of reading whole words as being as difficult as reading a foreign language.

The phonics method of teaching reading seemed to be gradually supplanting the ABC method toward the end of the nineteenth century in the United States. When you think about it, it was really only a small step to go from spelling the word 'cat' as 'see-ay-tee' to sounding out each letter, 'keh-ah-teh' says 'cat'; it was not a major innovation. But Mann's ideas about whole-word learning eventually gained more support than phonics. Huey (1908) concluded that the whole-word approach was a better way to learn to read. Huey wrote that new words were best learned by seeing them in a context that suggested their meaning, and not by focusing on words in isolation. He argued it was not necessary to pronounce all words correctly, as long as the child has grasped the overall meaning. If a child substituted a word that was different from the one on the page, yet still had a similar meaning, then this was 'an encouraging sign' (p. 349).

By the 1920s the whole-word 'meaning' approach seemed to have become the favoured approach. It found its best expression in the 'Dick and Jane' graded reading series, the Elson-Gray Basic Readers, whose main characters were Dick and Jane. These characters and their dog Spot came to represent the whole-word approach to reading. These were seen as real stories. They had 'family' characters and a plot. They used 'interest' words and were graded in difficulty. This type of reading series came to be known as 'basal' readers, and by the 1960s were staple reading material in almost all US schools (Balmuth, 1982).

### New Zealand reading 1900–1920: The ABC method

At the end of the nineteenth century in New Zealand, reading was still taught by using the ABC method, mostly with imported reading materials from Ireland, Scotland and England. Children started by learning the letters of the alphabet. Then they moved to reading two-letter words, three-letter words and so on. Price (1987) noted that 'the finely graded and structured reading was ingenious, but in the primers and infant readers it was excruciatingly boring to read, and difficult too' (p. 182). In 1900, New Zealand publishers Whitcombe and Tombs produced a new series, *The Imperial Readers*, although the stories still followed the traditional ABC approach. The first story in the First Primer began with 'I am on an ox. Lo! It is my ox.' The second story had three-letter words, such as 'A rat sat in a hat' (see illustrations below).

It is obviously difficult to write an interesting story using only two-letter words, but primers developed for Māori children in the

### Lesson B.

B. I am up on an ox.
c. lo! I am on my ox.
D. it is to go in ; so am I.
E. no, my ox is to go on.
F. am I by my ox?
G. no, I am on it ; so I am.
H. is my ox to go in ?
I. yes, it is to go in.
J. go in, my ox ; go in.

*'I am on an ox.' Page 6 from* The Royal Crown Primer, *published by Thomas Nelson, London, 1872.*

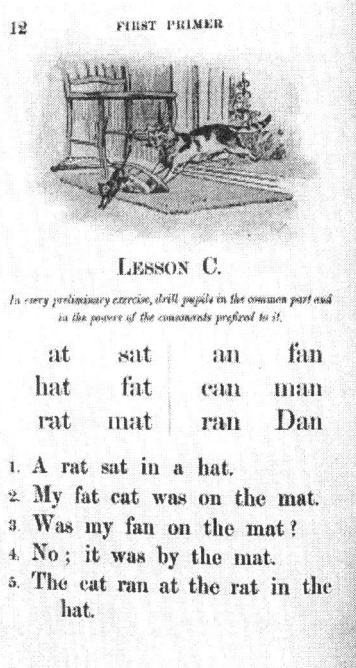

12          FIRST PRIMER

### LESSON C.

*In every preliminary exercise, drill pupils in the common part and in the power of the consonants prefixed to it.*

| at | sat | an | fan |
| hat | fat | can | man |
| rat | mat | ran | Dan |

1. A rat sat in a hat.
2. My fat cat was on the mat.
3. Was my fan on the mat?
4. No ; it was by the mat.
5. The cat ran at the rat in the hat.

*A rat sat in a hat.' Page 12 from the First Primer,* The Imperial Readers, *published by Whitcombe & Tombs, 1900. Reprinted with permission of Penguin Books (NZ) Ltd.*

1890s included words that teachers thought would be more relevant than the traditional 'I am on an ox.' Simon (1998) pointed out that in Native Schools, primers still included phonics but meaning was also stressed. In one reader, instead of the usual 'I am on an ox' and so on, Māori children read 'He is in my pa. If he is in my pa, I go to it. So do I. Do we go on? No. I am in my pa; so is he; he is in my pa. I go up to my pa. So do we' (p. 79). At the bottom of the page was a definition of 'pa' (a fortified place) and pronunciation clues: 'p-a, pa'.

In 1911 Whitcombe and Tombs replaced *The Imperial Readers* with *The Pacific Readers*. It was a new series, but the first primer still opened with a story of two-letter words, 'It is an ox. I am on it. Go up to my ox. Is he up on an ox? Yes. Is she on an ox? No, she is by me' (Price, 1992). This was very similar to the first primer of *The Imperial Readers*, published a dozen years earlier. Thus, prior to World War I, the method of teaching reading was still traditional, starting with the alphabet and then spelling out the letters of two-letter words, three-letter words and so on.

Looking back, learning to read was made more difficult because there were often not enough copies of the same reader to go around the class (Price, 1987). Also, children could not progress to the next class (or 'standard') unless they could read aloud the material in their current reader. Thus, there was an emphasis on rote memorisation so that pupils could pass their reading examinations. Ewing (1970) described the situation as follows: 'As the inspector's examination consisted of hearing each child read a few sentences from the reader in use in the class, the teacher naturally concentrated on this book. Unfortunately, the graded reader fitted so smoothly into the examination procedures that it became the only book used for reading lessons .... Had the inspector produced a different reader and asked the child to read from it, the number of failures would undoubtedly have increased, but teachers would have thought this an unfair innovation' (p. 66).

Price (1987) reviewed school inspectors' reports during that period. At many schools children were hardly able to read the simplest of material. Inspectors complained that children were made to memorise their text material so as to appear to be good readers. One inspector noted that '... children read as well with the book shut as open' (cited in Price, 1987, p. 188). Another complaint was that children would mindlessly chant their lessons in unison. A third complaint was that children were being asked to learn words by spelling them, even though this technique

*Classroom scene, probably a school in the inner city, 1919. Reprinted with permission, Alexander Turnbull Library, National Library of New Zealand.*

*Classroom scene, Woodcock's School, Rodney County, near Ahuroa. Reprinted with permission, Alexander Turnbull Library, National Library of New Zealand.*

distorted the sound of the word totally, as in 'tee, haitch, ee' spells 'the'.

To summarise, reading lessons in classrooms in the early part of the twentieth century involved lots of practice and drill in an atmosphere of fear and trepidation. Images of classrooms between 1910 and 1920 show children as not terribly happy. Class sizes also seemed quite large (see illustrations on previous page).

Ewing (1970) described it this way: 'Teachers "heard" the reading of individual children while all the others in the class, eyes firmly fixed on their own texts, followed word by word. On pain of punishment for failure, any pupil could be asked to "go on", or "give the next word". When a child stood up to read, he was often required to hold one hand behind his back in order to expand his chest and keep his back straight. Good expression and modulation in reading were qualities sought by the inspectors' (p. 66) (see illustration below).

Venezky (1995) noted that in colonial times in the United States there was also great emphasis on oral reading enunciation and good expression. Again, this reflected the needs of the time when it was very important to have good public speaking skills for professions such as law and the church. Oratory was very much part of the work skills needed for these positions. Oral reading of books and newspapers was common in families where not everyone might have been literate. These were not the days of radio and television. People were much more reliant

*A reading lesson? Christ's College, Christchurch, 1903.*

on the printed word for information about the world.

In colonial times in New Zealand, as in the United States, school was not a fun place to go. Children were not looked upon with kindness. According to Mathews (1966), children in United States schools were regarded as 'imps of Satan, and treated accordingly' (p. 78). It was the teacher's job to instil habits of discipline and obedience. In New Zealand, Price (1987) noted that 'It was widely held that positive education was completely the work of the school: "In the child there is a temple in ruins, which it is the aim of schools to remodel in all its positive beauty". There was no respect for the contribution of the pupil, whose interests and experiences counted for nothing' (p. 183).

### Reading 1920–1950: 'look and say' and phonics

What was teaching like in the years after World War I? Lowrie (1967) wrote a description of her years as an infant mistress from 1919 to 1949. In 1919 when she first started teaching, she was given a class of 60 to 70 children. She had a 'pupil teacher' to help her who had just left high school. She noted that infant schools were 'rather silent places' (p. 6), as children only spoke when spoken to. Children were

*Writing on slates. Makowhai School, 1909.*

not really unhappy, schools were just like that in those days. Children used slates and slate pencils; it was a few years after she started teaching that black-boards were introduced. She noted that one of the reading charts in her classroom had stories such as 'Is it an ox? It is an ox' (see illustration on previous page).

By the 1920s the ABC method was diminishing in importance. It had strong competition from the 'look and say' and phonics approaches. In 1895 Farnie had produced a manual for New Zealand teachers published by Whitcombe and Tombs that argued that the best 'modern method' (p. 44) of teaching reading was to combine the best elements of all three methods. In 1922 Whitcombe and Tombes published another reading series called *The Live Readers* that had a strong emphasis on 'look and say'. The author of the series was Miss Dorothy Baster, who had come to New Zealand from England with new ideas about reading (Price, 1997). In her teaching manual (Whitcombe & Tombs, 1922) she wrote: 'The method employed in this series of books is the complete reversal of the older Phonic method. In the "look and think" method of the *Live Readers* it is recognised that the average child has a good visual memory and finds no difficulty in retaining "word outlines" (p. 5).

The 1929 New Zealand Syllabus of Instruction (Education Department, 1929) recommended starting with a 'look and say' method, followed soon after by the teaching of phonics. The syllabus description was very

*Page from Book 1 of* Live Readers for the Modern Child, *published by Whitcombe & Tombs, 1922. Reprinted with the permission of Penguin Books (NZ) Ltd.*

clear in its attitude towards the ABC approach: 'It is hoped that the type of sentence common in the older books and reading sheets, such as "I am on the ox. Are you on? No, I am up" and similar absurd statements, has long since been abandoned in all schools' (p. 76). The syllabus recommended that children learn to read first with the 'look and say' method. When they had learned to recognise a few names and sentences, usually by the end of the first term of school, the teacher was to introduce phonics. The syllabus was very specific that skill in using phonics was the basis for a child being able to read independently without teacher help. Images of classrooms in the 1930s show blackboards with words that were a mix of look-and-say and phonics (see illustration below).

*Classroom scene, taken in Palmerston North, 1930s. Reprinted with permission, Alexander Turnbull Library, National Library of New Zealand.*

By 1930 in the United States, the situation seemed to be similar to New Zealand. Chall (1967) stated that by the 1930s the field had reached a 'consensus' (p. 13) about how best to teach beginning reading. The consensus was that children should start with meaningful texts that they could relate to and use the sense of the text to read 'whole' words. Only later should the whole words be analysed to discover letter–sound relationships.

Where did the idea of reading whole words come from? According to Anderson and Dearborn (1952), the whole-word (or 'look and say') method originated in ancient Greece with Aristotle and the principle of associative learning. It was described as a form of conditioning, in the same way as a cat thinks of food when you start opening a tin can. The printed word was the cue that made the child search his or her memory for the meaning of the word and its spoken form.

The 1930s was also a decade in which gestalt psychology was popular. The basic principle of this theory was that the whole was more than the sum of its parts (Crowder, 1982). The 'look and say' approach assumed that the child would initially identify a word by using gross strategies such as whether it was short or long. With practice, however, the child would gradually notice letter–sound correspondences (e.g. 'pet' and 'present' both start with the letter 'p', and both words have the same initial sound /p/). In this indirect way the child could infer the letter–sound rule that 'p' represented the phoneme /p/. In the 'look and say' approach, phonics was often introduced at a later point in the reading programme. For example, the teacher might take a known sight-word (e.g. <u>book</u>) and then

*Children reading. Newtown Schools, Wellington, 1939.*

write a list of similar words (e.g. big, but, bat), focusing on the initial /b/ sound of each word. The teacher would start with consonant sounds, then move to vowels and so on.

'Look and say' had been tried in the United States during the nineteenth century with good and bad results. Huey (1908) noted that the method went well at first, but broke down when children tried to read different reading material. Farnie (1895) also noted that a problem for 'look and say' was that 'the method is apt to engender a habit of guessing' (p. 43). Mathews (1966) noted that 'look and say' ideas fitted in well with the 'progressive' movement in education at the end of the nineteenth century along lines advocated by theorists like John Dewey, who argued that learning to read should be as pleasant as possible for children.

By 1930 New Zealand teachers had a wide range of materials to choose from. They could choose from the *Live Readers*, the *Beacon Readers*, and the *Progressive Readers*. The *Beacon Readers* were originally from the United States, but were adapted by the London publishing firm, Ginn. The *Beacon Readers* used both 'look and say' (with flashcards) and phonics. The first 400 or so words were to be learned as whole words. The primers included interest words such as 'mother' that were not necessarily simple to sound out. For example, a page from one of the first primers reads as follows: 'I can see my mother. I like my mother. Mother, Mother' (Grassam, 1922: 16). By delaying phonics in the early stages, the primers could start with more interesting stories. The *Beacon Readers* also had a programme for teaching phonics, although it was taught separately from the 'look and say' stories. The *Beacon Readers*

*Cover page*, Second Progressive Primer, *published by Whitcombe & Tombs, 1928–1931. Reprinted with permission of Penguin Books (NZ) Ltd.*

had some really interesting stories like *Chicken Licken* and *Three Billy Goats Gruff*, stories that are still popular with children.

In 1928, Whitcombe and Tombs published a new series, the *Progressive Primers*, that was very much a phonics-based reading series. There was a *Tiny Tots Primer* followed by a series of six *Progressive Readers* (see following illustrations). In 1940 a set of three 'Phonic Primers' was added to the series. The teachers' manual (Somerset, 1931) for the series was a wonderfully brief 64 pages. At the outset the manual stated that reading was about content and not sounds, and that words should be associated with 'ideas'. The manual recommended 'quick visualisation' of words in the initial stages until 30 words were learned; then the teacher was to introduce phonics. Although the manual made some concession to the importance of 'content', the suggestions for teaching were mostly phonics work. The *First Progressive Primer* itself was very phonic in terms of words used. Here is an extract:

May has a doll.
The doll has a doll's house.
A bed is in the doll's house.
The doll is not in bed.
Put the doll to bed, May.
The doll is in bed.
Hush! Hush!

26 ]

| *ie* |

### LITTLE BLACK PIG

| came | could |

"Grunt, grunt," said Little Black Pig. "I do not wish to stay in my sty. I do not wish to lie in the mud. I wish to fly. I think I can fly up to the sky. I shall try."

*'Little Black Pig.' Page from* Progressive Phonic Primers, *Book 2, published by Whitcombe & Tombs, 1928–1931. Reprinted with permission of Penguin Books (NZ) Ltd.*

There were competitors, but *Progressive Readers* dominated the market and they were what most schools used. Trevor (1941), New Zealand's first national reading adviser, surveyed 50 primary schools out of 329 in the Canterbury region. She noted that the Education Department only permitted schools to buy three published reading programmes: the *Progressive Readers*, the *Beacon Readers* and the *Live Readers*. The results of the survey showed that 'the great majority of teachers used two or more methods' (p. 38) of teaching reading, and that phonics was usually introduced in the latter part of the infant year. Trevor noted that 'the percentage of teachers using little or no phonics at all is very small' (p. 38). She reported that 74 per cent of the 50 teachers in the survey said they used both phonics and 'look and say' methods. Teachers still used the alphabetic ABC method, but only for teaching the names of letters. She found that 90 per cent (45 out of 50) schools used *Progressive Readers*, while only 28 per cent (14 out of 50) used the *Beacon Readers*, and 44 per cent (22 out of 50) used *Live Readers*. Twenty-seven schools (54 per cent) used a combination of the three published reading programmes.

Trevor thought infant mistresses were too conservative and 'loath to depart from the habits of a lifetime'(p. 61). She felt there was too much emphasis on phonics to the detriment of reading enjoyment. As

*Classroom scene, 1949. The children in this photograph were reading to their teacher from* Progressive Primers. *Reprinted with permission of the publishers, Learning Media Limited, Wellington.*

she put it, 'One teacher justified her early and subsequent use of phonics by saying, "Oh, but the children love them" – indeed a risky basis for deciding what is best for the child.' Trevor concluded, 'The so-called phonic method should not occupy the very dominant place it does in the teaching of reading in the group of schools studied' (p. 67). She recommended that the teaching of reading be adapted more to children's interests and experiences, away from the 'slavish pre-occupation with the mechanics of reading' (p. 68). She described infant classrooms in the Canterbury region as very unlike the homes that these five-year-olds had come from. There were few facilities for play, seat-work was excessive, and there was limited opportunity for adjusting to the individual needs of children. There was little opportunity for struggling readers to get appropriate instruction. Trevor noted, 'The children are put into groups as "repeaters" and find themselves doing the same work over again with younger children' (p. 66).

### 1950 to 1960: Janet and John

By 1950, the dominance of the *Progressive Readers* was coming to an end, although the end was unlikely to have occurred overnight. Classroom images, even in 1949, showed the *Progressive Primers* in use (see previous page). In 1949 the Education Department purchased a new reading series from England called *Janet and John*, published by Nisbet in London. *Janet and John* was an adaptation of an American reading series called *Jerry and Alice* published by Row, Peterson and Company (1938). Here are some lines from *Janet and John*, book 1, 'Here We Go':

> Janet
> John
> Come, John, come.
> Look, John, look.
>
> Little dog
> Come little dog.
> Come.
> Come and look.
> Janet, Janet.
> Come and look.
> See the little dog.

The concept of two children and a dog, although based on the *Alice and Jerry* series, was matched by the *Dick and Jane* series (Gray & Arbuthnot, 1958), which were also very popular in the 1940s and 1950s in the United States and Canada. Here is an extract from an early *Dick and Jane* primer:

> Jane said, 'Look!
> See how big I am.
> I am the mother.
> Dick is the father.
> Guess what Spot is.'
> (Scott, Foresman and Company, 1932: 12)

There were also similarities with the *John and Betty* series (Education Department of Victoria, 1951). Here is an extract:

> This is John.
> This is Betty.
> John can jump.
> Betty can jump.
> Betty can run.
> John can run.
> This is Scottie.
> Scottie can run.

The *Janet and John* stories revolved around a two-parent, two-child family and their dog. The purchase of the Janet and John series by the New Zealand Government was a big event. The teacher journal at the time, *Education*, published by the New Zealand Department of Education, had a copy of a page from the series in full colour ('The New Infant Readers', 1949). This was very unusual. At that time, most articles in *Education* were only illustrated in black and white. In the article, there was optimism that the new reading series would have the 'happy effect' of giving children 'at every stage a feeling of confidence and pleasure in their increasing ability' (p. 44).

There were four books in the *Janet and John* series, and seven in the New Zealand adaptation. The first book had 32 pages; the fifth book

Janet, Janet.
Come and look.
See the little dog.

*'Janet, Janet. Come and look.' Page from* Here We Go, *from the* Janet and John
*reading series by Mabel O'Donnell and Rona Munro, published by James Nisbet &*
*Co. Ltd, England (reprinted with permission).*

had 80 pages. New words were gradually introduced, at a rate of no
more than six new words in every 100. This was to avoid the problem
of children moving to a new book and suddenly finding it too difficult.
As Simpson (1949) put it, 'It sometimes happens that a child who has
been promoted to his first reading book sets out full of interest and
enthusiasm upon the adventure of learning to read. Later he may
meet difficulties, his interest flags, and reading becomes a worrying
and often a tearful business. In the past this was often due to the
deficiencies of the books – the uninteresting format, and the steepness
of the vocabulary progression. The *Janet and John* series attempts to
remedy these deficiencies' (p. 44).

The *Janet and John* series were similar in tradition to the *Live Readers* and the *Beacon Readers* in their use of the whole-word approach. In the *Janet and John* teaching manual (Education Department, 1956), teachers were advised not to teach any phonics until children had learned to recognise 400 words, which was about Book 4 of the series. Until then, teachers were asked to encourage children to use picture clues, length and shape of words, and context. In regard to context, the manual stated: 'Children should be taught, when they meet a difficulty, to read on to the end of the sentence and guess what the word is' (p. 22). The *Janet and John* approach was a remarkable change from the phonics of the *Progressive Readers*. For example, in 'Here We Go' (Book 1 of the *Janet and John* reading series), to recognise and remember the word 'kitten', children were asked to 'focus attention on the general shape or "pattern" of the word, noting that parts of it stick up "both at the beginning and middle"' (p. 48). When phonics activities were introduced later in the series, the approach was mostly to use 'word comparisons'. For example, to teach the word 'stood', comparison can be made with the word 'stop' which shared the same initial letters, and 'good', which shared the same final letters. In the New Zealand edition of the English series, phonics lists were provided in the last chapter of the teacher's manual. The lists were made of regularly spelled words from the *Janet and John* books (e.g. dug, jug, plug, snug).

An interesting aspect of the *Janet and John* approach was that children were not to be given a new book until they could read all the new words in the next book. The idea was to make reading the book a positive experience. It was suggested that teachers put the new words on the blackboard and review them with the class until they knew them. Thus, new words were learned before they were encountered in the next text.

Surprisingly, *Janet and John* have made a recent comeback in some English homes. *Janet and John* stories are the ones that baby-boomers remember with fondness from their school days. In an article in *The Daily Telegraph*, Parkin (1996) wrote that 'Lots of people think they are long dead, but *Janet and John* are in print and in some demand. Forty-seven years since they first appeared, the curly-haired boy and his pigtailed sister are still between limp covers, messing around in boats and on swings' (p. 21). Parkin goes on to say, 'Considering their age, they are remarkably free of prejudice. Mother is a bit of a shopper and Janet "helps". John makes a snowman, but she likes trains and is always in boats and up trees. True, the words "queer" and "darkie" appear in one book, but they are applied to dogs. Of course, it is a nostalgia trip for anyone who learnt with Janet and John. One look at the pictures of John in his all-over swimsuit, and Janet in her knicker-flashing Forties frocks, and a longing for a bottle of milk de-iced on the classroom boiler swept over me.' (p. 21).

The 'look and say' method underpinned the *Janet and John* reading series and other similar reading series in the 1950s. But this method was strongly criticised in a book called *Why Johnny Can't Read* (Flesch, 1955) that was published in the United States. Flesch criticised 'look and say' readers such as *Dick and Jane* for their lack of attention to phonics. The personal nature of the attack on 'look and say' elicited a defence from reading educators. An issue of *The Reading Teacher* in 1962 was entitled 'Johnny Can Read'. According to Crowder (1982), the essence of Flesch's argument was that 'Phonics gives a way of figuring out new words and connecting print, generally, with the spoken language already partially mastered. The whole-word system, typified in standard basal readers, was sacrificing these benefits in order to give children a cheap way of recognising the shapes of familiar words right off the bat' (p. 206).

Flesch's point was that the 'look and say' approach didn't help children discover links between letters and sounds. For example, the child might be able to read 'cat', but only because of an association with the 'cross thing' (t) at the end of the word. The child might read 'dog' because of the 'tail' (g) at the end of the word, without realising that the 'cross thing' was the letter 't', or that the tail was a 'g'. This kind of associative learning could eventually come unstuck. For example, if the child recognised 'dog' because of the 'tail' on the end, what happened when the child came across 'frog'? Wiley (1928) reported a number of errors of this type involving misreading of 'dog' as 'girl' because of the 'g'. This was the kind of criticism that was being levelled at reading materials that relied on a 'look and say' strategy for learning. Although children could learn to read that way, many might not.

### Beyond Janet and John: The 1960s

In 1960 the New Zealand Government decided to commission a new series to be produced in New Zealand. Price (1998) offered a financial explanation for the new series; that overseas funds were scarce and that the Prime Minister, Walter Nash, had rung the Education Department to ask if it was possible to publish a local reading series to replace *Janet and John*. John Ewing, Chief Inspector of Primary Schools, assured the Prime Minister that it could be done. The new reading series was called *Ready to Read*. Obviously the materials contained gender stereotypes: mother was in the kitchen; father was busy reading the newspaper. In some of the stories, the main characters lived in monocultural, middle-class surroundings. But gender stereotypes were also present in materials in other parts of the world at that time. Paul Smith (1991) wrote that in 1960s New Zealand, pupils went 'straight from school to a job or apprenticeship, to courtship, and engagement to the girl or boy of your dreams, to the home everybody assumed you would have simply because everyone else had one. For men, it was weekday work, weekend sport, and doing it themselves around their new homes; for women it was the kitchen and child-rearing in Nappy Valley' (pp. 7–8).

The new *Ready to Read* materials provided children with more story-like texts that related to their everyday lives, yet they weren't dramatically different from the readers of the 1950s. The images were still middle-class, with dad wearing a suit to work, picking up grandma at the airport and so on. But the stories had a New Zealand character and seemed more relevant to children's everyday experiences. The stories were graded in difficulty, written in so-called 'natural language', as opposed to sentences that were stilted or unnatural. The first primer titles were *Early in the Morning, Grandma Comes to Stay* and *The Fire Engine*. Here is an extract from *Early in the Morning*:

> Bill is asleep.
> 'Wake up, Bill,' said Peter.
> Sally is asleep.
> 'Wake up, Sally,' said Mother.
> Father is shaving.
> Father is here.
> Sally is here.
> 'Come to breakfast, Bill.'
> 'Come to breakfast, Peter,' said Mother.

Father is here.
Sally is here.
''Come to breakfast, Bill.
Come to breakfast, Peter,''
said Mother.

*'Father is here. Sally is here.' Page from* Early in the Morning, *from the Ready to Read reading series. Reprinted with permission of the publishers, Learning Media Limited, Wellington.*

There were 12 little books in the series and six miscellanies. The little books were graded in four different colours, with three of each colour: red, yellow, blue and green. The Department of Education (1969) published a vocabulary chart to assist teachers to know which words were used in each book. The teacher's manual (Simpson, 1962) gave suggestions for teaching phonics. The recommended procedure was to compare a new word with a known word of similar form. For example, in the first little book of the series the word 'shaving' appeared; in the second was the word 'shouted'. Teachers were encouraged to relate the new word 'shouted' to the previous known word 'shaving' and get children to note that both words started with 'sh'.

The instructional approach emphasised a wide range of reading strategies, but particularly use of context and picture clues for identifying unfamiliar words. Simpson (1962) stated: 'Reading for meaning should be thought of as a habit to be insisted on rather than as a skill to be taught. A child who has learned from the beginning to expect all reading to make sense, and who has not been allowed to get away with mere word calling, will be unlikely to make nonsensical guesses at a new word. He will instinctively use all the clues in his possession – the picture, his understanding of the situation in the story, the context in which the word occurs, and its phonetic elements. And if his first guess is wrong, he will often correct it himself' (p. 48).

This was called 'the method of teaching from the books as the need arose' (Simpson, 1962: 22). The aim of the new series was for children to learn to read by starting with the story and working out new words by focusing on meaning first. Rather than teach letters, sounds and words first, the teacher was to start with a book (a little book – about ten pages). What if children came to a word they could not read? Simpson (1962) argued that if the sentence was 'Today is Timothy's birthday', children might be able to read the printed word 'to', but not the printed word 'today'. Yet by using picture clues and reading the text again, they could guess the word correctly. According to Nalder (cited in Openshaw, 1991), Myrtle Simpson got the idea that children could learn to read 'using their natural language, through the experience of reading and talking through a story with an adult, probably a teacher or mature reader. Rather than having to be taught the words and taught phonics, they developed a reading system for themselves.'

In the *Ready to Read* reading series, phonetic analysis occurred when the teacher felt the children were ready for it and when there was an opportunity in the text material to illustrate a phonic principle. Phonics was taught when the child needed it, not as a matter of course. There was no sounding-out of words. Marie Clay (1967) reported a one-year longitudinal study of children learning to read with the new *Ready to Read* series. She concluded that children were able to learn to read this way, although she also indicated that some children were very slow to get under way and that this might be problematic.

The *Ready to Read* series was similar in many ways to the *Janet and John* series, in that the stories were graded, there were many 'interest' words that were not easy to sound out (e.g. mother, engine, aeroplane), and there was a strong emphasis on reading for meaning. Many of the characters in the stories were still monocultural and middle class, but *Ready to Read* was different in that new words were no longer pre-taught. Instead, they were taught in the process of reading the story. In *Janet and John*, new words had to be learned before reading the book. The *Ready to Read* series had moved toward much more use of context clues and visual clues in the story itself when children were unable to identify words. Another difference was the rate of introduction of new words in *Ready to Read* – a rate of one new word for every ten words. *Janet and John* had a rate of one new word in 20 (Randell, 1998). This meant that in the *Ready to Read* series the difficulty level from one primer to the next was greater. As a result, commercial publishers such as Price Milburn were asked to produce additional little books to make it easier for children to practise and learn the words of the new readers by reading them again and again in different stories (Randell, 1998).

## The 1970s

In New Zealand in the 1970s, the ideas of Myrtle Simpson (1962) were extended. The focus became very much learning to read by reading. Teachers were encouraged to use enlarged copies of stories (i.e. Big Books) so that all children could see the print when the teacher was reading to them. This was called the 'shared book approach' (Holdaway, 1979). In this approach the teacher read the blown-up copy of the storybook to the class and modelled certain strategies, such as predicting what a new word might be. Another recommended strategy was to look at the initial letters of the new word to see if the letters matched up with predictions.

These ideas were in line with researchers such as Ken Goodman (1970) in the United States and Frank Smith (1971) in Canada. In their writings they were giving theoretical support to the contextual approach. Goodman (1977), for example, argued that reading and listening were very similar: 'We understand that the listener or reader samples from the speech or print, predicts and assigns underlying structure and seeks meaning as efficiently as possible' (p. 312). Goodman analysed the reading errors made by children, which he called 'miscues', and concluded that many of their errors were meaningful. He argued that children should be encouraged to read for meaning, not necessarily for accuracy. They should be risk-takers, using context to help them read the meaning. It did not matter if they did not read the exact words on the page, as long as what they did read made sense. This was not 'look and say', and it certainly was not phonics. It was a theory that put a lot of emphasis on the power of context to help children read. In 1970, he published an article that reflected this view of the reading process, called 'Reading: A Psycholinguistic Guessing Game'. Thirty years later this theory is under much discussion because it now seems that poor readers rely on context more than good (Nicholson, 1991). Yet in the 1970s, the theory was very persuasive and fitted well with the New Zealand approach.

Children were encouraged to cope with difficult words by (a) reading to the end of the sentence, (b) re-reading up to the difficult word and then using meaning and syntax to guess what the word might be, and (c) using the first letter or letters to help. Teachers either used commercially produced Big Books or else made their own enlarged copies by hand. The approach also allowed for 'phonics in context'. For example, the teacher might place a frame around a word on the page of the Big Book, so that children could focus on a specific word (Holdaway, 1979). They might look at the initial letter, and work out what the word must be. This small amount of phonics was done in the context of reading. There was no listing of words in isolation.

During the 1970s, changes in reading materials and methods reflected changes in thinking about schooling. There was more emphasis on what the child brought to school in terms of their own language and experiences. For example, Sylvia Ashton-Warner's (1963) book *Teacher* emphasised the importance of getting children to talk about their own lives and using this as a basis for reading instruction. Ashton-Warner was a New Zealander who had taught Māori children in a country school in the 1950s. She found that a language experience approach was a way of bridging cultural differences. The children in her classroom wrote their own stories about their experiences. Ashton-Warner even produced primers for her Māori pupils, on topics that were relevant to their own lives. Only later did children move to the government-produced reading materials of the school such as *Janet and John*. Ashton-Warner elicited what she called 'organic' vocabulary from the Māori children she taught. The term 'organic vocabulary' referred to the words and expressions these children used to describe their innermost feelings. It was a powerful approach, although in hindsight it is not clear how much the approach contributed to children's reading progress. Ashton-Warner did a range of things in her teaching of reading, including teaching letter–sound relationships. She was a charismatic person and a dramatic teacher and writer. She produced some intriguing and powerful writing from her pupils. But she never reported grades or other reading data to verify the success of the approach.

Interestingly, when teachers used the language experience approach in the 1970s, a concern for many teachers was whether or not they should write down exactly what children said, even if it was ungrammatical (e.g. 'He ate too much foods.'). Another concern was whether the teacher rather than the child should write the story. Sylvia Ashton-Warner (personal communication, February 2, 1981), however, noted that 'This has never been part of my work at any stage, in any country. I've never written down a story dictated by a child. The only words for first reading are the words put on paper by the child himself, however few.'

Ashton-Warner raised issues that are still alive today. Should children write from their own experiences? Should they read books that use their own dialect form? Should they read materials that reflect the way they talk and the way they live? Ashton-Warner produced her own reading materials for Māori children using the children's own words. She called these books 'transitional readers'. The Department of Education at the time rejected them. It would be interesting to re-read the materials, but unfortunately she gave her only copies to a local teacher and they were accidentally destroyed. Hood (1990), in her biography of Ashton-Warner, recounted an interview that Hood held with a retired school inspector who explained to her why the readers were not viewed as suitable for children: 'The inspector said it [one of the readers] contained expressions from the pa [village] like, "I'll chop off your head!", which he felt was not the sort of thing that little children should be reading' (p. 50).

Was Ashton-Warner on the right track? The issue of dialect readers is still debated today. A school district in Oakland, California recently decided to use African-American dialect in their teaching. The argument is that using children's own way of talking acknowledges the value and legitimacy of their language. However, critics (e.g. Delpitt, 1988) argue that by emphasising African-American dialect, schools deny these children the opportunity to learn standard American English, which is the language of power in the United States.

*Whole language: The 1980s and early 1990s*

In the 1980s and 1990s the trend has been towards relying more and more on the use of 'authentic' children's literature as a starting point for learning to read. This is sometimes called the 'whole language', 'real books' or 'literature' approach. The theory is that children should read materials that are well written rather than 'contrived' so that the vocabulary is limited or controlled in some way. When the New Zealand Department of Education revised the old *Ready to Read* in the early 1980s, they followed this new trend. In the new series of readers, published in 1985, teachers were told that: 'Reading for meaning ... doesn't mean that children should dispense with actively learning about grapho-phonic cues', but that grapho-phonic learning should occur 'in the course of real reading and writing' (Department of Education, 1985: 42). The term 'real reading' was explained as reading done on 'text which the reader genuinely wishes to understand – it is not done on artificial or contrived exercises' (p. 42).

The 1985 'revised' *Ready to Read* stories were more 'real' than the 1960s *Ready to Read* stories. The books were written by professional children's authors who were told not to be constrained by factors such as vocabulary control (Randell, 1998). The approach was to write authentic, real stories that children could read for meaning. The stories were intended to be very predictable, with repetition of key phrases to help children predict the upcoming text words. The term 'predictable texts' was used for this kind of writing. Children could easily remember the stories almost word for word after listening to them just one or two times. The words in the books were not necessarily easy to decode. This was seen as less important than that the books be written so that children could use sentence context and memory for the story to predict upcoming words and sentences. Considering the whole-language approach, memorable texts meant that children could read and re-read the texts, and quickly learn to recognise the printed forms of the words. A problem for the theory, however, was that children could rely on their memory for the text and not attend to the print (Gibbs & Nicholson, 1999; Randell, 1998). Titles of the new stories at the primer level included *I Can Read*; *Boots for Toots*; *Going to the Beach*; *Our Teacher, Miss Pool*; and *What Does Greedy*

Push, push, push.

*'Push, push, push.' Page from* Going to the Beach, *written by Margaret Mahy and illustrated by Dick Frizzell, from the Revised* Ready to Read *reading series. Reprinted with the permission of the publishers, Learning Media Limited, Wellington, 1999.*

*Cat Like?* Here are the first two lines of *What Does Greedy Cat Like?* (Cowley, 1996):

> Greedy Cat likes paper.
> Greedy Cat likes string.

The grading of the revised *Ready to Read* series was more complex than in the 1960s. Each reader had a colour wheel (*An Introduction to Ready to Read*, 1993). The colours on the wheel were magenta ('emergent reading stage'); red, yellow, dark blue, and green (early reading stage); orange, light blue, purple, dark yellow (fluency). The wheel was a metaphor for a clock face. The idea was that children would gradually work their way around the clock, from magenta through to dark yellow. The suggested ways to use the reader were either for shared reading (teacher and children read together), for guided reading (more challenging material, with more teacher guidance and questioning), or for independent reading (children read on their own, practising their newly learned strategies). For example, the book *What*

*Does Greedy Cat Like?* (Cowley, 1996) has a colour wheel with an S (Shared Reading) on the magenta portion, which indicates it is suitable for shared reading with beginners. It has a G (Guided Reading) on the red portion, meaning it can be used for guided reading with children who have reached the next step along the wheel. The book also has an I (Independent Reading) for the light yellow portion of the wheel, which means it is suitable for children who have reached the next step along the wheel. If you think of a clock, the yellow portion is about a quarter after the hour.

There are now 96 titles in the revised *Ready to Read* series (Learning Media Literacy chart, undated), with 32 at the emergent stage, 32 at the early stage and 32 at the fluency stage. Twelve of the titles have been published as Big Books and there are 11 poetry cards with traditional (e.g. 'Sing a song of sixpence') and contemporary nursery rhymes (e.g. 'Humpty Dumpty sat on a chair, While the barber cut his hair'). In the new *Ready to Read* series, one interesting difference was that there was no vocabulary chart to assist teachers in knowing which new words were being introduced in each book as occurred in the 1960s series.

The theory behind the new series was that children should start to read by using books. In *Developing Lifelong Readers* (Mooney, 1988), published for the Ministry of Education, it was argued that 'Children do not learn to read in order to be able to read a book, they learn to read by reading books' (p. 3). It was argued that the 'wholeness' of reading (Mooney, 1988: 3) could only be achieved by reading for meaning. Reading was a meaning-getting process. By starting with the book itself, children would take advantage of picture clues and the language of the story to predict meaning. Letter–sound rules had a part to play, but mostly as a support strategy to confirm meaning. In *Reading in Junior Classes* (Department of Education, 1985) it was argued that children sample the text, predict what will happen, confirm their predictions and self-correct if their predictions don't fit with the sampled text. Advice for teaching children how to sample was given: 'Helping beginning readers to sample effectively means showing them how to attend only to those details of meaning and print which are necessary to make predictions, and to confirm or correct them' (Department of Education, 1985: 32). Children would take advantage of grammatical and meaning cues so that only a brief examination of 'grapho-phonic' cues was needed to confirm their guesses. It was argued that a beginning reader used exactly the same reading processes as a skilled reader. It was also stated that 'A slow-progress reader uses the same process as a high-progress reader. The only difference between them is how well each uses the process' (Mooney, 1993: 4).

### The late 1990s: Whole language versus phonics

Whole language became an influential reading approach around the world in the 1980s and 1990s. The approach was very similar to that which had been emerging in New Zealand from the 1960s onward. Yetta Goodman (1989), a proponent of whole language in North America, noted that 'With a holistic and progressive educational policy, New Zealand, influenced by John Dewey, disseminated a view of reading instruction that has had a lasting influence on the teaching of reading in the whole-language movement' (p. 118). The ideas underlying the revised *Ready to Read* series were similar to those of whole-language writers in North America (e.g. Goodman, 1970, 1976; Smith, 1971, 1973, 1975). Ken Goodman (1992) stated that "*Reading in Junior Classes* (Department of Education, 1985), the official New Zealand reading manual for junior school teachers, draws heavily on my work and that of other Americans" (p. 195). How popular did whole language become during the 1980s and 1990s in other countries? Here are a couple of indicators. Goodman (1992) noted that 'New Zealand and Australian publishers are selling more materials in the United States currently than they do in their own countries' (p. 195). Goodman also noted that his book *What's Whole in Whole Language* (1986) had at that time sold over 200,000 copies.

As we will later see, whole-language reading theory has been contested in the 1990s. The whole-language idea that a beginner reader uses the same reading processes as a skilled reader has also been challenged. However, it could be argued that the whole-language teaching approach may still be effective for many children even though the theory behind the method may not be correct. Juel (1995) has argued that the whole-language messenger (i.e. the theory of how children learn to read) might be wrong, yet the message (i.e. what the theory says about how to teach reading) may be correct. When reading 'real books' that are easily memorable, it is possible that children can intuitively discover letter–sound rules while reading and re-reading these books, thus making their own connections between letters and sounds without the specific help of the teacher. For example, children might note that the printed words 'sat' and 'mat' in the sentence 'Greedy cat sat on the mat' (from the story *Greedy Cat* by Joy Cowley, 1995) both end with the letters -at, and that this letter pattern in each word represents the spoken syllable /at/. Thus it can be argued that the revised *Ready to Read* series still enabled many children to learn to read. Is the approach as effective as it could be? We will come back to this issue later.

## Conclusion

What should we make of this short history of reading and writing? The history of our alphabetic writing system showed that there was a movement from using pictures to represent single objects, to using pictures to represent ideas, to using pictures to represent syllables. Along this path pictures became more symbolic, so that they no longer looked like the objects they originally represented. A final step in the history of the alphabet was to use symbols to represent phonemes. The alphabetic writing system, then, developed as a system for recording phonemes, the distinctive sound units within words. Thus, for thousands of years reading was taught by teaching the sounds that the alphabet stood for. Yet, over time, the ways words were pronounced began to diverge from the ways they were spelled. For example, the English writing system now has many words that have some irregularity in their spelling. There are also many borrowed words in English. The writing system is also morpho-phonemic, meaning that the spelling system is intended to reveal both sound and meaning. English spelling is basically phonemic, but not all words are easily 'sounded out'. This helps to explain why trends in reading instruction have tended, over the centuries, to swing from a meaning emphasis to a sound emphasis.

In the last hundred years in New Zealand, and in other countries as well, teaching methods have moved away from a bottom-up focus – that is, an exclusive emphasis on teaching how to sound out words. From at least the 1920s through to the 1940s, primers for children in New Zealand had a strong emphasis on phonics. Phonics was not too big a jump from the old ABC method. Primers had simple stories with words that were easy to sound out. In the 1950s the 'look and say' approach was given more emphasis, and phonics instruction was de-emphasised. From the 1960s on, especially in New Zealand, there has been much more emphasis on learning to read top-down; that is, starting with a story and learning to read by reading.

Where are we now? In many countries such as England and the United States, governments are making strong efforts to raise literacy levels. The reason is probably not so much a concern about the effectiveness of different reading methods, but concern with improving the competitiveness of their economies in an increasingly technological world. In the United States there has been a return to more traditional methods such as teaching phonics. Likewise in New Zealand, the recent Literacy Task Force government report noted that 'there is sound research that indicates that children should not rely on context as the primary or only strategy for working out unknown words but should also develop the use of word-level skills and strategies' (Report of the Literacy Task Force, 1999: 14). It seems that changes are occurring that represent not so much a pendulum swing back to phonics as a pendulum that has stopped swinging and is sitting in the middle.

## References

Adams, M.J. (1990). *Beginning to read: Thinking and learning about print*. Cambridge, MA: MIT Press.

Akmajian, A., Demers, R.A., & Harnish, R.M. (1984). *Linguistics. An introduction to language and communication* (2nd ed.). Cambridge, MA: MIT Press.

Anderson, I.H., & Dearborn, W.F. (1952). *The psychology of teaching reading*. New York: Ronald Press.

Ashton-Warner, S. (1963). *Teacher*. New York: Simon & Schuster.

*An introduction to Ready to Read*. (1993). Wellington, New Zealand: Learning Media.

Balmuth, M. (1982). *The roots of phonics. An historical introduction*. New York: McGraw Hill.

Bennett, J. (Producer) (1980). *The story of the alphabet*. London: Parker Films.

Boltz, W.G. (1996). Early Chinese writing. In P.T. Daniels & W. Bright (Eds.), *The world's writing systems* (pp. 191–199). New York: Oxford University Press.

Bond, G.L., & Dykstra, R. (1967). The cooperative research program in first-grade reading. *Reading Research Quarterly*, 2, 1–142.

Bonfante, L. (1996). The scripts of Italy. In P. T. Daniels & W. Bright (Eds.), *The world's writing systems* (pp. 297–311). New York: Oxford University Press.

Calfee, R.C., & Patrick, C.L. (1995). *Teach our children well*. Stanford, CA: Stanford University Alumni.

Chall, J.S. (1967). *Learning to read: The great debate*. New York: McGraw Hill.

Chomsky, N. (1957). *Syntactic structures*. The Hague, Netherlands: Mouton.

Clay, M.M. (1967). The reading behaviour of five-year-old children: A research report. *New Zealand Journal of Educational Studies*, 2, 11–31.

Coe, M.D. (1992). *Breaking the Maya code*. New York: Thames & Hudson.

Corballis, M.C. (1999). The gestural origins of language. *American Scientist*, 87, 138–145.

Cowley, J. (1996). *What does Greedy Cat like?* Wellington, New Zealand: Learning Media.

Cowley, J. (1995). *Greedy Cat*. Wellington, New Zealand: Learning Media

Crowder, R.G. (1982). *The psychology of reading*. New York: Oxford University Press.

Dahl, R. (1982). *The BFG*. London: Puffin.

Daniels, P.T. (1996). The study of writing systems. In P.T. Daniels & W. Bright (Eds.), *The world's writing systems* (pp. 1–18). New York: Oxford University Press.

Daniels, P.T. (1996). The first civilizations. In P.T. Daniels & W. Bright (Eds.), *The world's writing systems* (pp. 21–32). New York: Oxford University Press.

Delpitt, L.D. (1988). The silenced dialogue: Power and pedagogy in educating other people's children. *Harvard Educational Review*, 58, 290–298.

Department of Education (1969). *Ready To Read vocabulary chart*. Wellington: Author.

Department of Education (1978). *On the way to reading*. Wellington: Author.

Department of Education (1983). *Ready to Read*. Wellington, New Zealand: Author.

Department of Education (1985). *Reading in junior classes: With guidelines to the revised Ready to Read Series*. Wellington: Author.

Education Department (1929). *Syllabus of instruction for public schools.* Wellington: Author.

Education Department (1956). *Reading in the infant room. A manual for teachers.* Wellington: Author.

Education Department of Victoria (1951). *John and Betty. The earliest reader for the little ones.* Melbourne: Author.

Ewing, J.L. (1970). *The development of the New Zealand primary school curriculum 1877–1970.* Wellington: New Zealand Council for Educational Research.

Farnie, T.C. (1895). *Manual of school method.* Christchurch: Whitcombe & Tombs.

Flesch, R. (1955). *Why Johnny can't read.* New York: Harper & Row.

Flesch, R. (1981). *Why Johnny still can't read.* New York: Harper & Row.

Gelb, I.J. (1963) . *A study of writing* (2nd ed.) Chicago: University of Chicago Press.

Gibbs, C. & Nicholson, T. (1999). When you've heard it all before and still can't read. *Effective School Practices*, 17, 78–84.

Goodman, K.S. (1970). Reading: A psycholinguistic guessing game. In H. Singer & R.B. Ruddell (Eds.), *Theoretical models and processes of reading* (1st ed., pp. 259–272). Newark, DE: International Reading Association.

Goodman, K.S. (1976). Behind the eye: What happens in reading. In H. Singer & R.B. Ruddell (Eds.), *Theoretical models and processes of reading* (2nd ed., pp. 470–496). Newark, DE: International Reading Association.

Goodman, K.S. (1977). Acquiring literacy in natural: Who killed Cock Robin? *Theory Into Practice*, 16, 309–314.

Goodman, K.S. (1992). I didn't found whole language. *The Reading Teacher*, 46, 188–199.

Goodman, Y. (1989). Roots of the whole language movement. *The Elementary School Journal*, 90, 113–127.

Grassam, E.H. (1922). *The Beacon Readers Teachers Manual*, Aylesbury, England: Ginn.

Gray, W.S., & Arbuthnot, M.H. (1958). *Fun with Dick and Jane.* Toronto: W.J. Gage.

Growth in the garden (1999, January 27). *Education Week.*

Holdaway, D. (1979). *The foundations of literacy.* Sydney, Australia: Ashton Scholastic.

Hood, L. (1990). *Who is Sylvia? The diary of a biography*. Dunedin, New Zealand: John McIndoe.

Huey, E.B. (1908/1968). *The psychology and pedagogy of reading*. Cambridge, MA: MIT Press.

Juel, C. (1995). The messenger may be wrong, but the message may be right. *Journal Research in Reading*, 18, 146–153.

*Learning Media literacy K-3 programs*. Wellington, New Zealand: Learning Media.

Leu, D.J., & Kinzer, C.K. (In press). The convergence of literacy instruction and networked technologies for information and communication. *Reading Research Quarterly*.

Liberman, A.M. (1996). *Speech. A special code*. Cambridge, MA: MIT Press.

Liberman, A.M. (1997). How theories of speech affect research in reading and writing. In B.A. Blachman (Ed.), *Foundations of reading acquisition and dyslexia* (pp. 3–19). Mahwah, NJ: Lawrence Erlbaum.

Literacy strategy underway (1999, 25 January). *Education Gazette*, pp. 1, 3–5.

Lowrie, F.E. (1967). Infant schools yesterday and today. *Education*, 16, 6–10.

Mair, V.H. (1996). Modern Chinese writing. In P.T. Daniels & W. Bright (Eds.), *The world's writing systems* (pp. 200–208). New York: Oxford University Press.

Mathews, M.M. (1966). *Teaching to read: Historically considered*. Chicago, IL: University of Chicago Press.

Michalowski, P. (1996). Mesopotamian cuneiform. In P.T. Daniels & W. Bright (Eds.), *The world's writing systems* (pp. 33–72). New York: Oxford University Press.

Ministry of Education (1999). *Report of the Literacy Task Force*. Wellington: Author.

Mooney, M. (1988). *Developing life-long readers*. Wellington, New Zealand: Learning Media.

Nicholson, T. (1991). Do children read words better in context or in lists? A classic study revisited. *Journal of Educational Psychology*, 83, 444–450.

O'Connor, M. (1996). Epigraphic Semetic Scripts. In P.T. Daniels & W. Bright (Eds.). *The world's writing systems* (pp. 88–107). New York: Oxford University Press.

Openshaw, R. (Ed.) (1991). *Schooling in the 40s and 50s: An oral history (Research Resources No. 1)*. Palmerston North, New Zealand. Massey University, Educational Research and Development Centre.

Parkin, J. (1996, October 23). Janet and John – Read on. When it came to teaching her daughter to read, Jill Parkin found ... *Daily Telegraph*, p. 21.

Pinker, S. (1994). *The language instinct. How the mind creates language*. New York: Morrow.

Price, H. (1975). Lo! I am on an ox! *Education: A magazine for teachers*, 24 (unpaginated).

Price, H. (1987). Reading books and reading in New Zealand schools, 1877–1900. In R. Openshaw & D. McKenzie (Eds.), *Reinterpreting the educational past: Essays in the history of New Zealand education* (pp. 181–192). Wellington: New Zealand Council for Educational Research.

Price, H. (1992). *School books published in New Zealand to 1960*. Palmerston North, New Zealand: Dunmore Press.

Price, H. (1997). *The teaching of reading in New Zealand in the twentieth century*. Unpublished manuscript.

Price, H. (1998). *Ready to Read. A memoir*. Unpublished manuscript.

Randell, B. (1998). *Shaping the PM story books*. Unpublished manuscript.

Rayner, K., & Pollatsek, A. (1989). *The psychology of reading*. Englewood Cliffs, NJ: Prentice Hall.

Report of the Literacy Task Force (1999). *Advice to the Government on achieving its goal that 'By 2005', every child turning nine will be able to read, write and do maths for success'*. Wellington: Ministry of Education.

Row, Peterson & Company (1938). *The Alice and Jerry Basic Readers*. Evanston, IL: Author.

*Shared Reading* (1983). Wellington, New Zealand: Department of Education.

Scott, Foresman, and Company (1932). *Elson basic readers. Contents and sample pages*. Chicago: Author.

Simon, J. (Ed.) (1998). *Nga Kura Maori. The Native Schools system, 1867–1969*. Auckland: Auckland University Press.

Simpson, M. (1949). Preparing to use the new books. *Education*, 6, 46–47.

Simpson, M.M. (1962). *Suggestions for teaching reading in infant classes*. Wellington: Department of Education.

Smith, F. (1971). *Understanding reading*. New York: Holt, Rinehart & Winston.

Smith, F. (1973). *Psycholinguistics and reading*. New York: Holt, Rinehart & Winston.

Smith, F. (1975). The role of prediction in reading. *Language Arts*, 52, 305–311.

Smith, J.S. (1996). Japanese writing. In P. T. Daniels & W. Bright (Eds.), *The world's writing systems* (pp. 1–18). New York: Oxford University Press.

Smith, P. (1991). *Twist and shout: New Zealand in the 1960s*. Auckland: Random Century.

Somerset, G.L. (1931). *The teaching of reading to infants. A guide to the method of the Progressive Primer series*. Christchurch: Whitcombe & Tombs.

Swiggers, P. (1996). Transmission of the Phoenician script to the West. In P.T. Daniels & W. Bright (Eds.), *The world's writing systems* (pp. 261–270). New York: Oxford University Press.

The New Infant Readers (November, 1949). *Education: A magazine for teachers*, 2, p. 45.

Thompson, G.B. (1997). The teaching of reading. In *Encyclopedia of Language and education* (Vol. 2, Literacy).

Thompson, G. B. (1999). The processes of learning to identify words. In G.B. Thompson & T. Nicholson (Eds.), *Learning to read: Beyond phonics and whole language* (pp. 25–52). New York: Teachers College Press.

Trevor, R. (1941). *Reading in infant classes. The approach to reading in a group of Canterbury schools, considered in relation to recent developments overseas*. Unpublished Master's thesis, University of Canterbury.

The Janet and John books (1949). London: James Nisbett.

Threatte, L. (1996). The Greek alphabet. In P.T. Daniels & W. Bright (Eds.), *The world's writing systems* (pp. 271–280). New York: Oxford University Press.

Venezky, R.L. (1995). The history of reading instruction. In A.C. Purves (Ed.), *Encyclopedia of English studies and language arts*. New York: Scholastic.

Whitcombe & Tombs (1922). *Teachers' key to the Live Readers. An exposition of the best method for teaching reading to infants*. Christchurch: Author.

Wiley, W.E. (1928). Difficult words and the beginner. *Journal of Educational Research*, 17, 278–289.

# 3

# WHOLE LANGUAGE AND PHONICS: THE DEBATE

A friend of mine told me the following story. He had received an invitation to a book launching. The book was entitled *Sacred Soil*.

> His son, who was 12 years old, asked, 'Dad, what's this?'
> 'It's an invitation to a book launch.'
> 'Hmm. Scarred Soil.'
> 'No, it's not 'scarred'.'
> 'Scared Soil?'
> 'No, spell it out.'
> 'S-C-A (hesitation) No, S-A-C. Sack-red. Oh, Sacred.'

My friend wondered about this. His son had learned to read in a classroom which emphasised 'whole language'. He had misread 'sacred' but when asked what made him think 'scarred' he said that the cover of the book was illustrated with lots of cuts and lines (the book was about the New Zealand land wars.) In that context, 'scarred' was a meaningful error. He had shown good use of context, visual cues and some letter cues. But my friend could not help wondering, would his son have made this mistake if he had been taught in a phonics classroom? The aim of phonics is to read words correctly the first time you see them. His son would have read the word correctly. But would he have missed out on the visual cues, the scarred landscapes left by the New Zealand wars? These are the sorts of questions that arise when you come to discuss the pluses and minuses of phonics and whole language. Each method claims that it has qualities that the other method lacks. Each method claims that it produces a better kind of reader.

## Misconceptions

The popular opinion of the whole-language method is that children are taught to skip and guess as they read, without learning how to decode. The popular opinion of phonics is that children are taught to sound out words, without ever getting to read. Yet many children learn to read in whole-language classrooms, and phonics teachers are also very successful.

In the reading debate the observer views the differences in simple terms, looking at how children are affected by the different teaching methods. But to what extent are these ideas oversimplified? For example, an article in *Newsweek* magazine (Hancock & Wingert, 1996) used a very simple chart to summarise the pros and cons of whole language and phonics:

| Whole Language | Phonics |
|---|---|
| *Advantages*<br>• early emphasis on literature makes reading fun from the start<br>• words are learned in context with a goal of increasing overall understanding | *Advantages*<br>• strategies are learned for decoding new words<br>• tutoring may help bring kids with early reading problems up to grade level |
| *Disadvantages*<br>• if words are 'skipped' they may never be learned<br>• teachers often don't fully teach kids how to decode the alphabet | *Disadvantages*<br>• teachers may rely on 'skill and drill'<br>• emphasis on decoding practice may turn children off literature |

## The New Zealand Reading Approach

In the 1970s in New Zealand the natural language approach (later to be called 'whole language') was taking hold. It was a child-centred approach that built on the contexts and experiences the child already had. John Slane (1975), a New Zealand inspector of schools, argued that learning to talk had parallels with learning to read. First, he argued that children learn to talk in an atmosphere of parental support. The infant is never criticised for not talking properly. Second, the child wants to talk, to be able to talk with others. The child is motivated. Slane argued that schools did not provide these conditions. He blamed this on the 'experts' and the 'publishers' (p. 4). Reading was made competitive in schools. Children often had to read aloud in a group, which could be very distressing. Children were criticised by teachers and corrected if they were wrong. Unlike the home environment, in school, children were not allowed to make mistakes. Their approximations and efforts were not listened to. Slane argued that 'experts' had created stories for children to read that were controlled, limited and boring. He argued that this was a turn-off for children and was likely to kill the natural motivation that they already have for wanting to learn to read. Children needed 'memorable' (p. 6) stories that would motivate them to want to read.

Slane was critical of reading materials that heavily emphasised phonetic and structural analysis and 'rules of reading' (1975: 7). Slane concluded that children should be allowed to make errors and correct these errors themselves, in their own time. The child would learn to read by reading. He recommended that the teacher should be helping children to become independent, to teach themselves. Instead of teaching children phonetic and structural rules that don't work, he recommended that teachers should teach strategies with which children could help themselves:

'Try that sentence again.'
'Try reading on.'
'What word do you think would make sense there?'

Holdaway (1972), a teacher and reading adviser in New Zealand, had similar ideas about reading. First, he argued against 'teaching' reading, in that the idea of 'instruction' was a Western middle-class assumption about how children learn. Second, he questioned the idea of 'correction as a primary focus of teaching' (p. 8). He argued that the idea of 'correction' ran contrary to the way children learned to talk, which was to learn by approximating and self-correcting. Correction was negative feedback. Third, he argued against competition in the classroom, saying that it was designed to create an 'élite' (p. 8). He suggested that it was one reason why a quarter of children develop a 'failure complex' (p. 8). Fourth, he questioned the assumption that children only learn what the teacher teaches. He thought that a lot of what is taught is a turn-off for children, that forcing them to learn what is in the curriculum stops the natural learning process. Fifth, he questioned the assumption that learning is 'work' (p. 9). He felt that the work ethic in schools (e.g. 'get on with your work', 'work harder') signalled to children that reading is not about enjoyment, about meaning or about making mistakes. He argued that it sends a message to many children that they should feel inadequate and guilty.

Clay (1972) wrote a paper called 'Can we reduce failure to two per cent?' It was another indicator of a change in thinking about reading in the 1970s. She drew on her own research with New Zealand children in Auckland, arguing that to reduce the failure rate teachers must 'pick up and deal with each pathological effect as it occurs' (p. 26). The use of the term 'pathological' was a reference to work done in medicine to reduce infant mortality. She argued that infant mortality rates did not fall as a result of drastic changes in the health system, but in attending to specific negative agents that affected infants directly.

In learning to read, she argued that in every classroom a few children will become 'confused or tangled' (p. 27) and their problems go unnoticed. Clay argued for early identification of these confusions. In the 1970s, typically what happened was that all efforts were made to teach every child to read in the first three years of school. After that, if the child still struggled, he or she would be referred to a remedial clinic. Yet her research showed that it was possible to identify children in need of help well before that. She followed the reading progress of 100 five-year-olds in their first year of school. At age six, she ranked all 100 children according to what level of book they were reading. She found that this measure, which she called book rank, correlated very highly with reading tests at age seven ($r = .80$) and age eight ($r = .80$), so where a child was at six years of age in reading was very likely to be where the child would be at ages seven and eight. She found that the most important predictor of reading success in the first year of school was the ability to identify the letters of the alphabet. But she also felt that this was only one part of the key to success: children had to 'develop an effective set of strategies for discovering cues and relating cues' (p. 28).

Clay concluded that 'What is required is a system of strategies that work with all the intricacy and precision of a Rolls-Royce engine and not the inefficiency of a neglected Model T Ford' (p. 28). She felt that the best way to know whether a child's system of strategies was working well was to make regular records of the child's reading. The child should be monitoring and correcting his or her own reading. The child was to be encouraged to search for cues and check them. Teachers should keep graphs of children's progress in book levels across the school year to ensure that children are moving ahead. If children were not making progress, it might be because they were being progressed too quickly or used 'inefficient' cues (p. 31). She argued that schools should be committed to the concept of prevention, which meant small class sizes, time for observation of reading, a check of the child's progress at age six and a teacher who is 'well versed in individualised teaching techniques' (p. 32). She also hinted that, given the significance of the first year of school, teachers of those classes should be carefully selected.

These principles of child-directed learning, as set out by Slane (1975), Holdaway (1972) and Clay (1972), were very influential in determining the kinds of reading programmes offered in New Zealand classrooms during the next two decades. Notice that the key factors were the child being allowed to learn, to be allowed to make approximations, to be encouraged to be independent learners, and to develop an efficient system of strategies for reading. On the teacher's side, there was emphasis on understanding each child's needs, monitoring reading progress regularly, attending to ineffective strategies as soon as they occur, and having the skills of individualised teaching. These principles were incorporated into 'Reading in Junior Classes' (Department of Education, 1985) and later in 'The Learner as Reader' (Ministry of Education, 1996a). They were ideas that were also reflected in the whole-language approach in the United States and other countries.

### The New Zealand Approach in Action

The New Zealand approach in the 1960s was built on a series of graded readers called *Ready to Read*, which were updated in the 1980s (Ministry of Education, 1985). The New Zealand Government currently distributes enough copies for every child in every primary school in the country. Schools can and do buy other reading materials from other companies, but *Ready to Read* is the staple programme in schools. These graded reading materials are organised into three basic levels: *emergent*, where the reader is just starting to come to grips with the writing system and the nature of books; *early*, where the beginning reader starts to integrate three sources of information – meaning, structure and graphophonic; *fluency*, where the reader's attention to print detail diminishes and emphasis is on reading for a purpose. Reading stories and other texts to children is also part of the approach. The idea is to read stories regularly so that children enjoy reading for its own sake, and along the way learn some new words and ideas as well. Writing is also important. Shared writing, where the teacher models the process of writing and shows children how to spell, is part of the approach. Through writing and inventing spellings on their own, children are taught to listen to sounds in words and link these sounds to alphabetic letters. Writing is seen as an important way of acquiring knowledge of graphophonic cues – that is, letter–sound correspondences.

*Emergent stage.* Within each of the three basic reading levels – emergent, early and fluent reading – the teacher uses three different teaching approaches. The first is 'shared reading' with the emphasis on encouraging children to think what the primer might be about. Shared reading usually involves reading a book to the whole class. Often, a Big Book is read to the class. The teacher asks some preliminary questions. The rest of the shared reading is pretty much a straight reading of the text, perhaps with the occasional question to anticipate what might happen next. Children can follow up the shared reading by re-reading the text with the help of a read-along cassette or by reading to each other.

The next phase is 'guided reading'. The shared book reading is more in-depth, where children and teacher engage in more detailed discussion of the story before it is read, while it is being read and after it is read. Guided reading is usually done in small groups. Children are expected to integrate strategies during the shared reading. Meaning cues, grammatical structure cues and graphophonic cues are all attended to. Graphophonic cues are given more attention because the teacher points to each word while reading the story with the children.

The final stage at the emergent level is 'independent reading', where the child is expected to be able to read without teacher help. The teacher takes the child through the first one or two pages of the reader, and then lets the child complete the reading of the text. Usually the book given to the child is short, very predictable and memorable. The teacher is expected to monitor the child's reading to ensure that the child is 'not left to flounder' (Learning Media, 1985: 105)

*Early stage.* These three phases of reading instruction – shared, guided and independent – are used not just at the emergent stage, but at the 'early' and 'fluent' stages as well. At the 'early' stage, the shared reading is a little more challenging, in that the beginning reader is coping more effectively with text. The text materials are also more challenging in terms of word length, grammatical structure, predictability, vocabulary and ideas. Thus the shared reading involves more detailed discussion and questioning by the teacher before, during and after the reading. The questions still focus on predicting what will happen, drawing together children's prior experiences to help them understand the meaning of the story. The guided-reading phase is done in small groups, giving the teacher a chance to adapt the instruction to the needs of the group. The teacher may focus on enjoyment and discussion of the story, or on reading the words, perhaps asking children to read with their fingers under each word as they say it. Independent reading at the early stage means that the child will be able to read a more challenging story on his or her own and there is an expectation that the child is showing more awareness and knowledge of meaning, grammatical and graphophonic cues while reading. The idea is to get children predicting while they read, but at the same time verifying and confirming their predictions by reference to text cues.

*Fluency stage.* Shared reading at the 'fluency' stage is again more challenging. Children at this stage are reading quickly and accurately, which is the hallmark of fluency, and understanding what they read. They immediately recognise familiar vocabulary and pay less attention to print details. The main focus is on meaning and enjoyment. Shared reading of challenging text, for example, may involve looking at topics such as myths and legends, which are outside the everyday experiences of children. Children are encouraged to think about the nature of myths and legends and how they differ from other stories. Guided reading in small groups is designed to encourage more detailed reading, re-reading of specific parts of the text, quizzing children's understanding of what the text intends, and so on. Independent reading at the 'fluency' stage is designed to get children thinking while they are reading. The teacher will raise some open-ended questions for children to think about while reading 'outside the square' about the meaning of the text.

The important feature of the New Zealand approach as reflected in *Ready to Read* materials is the emphasis on learning to read in context. Instruction occurs in the context of reading of text. Children are given a lot of teacher assistance initially (emergent stage), but are gradually expected to become independent learners, making sure that predictions are consistent with grammatical and graphophonic cues (early stage). When children are able to read accurately and quickly on their own, they are thought to be at the fluent stage. Writing is also an important feature of the approach. Reading and writing are thought to be of help to each other. Children get ideas through reading; they learn a lot about letter–sound correspondences through their attempts at spelling. Children are expected to begin writing something, almost from the beginning. They are encouraged to invent their own spellings (first draft), to verify their spellings if possible (second draft), but always to write for meaning.

### Whole Language – Other Perspectives

In Australia, Turbill and Cambourne (1996) write that a whole-language teacher is a 'humanist at heart, who has a constructivist view of knowledge and learning operating within a postmodern society!' (p. 95). They note that labels are easily attacked and can be misunderstood, but that if there have to be defining labels, these labels define the whole-language teacher. Ken Goodman is said to be the founder of whole language in the United States, although his reply is that 'whole language found me' (Goodman, 1992: 188). What does 'whole' mean? Goodman (1989) writes, 'Whole language starts with the premise that the whole is more than the sum of its parts' (p. 208). He does not like reducing reading to 'skills'. Instead, he argues that reading and writing should always be in context. The 'whole' text is easier to read. Goodman and Goodman (1981) wrote that 'a story is easier to read than a page, a page is easier than a paragraph, a paragraph easier than a sentence, a sentence easier than a word, and a word easier than a letter' (p. 438).

Goodman (1992) described the process in terms of learning principles, such as 'starting where the learner is' and creating classrooms that are 'communities of learners' (p. 209). He says that whole language rejects teaching reading from part to whole (which puts it in conflict with the phonics approach). Instead, Goodman says that whole language insists on 'real reading and real writing from the beginning' (p. 210). A key point in this view of reading is that 'readers predict as they read, and use cues from their reading to confirm or disconfirm their predictions' (p. 212). Children develop skills in prediction by reading real texts written by children's authors, who write in a way that allows children to use real language as the basis of their predictions.

Goodman (1989) wrote that 'whole language *does* support the learning of phonics' (p. 215), but qualified this by saying that 'direct instruction in phonics is neither necessary nor desirable' (p. 215). Goodman also wrote that children 'learn spelling without direct instruction if they read and write' (p. 212). It is a belief of whole language that children learn phonics rules as part of the process of writing for themselves. Whole language very much sees the child as in control, as capable of inventing reading and spelling for themselves by reading and writing 'authentic' text, and by becoming sophisticated in the use of prediction, followed by use of print cues to confirm or disconfirm predictions.

Whole-language educators believe that children use their knowledge of language and its structure in order to learn to read. It is believed that just as children need to be surrounded by oral language in order to learn to talk, they also need to be in a rich language environment to become a reader. Mickelson (1993) defined whole language as 'the application of language acquisition theory to classroom practice' (p. 111). She cited Frank Smith (1971: 4): 'Children learn to read by reading and by being read to. Drills, exercises and rote learning play little part in learning to read.' She cited Vygotsky (1962), who argued that children can learn new things on their own as long as we provide assistance as needed. This assistance is like scaffolding. The child is given support until it is no longer needed.

Children are seen as 'readers' and 'writers', with opinions and ideas of their own that are important to capture. Teaching targets observed needs, and works within the child's 'language world' to promote literacy as functional and enjoyable. Authentic contexts are given for all writing. Quality children's literature is sought for reading. Children are encouraged to self-evaluate and self-monitor their own reading and writing as part of a language community in the classroom. This literacy-community feeling is created by providing a print-saturated environment. There are examples of writing everywhere. Books are everywhere. It is this experience of being in a community of readers and writers that enhances a child's ability to read and write. The key motivation to read and write will be that writing and reading is real and functional. The enjoyment of high-quality stories is in itself a powerful motivating force to read.

### Misconceptions about whole language

There are also some things that whole-language teachers say are common misconceptions. First, they *do* teach skills. They teach them when the need arises, and in the context of reading and writing. Second, they *do* evaluate, but they do it by way of recording children's reading and writing, analysing the extent to which children are acquiring the three main strategies of reading: meaning, structure (or grammar), and graphophonic strategies. They create portfolios of children's oral reading behaviours by carrying out 'running records', which are recording procedures for documenting the strategies children use when they are reading. They also keep examples of children's writing. They monitor children's knowledge of the alphabet and ability to write sentences from dictation. They also keep notes of their own observations of children at work, and instances of children's interactions that seem important to record. Third, it is argued that they *do* have structure, in that reading is taught when the child is ready. They provide help as the child needs it. Children have 'conferences' with the teacher to talk about their work, they read to the teacher on a regular basis, and the teacher works with them as they write stories.

Weaver (1996) contends that whole language is a 'constructivist' view of learning. Children aren't passive learners. They can learn for themselves, but not when reading is reduced to unnatural primer language like 'The cat in the hat'. Children need whole, natural language. Weaver also stressed that skills are taught in whole language but they are taught in context, through reading and writing. Phonics skills are taught while children are doing real reading and real writing. Teachers read Big Books with children, re-reading and discussing them. The teacher will highlight words that have phonics similarities as long as they crop up in the context of reading. Children also learn letter–sound rules through their writing and spelling.

*Whole language and writing*

Whole language emphasises writing as a vehicle for learning letter–sound rules. Children are given opportunities to write about topics they select for themselves, and they are encouraged to invent their own spellings. There is lots of sharing of writing with children reading their stories to one another, the teacher modeling how to write and giving individual guidance where needed. Children are *not* given formal spelling lessons and are not asked to memorise lists of words (Ministry of Education, 1996b). Instead, they are taught skills and strategies which will enable them to work out by themselves the spellings of unknown words. If they do not know how to spell a word, they are encouraged to 'have a go', to write down all the sounds they can hear in the word, to 'approximate' the correct spelling.

In a whole-language writing lesson, children are helped to invent their spellings by creating their own personal dictionaries of words they use frequently. Teachers encourage children to listen to phonemes in words as they attempt to spell them. For example, here is a suggested dialogue between teacher and pupil (Ministry of Education, 1996b: 67):

Teacher: What are you writing today, Jade?
Jade: Tommy and I broke the kitchen window.
[What happened was that Tommy kicked a rugby ball to Jade, she missed it, and it broke the kitchen window.]
Teacher: How will you spell broke?
Jade: I don't know.
Teacher: Say it slowly and listen to what you can hear.
Jade: br-o-k.
Teacher: What can you hear?

Jade: k?
Teacher: Great! Where does that come in the word? You listen: br-o-k.
Jade: At the end?
Teacher: Great! Put it down. Now let's listen again and see if we can get the start.

The teacher might encourage Jade, in this example, to think of another word that she knows, that has 'br' (e.g. 'breakfast). If the child still has trouble, the teacher might write the letters for her. Jade can probably spell the words 'I' and 'the' for herself. The teacher will let her work on 'kitchen' on her own, and come back later to help out. Jade is writing an authentic story. She is not circling letters on a worksheet or practising lists of words. Jade is taking ownership of her work. Jade is responsible for her own learning. The teacher is a coach and helper, not telling Jade what to do. Jade is taking risks, learning to write on her own. Skills taught in this way are learned effortlessly in the whole-language view. Context supports the learner, as she grapples with the spellings of new words.

Children also learn letter–sound rules while reading. In a whole-language classroom, children are encouraged to use graphophonic cues as one strategy for identifying a new word, but they are not encouraged to use sounding-out strategies as the first line of attack. Children are taught that when they meet a new word they should think about the probable meaning of the word, perhaps even read to the end of the sentence to clarify the meaning of the word. They can then verify the probable meaning by checking the first one or two letters of the word.

### Whole-language theory and New Zealand

Goodman wrote that 'reading, like listening, is a sampling, predicting, guessing process' (1970: 15). The belief is that the reader relies more on prediction and less on decoding the print. Goodman wrote, 'As the child develops reading skill and speed, he uses increasingly fewer graphic cues' (1967: 133). This is a very important aspect to whole language. For example, the New Zealand English Curriculum for levels 1 and 2 (Ministry of Education, 1994) states, 'students are encouraged to sample and predict, make approximations, and use cue sources to cross-check and confirm their understanding' (p. 77).

This is where whole language sees itself as different from phonics. In phonics, the first strategy is to sound out. The sounding out might be incorrect, but the child can revise this rough sounding out by using sentence context. In phonics, using context is a back-up strategy after sounding out, whereas in whole language it is the opposite. In whole language, sounding out is seen as a fickle friend because many words are spelled irregularly. In phonics, context is seen as a fickle friend because very few words can be accurately guessed from context.

### Whole-language strategies

Routman (1991, see also Pressley, 1998: 23) lists some of the strategies taught in whole language when children come to a difficult word:

* Skip the difficult word. Read on. Then go back.
* Re-read from the beginning of the sentence.
* Substitute a word that makes sense.
* Look for a known chunk of the word.
* Look for picture clues.

Pressley (1998) points out that there are problems with these recommendations in that they do not fit with research on what good readers actually do (Tunmer & Chapman, 1998). Sounding out words is what good readers do, yet this strategy is not on the Routman list. This reflects the whole-language emphasis on using context clues as the first strategy when they come to an unfamiliar word.

Whole-language educators say that they do teach phonics. Teaching phonics in a whole-language classroom can be done in the following ways (Weaver, 1996):

* In Big Book reading, draw children's attention to beginning and ending sounds of words. The teacher may cover up parts of a word, so that children focus only on one letter and its sound. The teacher may say the word slowly so that children hear the sound that the letter makes. This promotes phonemic awareness in a natural way, while reading in context.
* Charts of word families and words that start the same way can be used, but the words must come from the Big Books. Some Big Books

will have words with similar rhymes, like <u>cat</u>, <u>sat</u> and <u>mat</u>. These words occur in the story *Greedy Cat* (e.g. 'Greedy cat sat on the mat by the fridge'). The teacher can write these words on a chart to illustrate the <u>at</u> word family. This is acceptable in whole language because it teaches a phonics rule that is grounded in the context of a Big Book.

- Talk about letters and sounds as you teach children to write. The teacher asks the child to say the word slowly and to listen to beginning and ending sounds. The child then writes down the letters that correspond to those sounds. If they know the sound, they will be able to relate it to a letter that has the sound as part of its letter name. Or they may consult an alphabet card that has illustrations with each letter. The illustrations are a key to the sounds of the letters. The child can thus locate the appropriate letter for each sound they spell. In whole-language classes, writing is encouraged. This aspect of the writing lesson can help a child work out letter–sound correspondences. It is acceptable because children are engaged in a purposeful task.

These suggested activities provide contexts in which phonics teaching can occur. Is it possible, though, that the 'whole' can somehow obscure the parts? Is it possible that children can reach the 'whole' of reading by focusing on the parts separately? If reading is an orchestration of many finely honed skills, then maybe it is a good idea to work on them separately, so that the child does not have to compensate for weak skills by relying on other skills. This is the kind of thinking that underlies phonics.

### What is Phonics?

What advantage might phonics have over whole language? Adams (1990) made the point that most of the content words we read are unique and do not occur very often. How is the child to read these words if they have never seen them before? Carroll *et al.* (1971) found that 5,000 words accounted for 90 per cent of words in children's reading material. But the 5,000 frequent words were only five per cent of the total number of different words in children's reading materials. There were at least 80,000 other words that occurred very rarely in text, about one or two times per million words. These are the key words of reading, important for understanding (e.g. fever, disease, infection, medicine, penicillin, germs).

Phonics seems to come in many shapes and sizes (Adams, 1990). But let's look at one standard way of teaching phonics (a detailed explanation of how to teach phonics is in the appendix to this chapter):

- Children learn the sounds of the 21 consonants, not their names.
- Children learn to listen to the beginning and ending sounds in words.
- Children learn to write the letters of the alphabet by tracing them and making them in sand.
- Next the five short vowel sounds are taught
- Then come three-letter words. Adams (1990) suggests using phonograms (e.g. c-at). There are 27 phonograms to be learned.
- At the end of this initial teaching, children can recognise more than 150 words.
- Next are four-letter words, using longer phonograms (e.g. s-<u>and</u>, j-<u>ump</u>).
- After that are consonant digraphs (e.g. ch, sh, th) and blends (e.g. cr, sl).
- Finally, the five long-vowel sounds and the 'silent e' pattern are taught.

Notice the difference between this and whole language. There is often no reading of books in the early weeks of phonics teaching. Children learn the sounds of letters, then they sound out three-letter words, four-letter words, and so on. There is a hierarchy of learning, moving from the easy rules to the harder ones.

### Problems with phonics rules

How does phonics deal with words that are spelled irregularly? Groff (1983) carried out a study where he read a series of sentences aloud to children and in each sentence deliberately mispronounced a word. He was simulating the situation where a child had applied phonics rules but did not read the word correctly (e.g. read <u>find</u> as 'finned'; read <u>have</u> as 'hayv'). Groff found that 90 per cent of the time the children who listened to him read these incorrect words were able to figure them out, using the sentence context. Groff concluded that many words can be successfully read with phonics, as long as the child uses context as a back-up. The results of his study put some perspective on the much-cited studies of Clymer (1963), who found that many phonics rules did not work well because there were many exceptions. Yet Clymer may have been too strict on phonics. He did not take into account that context clues from the sentence might be a powerful back-up to sounding out.

### Other problems for phonics?

Adams (1990), although supportive of teaching phonics, has pointed out some problems:

- Many children don't know their alphabet. Phonics may be very frustrating for them.
- It is difficult to teach children letter 'sounds' when the names of the letters are often quite different to their sounds.
- Many words are irregularly spelled and are not easily sounded out (e.g. 'friend', 'laugh').
- Children learning phonics are often not given books to read until they have learned how to sound out words.

### Will Children Read Differently Because of Whole-Language or Phonics?

In a survey of 25 whole-language teachers, Nicholson and Lam (1998) found that the teachers did not usually recommend sounding out as the first line of attack for unfamiliar words. They preferred the child to think of a meaningful response, then use letter clues as a back-up. This is consistent with the whole-language way of thinking about the reading process. In contrast, phonics teachers would argue that the child should do it the other way around, use letter clues first to come up with an approximation to the spoken form of the word, and then use context clues to assist in working out the parts of the word that can't be sounded out.

Thompson (1999) argued that in whole language, where children are encouraged to do a lot of reading and re-reading of books, there are opportunities for children unconsciously to store the visual forms of words in memory, so that when they see the same words again they will recognise them from their memory of what the words look like. This is particularly possible in the New Zealand whole-language approach where children follow a carefully sequenced series of graded reading materials which are read and re-read (Thompson, 1993). Teachers are also encouraged to monitor children's oral reading progress on a regular basis, using 'running records'. What happens is that the child reads and the teacher records the number of words read correctly, and uses a special coding scheme to record the nature of incorrect responses made as children attempt words (e.g. 'hanging' misread as 'holding'). Teachers, sometimes on a daily basis, carry out these running records of children's reading of text and analyse the extent to which children are using the three main cueing systems: meaning, syntax and graphophonics. In addition, accuracy rate is calculated by the teacher, as well as the extent to which self-correction is taking place, which is where the child initially makes a mistake but then corrects.

Whole-language teachers are supposed to ensure that children read stories with at least 90 per cent accuracy. Anything less is said to detract from meaningful reading. The extent of self-correction indicates whether the child is using the three-cue system in the way intended, which is to cross-check the semantic and syntactic cues (e.g. 'holding' – does it make sense?) against the graphophonics cues (e.g. 'holding' – does it look the same as 'hanging'?). Lots of self-correction is said to indicate a healthy cross-checking of cue systems. This close monitoring of children's reading by teachers ensures that their reading accuracy and ways of identifying words are checked on two dimensions:

- Are they balancing the three-cue systems?
- Are they reading at high accuracy levels?

The net effect is that children's reading and re-reading of text material in the whole-language classroom should be at a quite high accuracy level, which in turn gives children high levels of accurate feedback about words. Whole-language writers stress that children should get accurate feedback about what the words on the page are. Techniques such as listening to stories read aloud on audiotape and 'buddy reading' where one child reads aloud to another all are intended to contribute to accurate feedback. Thompson (1999) has argued that this repeated correct matching of written and spoken words, again and again through reading, builds and strengthens orthographic visual storage of written words in memory. The whole-language practice of using 'predictable', memorable text where words are easy to guess, also provides opportunity for the build-up of orthographic memory for the visual forms of words.

In addition to orthographic storage – that is, visual storage of words – there are opportunities for children unconsciously to learn letter–sound correspondences by noting the sounds that letters make in various positions within words. For example, a child may be able to read words like 'happy', 'baby', 'you' and 'yellow' by recalling their visual forms from memory. But the child may also have formed, unconsciously, some letter–sound correspondences for each letter as well. For example, the child may have implicitly inferred that the letter *y* in each of these words has two different sounds, depending on whether it is the first letter or the last. A child may, without being told by the teacher, induce a rule that *y* at the end of the words has the 'ee' sound, but at the beginning of the word has a 'yeh' sound. Thus, without being directly taught letter–sound rules, children can acquire them in whole language through reading text. This source of knowledge is referred to as 'induced sublexical relations' (Thompson, 1999).

The difference between phonics and whole-language instruction is that when attempting an unfamiliar word, the phonics reader will use letter–sound rules to sound out an unfamiliar word, whereas the whole-language reader will use sublexical letter–sound patterns. If a whole-language reader has, for some reason, learned some phonics as well (perhaps from parents or the teacher), then the child has two knowledge sources available, both sounding-out rules from phonics and sublexical relations from whole language. These are the two main sources of knowledge but there are two other knowledge sources as well, identifying new words by making analogies to known words or word-parts (e.g. relating the -ent in went to the -ent in apartment) and identifying new words by using context clues. Thus, there are the four possible sources of knowledge available to children.

Is it possible that children might use all four knowledge sources? If a child attended a school where there was a mix of teaching methods – where both phonics and whole language were taught – would they not be able to build up a range of knowledge sources for identifying unfamiliar words? This may well be possible, although research suggests that children's strategies differ depending on the instructional emphasis of the school. Children can develop all four knowledge sources, no matter how they are taught, but the emphasis of the teaching seems to influence the extent to which children will rely on a particular knowledge source. Connelly, Johnston and Thompson (1999) reported data from 82 five- and six-year-old children: 41 in Scotland, where phonics is the preferred approach, and 41 in New Zealand, where whole language is used. The children in both countries were matched with each other in word reading ability, intelligence and vocabulary, so the Scottish sample and the New Zealand sample were virtually identical in terms of their ability to read words. What the researchers were interested in was *how* they read.

The Scottish and New Zealand children were asked to read a list of isolated words, as well as words in text. They were assessed on their comprehension of the text they read. They were asked to read a list of non-words. They were also assessed for spelling and phonological awareness. The results were striking. There were several differences in reading strategies between the Scottish and New Zealand children. When faced with an unfamiliar word the Scottish phonics children tended to 'attack' it by sounding it out. They were better at reading non-words, presumably because these words have regular spellings and could be sounded-out easily. They also made more nonsense mistakes in their reading, presumably due to their efforts to identify words via their letter-sounds.

In contrast, the New Zealand children were better at reading irregularly spelled words. They were also more likely not to give a word at all if they did not know it. The researchers called these attempts 'refusals' (Scottish children = 11 per cent refusals; New Zealand children = 46 per cent refusals). In other words, the New Zealand whole-language children were reluctant to sound out unfamiliar words, even though they did have some sounding-out skills. We know this because of their ability to decode some of the non-words in the non-word test (e.g. blum). They were not as good as the Scottish phonics children on this task (Scottish = 39 per cent correct; New Zealand = 17 per cent correct) but they did show some skills. The New Zealand whole-language children were faster at reading than phonics children, but phonics children had slightly better comprehension than whole-language children (Scottish children one month below average for their age, using British norms; New Zealand children five months below average for their age, using British norms). There was no clear difference between either group in spelling. Also, both groups had similar levels of phonemic awareness.

These data suggested two things. First, children in New Zealand and Scotland had acquired similar levels of word reading skill, although taught with very different methods. Second, children's reading strategies were influenced by the way they were taught. The Scottish phonics reader tended to 'attack' words, although this slowed their reading. The New Zealand whole-language reader tended to rely on words stored in memory. This access to the stored visual form of the word was quick, which explained why they were faster readers. However, if the word was not recalled from memory, they tended to say nothing rather than attack it. This presumably also made for faster reading since extra time was not spent sounding out. The Scottish and New Zealand children were all matched for word reading ability (not for reading comprehension), so no judgement can be made that one group was superior to the other in terms of word level skills. But they were different in their reading strategies, and there was a small difference in comprehension, favouring the Scottish children.

**Can Whole Language Be Improved?**

Replicating the Groff (1983) study, Tunmer and Chapman (1999) reviewed data from their own research with 67 six- and seven-year-old children in New Zealand which showed that a combination of graphophonemic information plus context can be very effective in identifying words that are spelled irregularly. Eighty words were deliberately mispronounced by the researchers. The mispronunciations were intended to simulate the sorts of mistakes that would be made if a child was trying to sound out an irregularly spelled word. The task for the children was to guess what the words really were. Children were able to guess 25 per cent of the meanings of these irregularly spelled words without any sentence context help at all (e.g. they guessed that 'stow-match' really meant 'stomach'). When given a sentence context for the word (e.g. 'The football hit him in the stow-match'), children were able to guess even more of the words, and were correct 66 per cent of the time.

In another experiment by Tunmer and Chapman (1999), 289 six- and seven-year-olds were asked to read 80 irregular words in isolation and in sentence context. They found that children were better able to identify the irregular words in sentence context, but that the children who were better able to do this were the ones who had better phonological recoding skills. What happened was that the irregular words were too hard for the poor readers to decode, whereas the better readers were able to decode more of each word, and so had better letter–sound information with which to guess each word. This enabled them to identify the irregular words better in context. This pattern of results showed that when given the same words to read, good readers do better in context than poor readers, not because they are necessarily better at guessing, but because they are better at phonological recoding. For example, a good reader who can sound out a word to the point where it sounds like 'stow-match' is in a better position to guess its meaning in the sentence, 'The football hit him in the stomach', than a poor reader who can only decode 'stomach' as 'stotch'.

Tunmer and Chapman (1999) have argued that a weakness of whole language is that it fails to give sufficient emphasis to the development of phonological recoding abilities. Instead it encourages a reliance on contextual strategies, which research does not support as a primary strategy. While not arguing for direct phonics instruction, especially not as 'drill and skill', they argue for a metacognitive approach that teaches children strategies for identifying words, by showing them how to create word families (e.g. hat, mat, cat), by adding and deleting letter-sounds. Another strategy is to teach children to analyse words strategically, looking for rhyme patterns (e.g. -at, -ain) that they already know. For example, if they know the rhyme pattern -all in the known word <u>ball</u>, then they can use this to help decode an unfamiliar word like <u>stall</u> or <u>wall</u>. Poor readers often have difficulty in thinking metacognitively about words. They learn words like a grocery shopping list, without looking for patterns. The metacognitive approach tries to make use of letter patterns in known words so as to read unknown words.

## Conclusions

Whole language and phonics are different. Whole-language teachers argue that if we teach children to read for meaning, they will soon learn for themselves how to identify words. But a problem for whole language is that relying on contextual strategies is not a good prognosis for learning to read. Researchers have found that the beginner reader and the poorer reader rely on context, but the good reader is able to read words independently of context. The good reader does not need context (Nicholson, 1991; Stanovich, 1980). Phonics teachers in contrast argue that if we teach children how to identify words accurately, then reading with meaning will follow.

A problem for phonics is that some children do not respond to phonics teaching. Gough (1996) found that ten per cent of children did not respond to this method. These children also did not acquire one of the essential prerequisites for learning to read – phonemic awareness. He has argued that both whole language and phonics do not give enough attention to phonemic awareness. In his provocative paper 'A pox on both your houses', Gough argued that a better, third, way to teach reading would be to teach phonemic awareness in preschool, to the point where pre-schoolers could segment the sounds in words fully. Then they could learn the sounds of the letters of the alphabet, given that they now knew what 'sounds' were. Then, through their own invented writing they could teach themselves the letter–sound rules of English. Gough noted that 'invented spellings', that is, words spelled according to their sounds even though the spellings are inaccurate, reflect understanding of the alphabetic principle. He suggested that some teaching of phonics rules (not too much) would be useful to point children in the right direction. Once children have some ability to decode words, then the best thing to do is start reading. This is the aspect of whole-language classrooms that is most important – to have children read. Gough reported timing the number of minutes children spent reading in a first grade classroom during a one-hour reading lesson, and found that children were reading on their own for a total of less than five minutes.

It is difficult for a teacher to choose between phonics and whole language. Phonics does focus attention on skills, and skills are important. In phonics there is a feeling that if the skills are right, then you will play a better game. But you can overdo skills as well. This is why whole language seems attractive. Children read 'authentic' stories. They write what they want to write. They are not hung up on spelling accuracy. But at the same time, some children do not develop the graphophonic skills that they must have in order to succeed. They rely on the semantic and syntactic cueing systems to the detriment of the graphophonic system.

## How is the New Zealand Approach Different from Other Whole-Language Approaches?

Hughes (1999) surveyed 92 teachers from a random sample of 20 primary schools across Auckland. She found that the vast majority of teachers had views of the reading process that were consistent with whole language. For example, when asked to write about the advantages of whole language, the teachers sampled were able to list many advantages. When asked to write disadvantages, very few were listed. In contrast, when asked to write advantages of phonics, very few were given, but when asked to write about disadvantages, a great many were listed. Yet almost all the teachers reported that they also taught some phonics.

The New Zealand approach to reading can provide opportunities for the teaching of phonics. Clay's (1972) notion of an intricate and precise system of strategies and the avoidance of inefficient strategies leaves open lots of opportunity to work on graphophonic skills if these are needed. An example of this opportunity to improve on the current New Zealand approach is a study by Tunmer, Chapman, Ryan & Prochnow (1998). They conducted a six-year longitudinal study of children's reading development in the Manawatu region of New Zealand beginning in 1992. In 1996 they began an instructional modification of the regular whole-language reading programme. New entrants (five-year-olds) in seven schools were involved in the study, a total of 77 children. Their teachers were taught to use a 'metacognitive' approach that was neither whole language nor skill-and-drill. Additional materials were introduced into the programmes of the new entrant classrooms. These included packages (Byrne & Fielding-Barnsley, 1991; Goswami, 1995; Lloyd, 1992) aimed at teaching phonemic awareness skills, knowledge of familiar phonogram patterns, the sounds of the letters of the alphabet, and some simple word-reading and spelling skills of phonics. The results showed that children who received the modified instruction were significantly better in reading and in attitudes to reading than a group of children of the same age who had been assessed with the same set of reading measures in an earlier part of the study in 1993, but who had not received a modified teaching programme.

The New Zealand whole-language literature lacks some of the philosophical terminology of the Australian and North American versions. It seems less ideological and more pragmatic. Words like 'constructivist', 'postmodern' and 'the whole is more than the sum of its parts' are not part of the New Zealand literature. The features of the New Zealand approach that are similar to whole language are the notions of child-centred learning, reading for meaning, and multiple-cue strategies. The pragmatic quality to the New Zealand approach is inclusive of incorporating ideas and teaching strategies that will improve children's systems of strategies for reading. New Zealand teachers are very autonomous. They have much opportunity to make adjustments and fine-tune their reading programmes. There is already a New Zealand research base to suggest that teachers could get some good results with some modification of existing programmes to include more phonemic awareness, alphabet and word-reading instructional activities, and supplementing whole-language activities such as shared book reading, guided reading and independent reading. There is a great deal of opportunity for drawing good ideas from both whole language and from phonics.

# APPENDIX: WHAT IS PHONICS?

### (CONTRIBUTED BY DORIS FERRY)

Phonics is not reading. However, it is an essential skill for successful reading (Adams, 1990). Learning a coding system enables a pupil to sound out letters and letter combinations and arrive at the pronunciation of a word. In English some words defy phonic analysis and must be learned by sight. Since many of these words are the commonly used ones, a beginning reader needs to meet them frequently in well planned, carefully structured graded reading books.

Phonics is not phonetics, which is a study of the sounds of spoken language. And it is not phonemic awareness, which is awareness that spoken words are composed of phonemes (Nicholson, 1999). It is a practical subject which breaks the language into small portions that are easier for the pupil to learn. The phonics teacher must have an extensive overview of the entire phonic system, but judiciously teach only a simplified form to beginners. With time the teaching can become more refined as the pupil matures in knowledge. Words initially taught as 'sight words' may later be shown to be part of a group or a rule. This technique of successively revealing detail is common in many areas of learning.

Systematic and effective teaching of phonics must occur, but the actual teaching needs to be achieved without destroying the joy of reading. For a beginning reader there is a bonus in the excitement of acquiring a new skill as well as enjoying the meaning. These aspects are a compensation for the mechanical process of 'cracking the code'. Children as young as four can be developmentally ready to absorb phonics quickly, whereas for older children these same skills can be an uphill grind. Little children can often enjoy the repetitive aspect of phonic drill and the repetition in early readers, necessary for reinforcement. By concentrating on building up a store of sight words and phonic skills they can sometimes quickly progress to reading books with stories that are relevant to their experiences.

Phonics relies on reading materials that reinforce phonics skills. Phonics uses context to assist with word identification, although mainly to confirm the meaning of a word after the word has been sounded out. The choice of reading books is critical for phonics instruction. These readers must have a constrained vocabulary of phonic and sight words to allow the pupil to concentrate on the meaning. An example of a phonics-constrained type of book is Dr Seuss' *Hop on Pop*. The first sentence is, 'Up, pup. Pup is up'. These sentences at first glance seem uninteresting, but Dr Seuss' illustrations and zany humour make him one of the world's best known children's authors.

### Phonics instruction

Phonics instruction should be approached with the awareness that some words will always be learned as 'sight words' (also called 'outlaws'). All children do not need the same amount of instruction. This does not mean that they should be given perfunctory phonics and left to discover the rest of the system for themselves. The optimum amount of phonics instruction for each child is the minimum that will result in becoming an independent reader. However, much greater depth of phonics knowledge is required for spelling. Phonics can be taught from the beginning of a reading programme. For this reason the following instructions are primarily directed at teaching the beginning reader, not the remedial reader. Phonics instruction can continue throughout the primary school years. The following information covers only the amount taught in the first two to three years of schooling.

*Sequence of instruction*

- beginning and ending consonant sounds
- short vowels
- digraphs and consonant blends
- plurals
- long vowels
- hard and soft 'c' and 'g'
- long and short 'oo'
- effect of 'r' on a preceding vowel
- vowel digraphs
- syllabication.

Note: In the following pages, spoken words will be in quotation marks. Spoken segments of words will have slash marks (e.g. /k/). Printed words or letters for instruction will be underlined. For ease of reading the international phonetic proper way to represent 'cat' is /kæt/ but I will write the sounds as /cat/.

### 1. Beginning and ending consonants

Learning to handle the beginning consonants is the first step in the development of a coding system. A good exercise is the well known 'I spy with my little eye something beginning with the sound …?'. Have a picture of a zoo, where the pupil finds the animal with a given beginning sound. End sounds are a little more difficult. In teaching, the end sound may be slightly elongated but not distorted. Exercises are useful for learning beginning and end sounds. For example, use pictures of 'sun', 'leaf', 'door'. Put the letter card d alongside the pictures. Ask the pupil to put a circle around the picture whose name begins with the letter on the card (answer is 'door'). Another example is to write the letters f, b, n. Then put a card with the number 10. Ask the pupil to point to the letter that stands for the ending sound of the number (answer is n). From the outset, stress the importance of

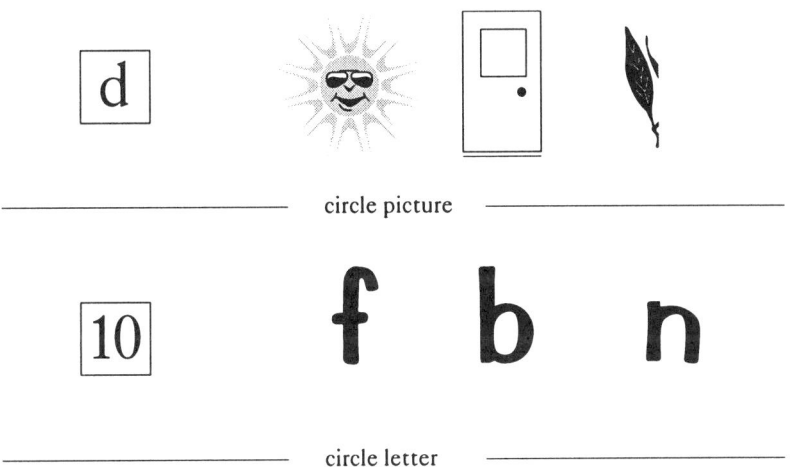

circle picture

circle letter

printing. Pupils begin by correctly forming the letters in sand (which is fun) and proceed to paper with ruled lines. Chalk-boards are useful for practice.

### 2. Short vowels

Show pictures of 'apple', 'egg', 'ink bottle', 'orange', and 'umbrella'. Write the short vowels that go with each picture, under each picture.

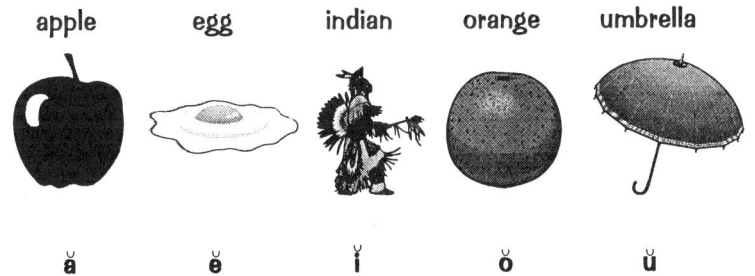

The short vowel sounds can be signalled with the breve mark ∪ as in căt written above each vowel. The long vowel sounds (e.g. the /a/ in 'cake') are the same sounds as in the names of the vowel letters and are usually taught later. The long vowel sounds can be signalled with the macron mark, which is a short horizontal mark ( – ) placed over the letter vowel in the printed word as in cāke. Children are ready now for three-letter words with consonants and medial short vowels. Do not teach these as sounds in isolation, eg. /c/, /a/, /t/ . Instead, use the phonogram[1] approach. In a phonogram pattern, the vowel combines with one or more consonants to form a rime. The rime is the part of the word that follows the initial consonant(s). For example, -at is a two-letter phonogram. To the children, call this the -at family.

This approach is recommended because vowel sounds can vary from one word to another. Wylie and Durrell (1970) found that vowel sounds were very stable and reliable if they were components of phonograms that were located at the end of words. Of 286 rime phonograms they studied, 95 per cent had consistent vowel sounds. Even more important, they found that by teaching just 37 high-frequency phonograms, pupils could in principle read nearly 500 words (see Table 3.1). Greaney and Tunmer (1996) found that teaching high-frequency phonogram patterns improved the word reading skills of below-average readers whose ages varied from nine to 11 years. These phonogram patterns can be found in Greaney (1994).

To ensure that you never hear the word 'boring' applied to phonics, be sure to have hands-on equipment and games. For example, use a magnetic board for placing letters and 'families' (e.g. -at, -og, -up). The -at family is demonstrated on the magnetic board by adding '-at' to appropriate consonants as the pupil pronounces each word.

| b | -at | m | -at |
|---|-----|---|-----|
| c | ↓ |  | ↓ |
|  |  | p |  |
| f |  | r |  |
|  |  | s |  |
| h |  | v |  |

Similarly, many other words can be formed by adding consonants to the following phonograms:

---

[1] A phonogram is a closed syllable which begins with a vowel, ends with a consonant, and which produces a single speech sound.

**Table 3.1: Phonogram Chart**

| -ack | -ail | -ain | -ake | -ale | -ame | -an |
|------|------|------|------|------|------|------|
| -ank | -ap | -ash | -at | -ate | -aw | -ay |
| -eat | -ell | -est | -ice | -ick | -ide | -ight |
| -ill | -in | -ine | -ing | -ink | -ip | -ir |
| -ock | -oke | -op | -ore | -or | | |
| -uck | -ug | -ump | -unk | | | |

| -<u>am</u> | -<u>ad</u> | -<u>ag</u> | -<u>an</u> | -<u>ap</u> | | |
|-----|-----|-----|-----|-----|-----|-----|
| -<u>et</u> | -<u>en</u> | -<u>eg</u> | -<u>ed</u> | | | |
| -<u>ip</u> | -<u>im</u> | -<u>ib</u> | -<u>ig</u> | -<u>ill</u> | | |
| -<u>ot</u> | -<u>ob</u> | -<u>og</u> | -<u>od</u> | -<u>oll</u> | -<u>ox</u> | |
| -<u>ub</u> | -<u>ud</u> | -<u>ug</u> | -<u>up</u> | -<u>um</u> | -<u>un</u> | -<u>ut</u> |

Another piece of hands-on equipment is a cardboard wheel for each phonogram where a circle with the consonants printed around its curcumference, turns on a base. As you turn the circle, each consonant links to a specific phonogram (e.g. r-at). As the wheel turns, different consonants appear in front of the 'at' (e.g. <u>r</u>, <u>p</u>, <u>b</u>, <u>c</u>, <u>f</u>, <u>h</u>, <u>m</u>, <u>s</u>).

Another hands-on idea is a set of cards with the word printed on one side and a picture depicting the word on the other side; for example, the word 'cat' on one side and a picture of a cat on the other. The cards are placed on the table picture side up and on a separate piece of paper the pupil writes the word and then turns the card over to verify that the spelling is correct.

Many long words have within them a three-letter word with a short vowel as a component. Pupils may easily recognise longer words in context simply by observing a three-letter word as part of a longer word.

At the end of this programme pupils can read and spell more than 150 words. These exercises can be a lot of fun. However, it is worth emphasising again that phonics taught remedially can be tedious.

The short vowels in four-letter words can also be taught through phonograms:

-<u>and</u>, -<u>ist</u>, -<u>est</u>, -<u>elt</u>, -<u>end</u>, -<u>ust</u>, -<u>ump</u>, -<u>ond</u>
e.g. <u>sand</u>, <u>hand</u>, <u>land</u>, <u>band</u>, <u>nest</u>, <u>rest</u>, <u>best</u>

At the same time you do this, teach the end-of-word sounds:

-<u>ng</u>, -<u>ck</u>, -<u>nk</u>
e.g. <u>bang</u>, <u>back</u>, <u>bank</u>, <u>sing</u>, <u>sick</u>, <u>sink</u>.

All this and following instruction can be taught with moveable magnetic equipment, reinforced with workbook activities and phonic reading books.

### 3. Digraphs and consonant blends

It is necessary to explain to pupils the difference between digraphs and consonant blends. With a consonant blend the two sounds are blended, that is, there are still two sounds (e.g. <u>tr</u>-, <u>cl</u>-), while in a digraph the two letters make a single sound (e.g. <u>ch</u>, <u>sh</u>, <u>th</u>, <u>wh</u>).

  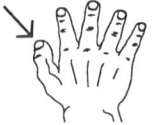 

### (i) Digraphs

Use pictures of key words (e.g. 'ship', 'whale', 'chick', 'thumb'). Show children which picture goes with which word. Write the words under the pictures. Underline their first sounds (e.g. <u>sh</u>, <u>th</u>, <u>ch</u>, <u>wh</u>).

| <u>sh</u>ip | <u>ch</u>ick | <u>th</u>umb | <u>wh</u>ale |
|------|------|------|------|
| <u>sh</u> | <u>ch</u> | <u>th</u> | <u>wh</u> |

The pictures can be displayed on the floor, or on a magnetic board. Here is <u>sh</u> as an example, used at the beginning and at the end of words:

| <u>sh</u> | <u>ip</u> | d<u>i</u> | <u>sh</u> |
|------|------|------|------|
| ↓ | <u>op</u> | f<u>i</u> | ↓ |
|   | <u>ut</u> | w<u>i</u> |   |
|   | <u>in</u> | s<u>a</u> |   |
|   | <u>ot</u> | m<u>a</u> |   |
|   | <u>ell</u> | r<u>u</u> |   |

Here the teacher will be aware of later additions such as <u>tch</u>, <u>ph</u>, <u>gh</u>, and the three sounds of <u>ch</u> (as in <u>church</u>, <u>chemist</u> and <u>machine</u>), although <u>ch</u> as in <u>chair</u> is by far the most common. There are also the two sounds of <u>th</u> (as in <u>think</u> and <u>them</u>). Initially, however, only the simple sounds should be taught to young children.

It may be possible for the teacher to invent funny sentences which use the 'sh' sound. These could be read to pupils to reinforce the 'sh' sound. A delightful dictionary by Scholastic (now out of print) had the 'sh' sound presented in amusing illustrations and sentences such as 'Show me a showered and shampooed sheep with shiny shoes and I'll show you a sheep in sharp shape'.

*(ii) Consonant blends (also called clusters)*

*a. Two-letter blends*

| | |
|---|---|
| r-clusters | fr, cr, br, gr, dr |
| l-clusters | gl, fl, bl, sl, pl, cl |
| s-clusters | sk, sp, sn, sw, sc, st, sm |

The entry for fl in the dictionary mentioned above is 'flamingo flapping, flamingo flying, flamingo doing flips in flight, flamingo doing a flat flop in the flowers'.

*b. Three-letter blends*

spl, str, spr, squ

*Digraphs combined with another letter*

thr, shr, sch, chr

For beginning pupils teaching is confined to the two-letter blends. For example, children are shown a picture of a 'clock' and asked to choose which consonant blend represents the first two phonemes in 'clock' (e.g. give a choice of cl, gl, bl). Again, for these use a magnetic board. Some examples of blends to illustrate:

| st ← op | pr ← am | sl ← ap | cl ← ock |
|---|---|---|---|
| ↓ | ↓  ↓ | ↓ | |
| dr | tr | sn | bl |
| pr | cl | tr | fl |
| cr | sl | cl | st |

Another technique for teaching consonant blends is a blends chart (Nicholson, 1999, see Table 3.2).

### 4. Plurals in s and es

There is a rule which says, 'es comes after s, ss, x, ch, sh, and tch'. Make it simple by clapping to hear the syllables.
Cats has one syllable: add s to cat.
Foxes has two syllables: add es to fox.

### 5. Long vowels

The long vowels are the letter names. So far only short vowels have been involved. Moving to the long vowels needs careful preparation. Pupils must hear the different sounds of the long and short vowels. Teachers could use different colours for the long (blue for long) and short vowels (red for short), or a symbol above the vowel (macron and breve) to indicate either it is a short (use the breve) or long sound (use the macron).

### (a) Silent e (also called magic e)

With magnetic letters, pupils add 'e' to short vowel words and change the breve mark to the macron, indicating that the vowel is now long. Thus prepared, 'silent e' becomes a real adventure.
Examples:

| mă̆t | māte | hŏp | hōpe |
| ră̆t | rāte | rŏb | rōbe |
| hĭd | hīde | cŭb | cūbe |
| rĭp | rīpe | tŭb | tūbe |
| bĭt | bīte | cŭt | cūte |

Combining digraphs, blends and silent e, pupils can now successfully sound out words like:
complete, athlete, concrete

### (b) The multiple spellings of long vowels

ai, ay, oa, oe, ow, ee, ea, ie, ue, ew

The same vowel sound can be spelled in a number of different ways. The chart below shows some of the common spellings of each of the vowel sounds. It must be admitted that the long vowel sounds and their various spellings present the greatest difficulty. For example, we have:

**Table 3.2: Consonant blends and digraphs (Nicholson, 1999)**

| | | |
|---|---|---|
| **bl** | **br** | **ch** |
| black<br>blind<br>blue<br>block | brain<br>branch<br>bread<br>bridge | cheese<br>chair<br>chase<br>chicken |
| **cl** | **cr** | **dr** |
| clown<br>class<br>clean<br>climb | crab<br>crane<br>cricket<br>cry | drum<br>drink<br>dream<br>drive |
| **fl** | **fr** | **gl** |
| flower<br>flag<br>flies<br>floor | frog<br>free<br>fresh<br>friend | glass<br>glove<br>glue |
| **gr** | **kn** | **ph** |
| grapes<br>grandma<br>grandad<br>green | knife<br>knee<br>knock<br>know | phone<br>photo |
| **pl** | **pr** | **qu** |
| plane<br>plate<br>play<br>please | present<br>pretty<br>prize | question<br>quiet<br>quick<br>quiz |

| | | |
|---|---|---|
| 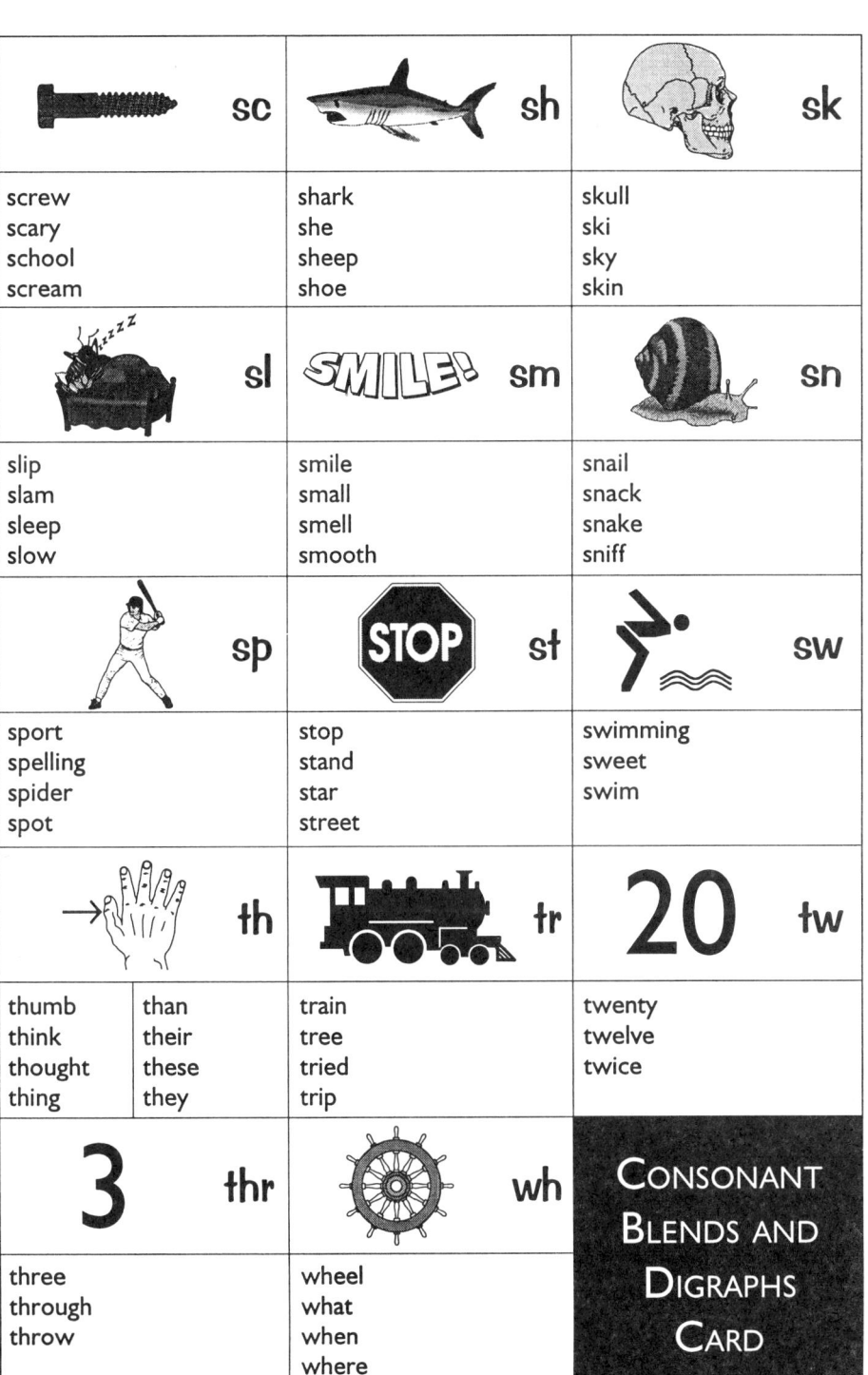 **sc** | **sh** | **sk** |
| screw<br>scary<br>school<br>scream | shark<br>she<br>sheep<br>shoe | skull<br>ski<br>sky<br>skin |
| **sl** | **sm** | **sn** |
| slip<br>slam<br>sleep<br>slow | smile<br>small<br>smell<br>smooth | snail<br>snack<br>snake<br>sniff |
| **sp** | **st** | **sw** |
| sport<br>spelling<br>spider<br>spot | stop<br>stand<br>star<br>street | swimming<br>sweet<br>swim |
| **th** | **tr** | **20 tw** |
| thumb   than<br>think   their<br>thought   these<br>thing   they | train<br>tree<br>tried<br>trip | twenty<br>twelve<br>twice |
| **3 thr** | **wh** | **CONSONANT BLENDS AND DIGRAPHS CARD** |
| three<br>through<br>throw | wheel<br>what<br>when<br>where | |

| | |
|---|---|
| sail | sale |
| road | rode |
| meet | meat |

You can practise these different spellings on a magnetic board, or use a scrapbook approach, with a page for each vowel sound.

The page can be divided into four columns. The different phonic patterns can be coded, as in red for vowels, green for consonants, blue for blends and underline silent letters. These cues can be useful in the initial learning stages. You can drop them later as pupils become more confident. As new words are dealt with, they can be written into the correct columns to fit the long vowel pattern, as shown in the examples below:

| ă | ā/e | āi | āy | |
|---|---|---|---|---|
| mat | mate | rain | day | |
| trap | plate | snail | play | |

| ĕ | ē/e | ēa | ēe | |
|---|---|---|---|---|
| pet | Pete | seat | tree | |
| bed | these | teach | sheep | |

| ĭ | ī/e | īe | y | |
|---|---|---|---|---|
| big | like | pie | my | |
| sick | bite | tie | why | |

| ŏ | ō/e | ōa | ōe | ōw |
|---|---|---|---|---|
| not | home | boat | toe | tow |
| dog | stone | road | goes | snow |

| ŭ | ū/e | ūe | ew | |
|---|---|---|---|---|
| cut | cute | due | new | |
| cup | tune | cue | few | |

Pupils can find it exciting to discover they can now spell even long words such as:

| | | | |
|---|---|---|---|
| continue | rescue | Tuesday | avenue |

Other long vowel sounds can be learned as phonograms:

| | | | | |
|---|---|---|---|---|
| no | go | so | | |
| me | be | he | we | she |
| old | bold | cold | sold | hold |

The following are some useful rules to guide teachers. Pupils may not need to know them word for word, but they should be aware that there are spelling patterns to follow:

**Rule 1.** After a short vowel, spell /k/ as ck. After a long vowel with silent e, spell /k/ as k only.

| | |
|---|---|
| back | bake |
| tack | take |
| snack | snake |

**Rule 2.** After a short vowel, double the consonant before adding the suffix. After a long vowel with a silent e drop the e and add the suffix.
Adding the suffixes ing and ed:

| | | |
|---|---|---|
| hop | hopping | hopped |
| hope | hoping | hoped |

**Rule 3.** At the end of a word the digraph ch becomes tch after a short vowel

| | | | | |
|---|---|---|---|---|
| catch | fetch | ditch | notch | Dutch |

The exceptions are: much, such, rich, which.
A pupil of mine once wrote the word clutch. His father, sitting in on the lesson, said 'I am a motor mechanic. In future I too will put t in clutch'. [It seemed that the father used to spell clutch as cluch.]

### 6. Hard and soft 'C' and 'G'

c has the hard sound of /k/ in cat, cage and can.
c has the soft sound of /s/ in city, cent and mice.

Phonograms are helpful:

face    race    place    rice    mice    nice

g has the hard sound of /g/ in gate, goat, dog, gum (if followed by a, o, u).

g has the soft sound of /j/ in gym, gem, giant (if followed by e, i or y).

At the end of a word the /j/ sound is written dge as in judge and bridge, but ge following n or r as in orange, large.

### 7. Long and short 'oo'

Examples:

| oo | oo |
|----|----|
| moon | book |
| spoon | good |
| rooster | stood |

### 8. Effect of 'r' on a preceding vowel

The ar and or present no problems. Use the phonic wheel approach described earlier. For most children er, ir and ur have the same sound and are more difficult. For example:

| ar | | er | | ir | | or | | ur | |
|----|----|----|----|----|----|----|----|----|----|
| f ↓ m | | t ↓ m | | b ↓ d | | f ↓ m | | b ↓ n | |
| sh | k | f | n | g | l | sp | t | h | t |

### 9. Vowel digraphs

These are two-vowel combinations that usually have a single sound:

ai and ay        oi and oy        au and aw

Pupils pronounce stimulus words, noting that each pair has the same sound:

ai and ay in rain and play
oi and oy in boil and boy

au and aw in Paul and paw

Some vowel digraphs have two sounds and are more difficult (e.g. ow as in cow and row; ea as in beach and bread). Hands-on techniques such as the phonics wheel  are useful or a digraph chart (Nicholson, 1999, Table 3.3 on the following two pages) could be used for practising these spelling–sound patterns.

### 10. Syllabication

This can be made easy with a game. Each player has a large card with 16 pictures where the number of syllables for the pictures vary. There is a spinning top with the numbers one to four. Players spin the top in turn and place a counter on a picture that has the same number of syllables as the spinning top indicates. The winner is the first player to cover all the pictures in the card. Pupils clap to count the syllables. Words like radio (3 syllables) and rhinoceros (4 syllables) are a challenge.

Another technique is to teach children that each syllable has a vowel. When they come to a long word, they should look for the vowels. A good idea is to underline the vowels. The syllable will include the vowel and one or more consonants before the vowel, and sometimes after it. For example, the word window has two vowels. It helps to draw a line just after the vowel, as in win/dow. Then sound out each syllable one after the other. If a word ends in an e, this may be a silent e. Tell children that the silent e may not indicate another syllable, since it has no sound (e.g. cho/co/late). There are exceptions to this silent e rule though (e.g. ter/rib/le), where e is not a silent e. Also, for vowel digraphs (e.g. team) tell children to count the two vowels as one.

### Review

Phonic dictation can be used to consolidate the work that has been done. Pupils can write sentences that have phonic patterns. Every mistake the pupil makes should be corrected. Pupils are given the correct answers and they make the corrections. Children actually enjoy dictation.

Phonic reading materials are important. They are sometimes called 'decodeable text' (see Figure 3.4 on p. 122). Juel and Roper-Schneider (1985) have argued that if children are taught phonics then it is

**Table 3.3: Vowel Digraphs (Nicholson, 1999)**

| Aa | al | ar | ai |
|---|---|---|---|
| | ball<br>call<br>fall<br>talk | car<br>far<br>park<br>party | mail<br>paint<br>rain<br>sail |
| | ay | | aw |
| | pray<br>day<br>play<br>say | | saw<br>law<br>raw |

| Ee | er | ea | ea |
|---|---|---|---|
| | butter<br>her<br>perfect<br>were | beach<br>read<br>seat | head |
| | ee | | ew |
| | teeth<br>bee<br>beetle<br>feed | | screw<br>few<br>new<br>grew |

| Ii | ir | ie | |
|---|---|---|---|
| | bird<br>Sir<br>birthday | piece | |

| | | |
|---|---|---|
| **or** horse<br>for<br>fork<br>more | **oa** boat<br>coat<br>goat<br>loaf | **oi** oil<br>boil<br>join<br>noise |
| **oy** boy<br>joy<br>toy | **oo** boot<br>roof<br>moon | **ou** house<br>found<br>shout |
| | **oo** book<br>cook<br>foot | **ou** soup |
| **ur** surf<br>fur<br>hurt | **ow** snow<br>tow | |
| | **ow** cow<br>owl<br>now | **VOWELS DIGRAPHS** |

**Figure 3.4: Example of decodeable text for beginners (Nicholson &
Lee, 1999)**

Nat the Rat

In the jet.
On the mat.
On the hat.
On the cap.
On the lap!

Get the net.
Not on mat.
Not on hat.
Not on cap.
Not on lap.

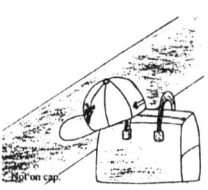

On the mat.
On the hat.
On the cap.
On the lap.

On the run.
In the net.
Not on jet.

Nat is sad.
Nat not bad.
Dad not mad.
Mum not sat.
Nat is glad.

important to reinforce these skills by using decodeable text (e.g. picture books like Dr Seuss' *Hop on Pop*) and lots of practice, so that children can successfully apply the phonics they have learned. Teachers should follow up the decodeable book reading with some open-ended questions to signal to the child that comprehension is also important.

## References

Adams, M.J. (1990). *Beginning to read. Learning and thinking about print.* Cambridge, MA: MIT Press.

Byrne, B., & Fielding-Barnsley, R. (1991). *Sound foundations: An introduction to pre-reading skills.* Sydney, Australia: Peter Leyden Educational.

Carroll, J.B., Davies, P., & Richman, B. (1971). *Word frequency book,* Boston: Houghton Mifflin.

Chomsky, N. (1957). *Syntactic structures.* The Hague, Netherlands: Mouton.

Clay, M. M. (1972). Can we reduce failure to two per cent? In D. Holdaway & V. Shumaker (Eds.), *Reading: A local and an international challenge* (pp. 26–32). Auckland: Auckland Council of the International reading Association.

Clay, M. M. (1991). *Becoming literate: The construction of inner control.* Auckland, New Zealand: Heinemann.

Clymer, T. (1963). The utility of phonic generalisations in the primary grades. *The Reading Teacher, 16,* 252–258.

Connelly, V., Johnston, R. S., & Thompson, G. B. (1999). The influence of instructional approaches on reading procedures. In G. B. Thompson & T. Nicholson (Eds.), *Learning to read: Beyond phonics and whole-language,* (pp. 103–123). New York: Teachers College Press.

Cowley, J. (1996). *What does greedy cat like?* Wellington: Learning media.

Department of Education (1985). *Reading in junior classes, with guidelines to the revised* Ready to Read *series.* Wellington: Author

Flockton, L., & Crooks, T. (1997). *Reading and speaking: Assessment results 1996,* Wellington, New Zealand: Ministry of Education.

Foss, D. J., & Hakes, D. T. (1978). *Psycholinguitics.* Englewood Cliffs, NJ: Prentice Hall.

Goodman, K. S. (1967). Reading: A psycholinguistic guessing game. *Journal of the Reading Specialist, 4,* 126–135.

Goodman, K. S. (1970). Behind the eye: What happens in reading. In

K. S. Goodman & O. S. Niles (Eds.), *Reading process and program*, (pp. 3–38). Urbana, IL: National Council of Teachers of English.

Goodman, K. S. (1989). Whole-language research: Foundations and development. *The Elementary School Journal, 90*, 207–221.

Goodman, K. S. (1992). I didn't found whole-language. *The Reading Teacher, 46*, 188–199.

Goodman, K., & Goodman, Y. (1981). Twenty questions about teaching language. *Educational Leadership, 38*, 437–442.

Goswami, U. (1995). *Rhyme and analogy.* Oxford: Oxford University Press.

Gough, P.B. (1996, February). *A pox on both your houses.* Paper presented to symposium on integrated direct instruction in reading, sponsored by the Language Arts Foundation of America and Oklahoma City Schools, Oklahoma City.

Greaney, K. (1994). *Vowel Phonograms Test/Teaching Kit.* Kanuka Grove Teaching Centre, Palmerston North, New Zealand

Greaney, K. T., Tunmer, W. E., & Chapman, J. W. (1997). Effects of rime-based orthographic analogy training on the word recognition skills of children with reading disability. *Journal of Educational Psychology, 89*, 645–651.

Greaney, K., & Tunmer, W.E. (1996). Onset/rime sensitivity and orthographic analogies in normal and poor readers. *Applied Psycholinguistics, 17*, 15–40.

Greaney, K., Tunmer, W.E., & Chapman, J.W. (1997). Effects of rime-based orthographic analogy training on the word recognition skills of children with reading disability. *Journal of Educational Psychology, 89*, 645–651.

Groff, P. (1983). A test of the utility of phonics rules. *Reading Psychology, 4*, 217–225.

Groff, P. (1983). A test of the utility of phonics rules. *Reading Psychology, 4*, 217–225.

Hancock, L. N., & Wingert, P. (1996). If you can read this ... you learned phonics or so its supporters say. *Newsweek*, p. 75.

Holdaway, D. (1972). Reading for the 70s: The challenge in New Zealand. In D. Holdaway & V. Shumaker (Eds.), *Reading: A local and an international challenge.* Auckland: Auckland Council of the International Reading Association.

Hughes, C. (1999). *Teachers' perceptions of the methods and practices employed in the teaching of reading and language arts.* Unpublished Master's thesis,

The University of Auckland.

Juel, C., & Roper-Schneider, D. (1985). The influence of basal readers on first grade reading. *Reading Research Quarterly, 20, 135–152.*

Juel, C., Griffith, P. L., & Gough, P. B. (1986). Acquisition of literacy: A longitudinal study of children in first and second grade. *Journal of Educational Psychology, 78,* 243–255.

*Learning Media Literacy K-3 programmes* (undated). Wellington: Learning Media

Lenneberg, E. H. (1967). *Biological foundations of language.* New York: John Wiley.

Lloyd, S. (1992). *Jolly phonics.* Essex, England: Jolly Learning.

Mickelson, N. (1993). Whole-language: Philosophy, implementation and evaluation. In C. J. Gordon, G. D. Labercane & W. R. McEachern (Eds.), *Elementary reading: Process and practice,* (pp. 111–122). Needham Heights, MA: Ginn.

Ministry of Education (1994). *English in the New Zealand Curriculum.* Wellington: Learning Media.

Ministry of Education (1996a). *Dancing with the pen.* Wellington: Learning Media.

Ministry of Education (1996b ). *The learner as a reader: Developing reading programmes.* Wellington: Learning Media.

Nicholson, T. (1991). Do children read words better in context or in lists? A classic study revisited. *Journal of Educational Studies, 83,* 444–450.

Nicholson, T. (1999). *At the cutting edge. Learning to read and spell for success* (2nd ed.). Wellington: New Zealand Council for Educational Research.

Nicholson, T. (1999). *Phonics blends and digraphs cards.* Unpublished manuscript, The University of Auckland.

Nicholson, T. & Lee, I. (1999). *Nat the Rat.* Unpublished manuscript, The University of Auckland.

Nicholson, T., & Lam, R. (1998). Whole-language teachers and phonics: Not 'do they?' but 'How much is enough?'. *Set: Research information for teachers,* 2, Article 6.

Pressley, M. (1998). *Reading instruction that works: The case for balanced teaching.* New York: The Guilford Press.

Routman, R. (1991). *Invitations: Changing as teachers and learners K-12.* Portsmouth, NH: Heinemann.

Slane, J. G. (1975). *Sense and nonsense in teaching reading.* Auckland: Auckland Council of the International reading Association.

Smith, F. (1971). *Understanding reading.* New York: Holt, Rinehart & Winston.

Stanovich, K.E. (1980). Toward an interactive-compensatory model of individual differences in the development of reading fluency. *Reading Research Quarterly, 21,* 32–71.

Thompson, G. B. (1993). Reading instruction for the initial years in New Zealand schools. In G.B. Thompson, W.E. Tunmer & T. Nicholson (Eds.), *Reading acquisition processes* (pp. 148–154). Clevedon, England: Multilingual Matters.

Thompson, G. B. (1999). The processes of learning to identify words. In G. B. Thompson & T. Nicholson (Eds.), *Learning to read: Beyond phonics and whole-language.* New York: Teachers College Press.

Thompson, G. B., & Fletcher-Flinn, C. M. (1993). A theory of knowledge sources and procedures for reading acquisition. In G.B. Thompson, W.E. Tunmer & T. Nicholson (Eds.), *Reading acquisition processes.* Clevedon, England: Multilingual Matters.

Tunmer, W. E., & Chapman, J. (1999). Teaching strategies for word identification. In G. B. Thompson & T. Nicholson (Eds.), *Learning to read: Beyond phonics and whole-language.* New York: Teachers College Press.

Tunmer, W.E., Chapman, J.W., Ryan, H.E., & Prochnow, J.E. (1998). The importance of providing beginning readers with explicit training in phonological processing skills. *Australian Journal of Learning Disabilities, 3,* 4–14.

Turbill, J., & Cambourne, B. (1996). Guest editors' introduction. *The Australian Journal of Language and Literacy, 20,* 94–98.

Vygotsky, L. S. (1962). *Thought and language.* Cambridge, MA: M.I.T. Press.

Weaver, C. (1996). *On research on the teaching of phonics.* Fact sheet. Heinemann

Wyllie, R.E., & Durrell, D.D. (1970). Teaching vowels through phonograms. *Elementary English, 47,* 787–791.

# 4

# THE SEARCH FOR THE BEST READING METHOD

In 1967, a landmark book was written by Jeanne Chall at Harvard University, called *Learning to Read: The Great Debate*. This book reviewed all the research up to that time which had compared one reading method with another. The aim was to identify which reading method had best stood the test of time. In 1998, 31 years later, the United States Congress established a National Reading Panel of experts to do again what Jeanne Chall had done in the 1960s. The purpose of the panel is to identify research-based findings on how best to teach children to read, and to present a report to the Secretary of Health and Human Services, to the Secretary of Education, and to the United States Congress. As part of their task, the panel of experts not only read research comparing phonics and whole language, but they also talked with parents, teachers and literacy organisations throughout the United States. The panel has yet to report its findings (Shanahan, 1999). What are those findings likely to be? Let's do our own review of the research.

## A Look Back At the 1960s

In 1955 Rudolf Flesch published an influential book called *Why Johnny Can't Read* aimed at parents. It was highly critical of the prevailing whole-word method of teaching reading at that time. The book opened with

'A letter to Johnny's mother'. Flesch had been teaching Johnny some phonics, and now Johnny was beginning to make real progress. Thus the starting point for the book was to tell Johnny's mother why Johnny was unable to read. The reason? It was because Johnny had not been taught with phonics.

This case for phonics found academic support in *Learning to read: The great debate* (Chall, 1967). Chall reviewed research on the main approaches to teaching reading. She also reported the results of visits to many classrooms to observe the teaching of reading. She concluded that teaching methods which stressed the 'code' (i.e. letter–sound correspondences) were superior to those that stressed reading for meaning, as in the whole-word method.

In 1967, the same year that Chall's book appeared, the results of a nationwide research study called the 'Cooperative Research Programme in First-Grade Reading Instruction' (Bond & Dykstra, 1967) were also published. The project (which later came to be known as the 'First Grade Studies') compared the relative effectiveness of several different methods of reading instruction with the mainstream basal method. The methods included phonics, individualised reading, language experience, basal plus phonics, linguistic reading and the initial teaching alphabet. The First Grade Studies involved 27 projects at different sites around America. Fifteen of these projects specifically compared reading methods. Each project had its own director and was stand-alone. All projects used experimental and control groups. All projects ran for the same period of time, 140 school days (seven school months).

The basal was the control method because basal reading programmes were in 95 per cent of American schools at that time. The basal reading method used readers that were graded in difficulty, with slow introduction of new vocabulary, lots of repetition of words, and introduction of phonics only after children had acquired a certain number of sight words. Another feature of the basal programmes used in the First Grade Studies was that they were all commercially produced.

The results of the First Grade Studies were not clear-cut. For one thing, the results were not consistent across projects. A reading method could do very well in one site, yet not do very well in another. Why should this happen? One possibility is that the teachers using a certain method in one research site may have been better teachers than the teachers using the same method in another research site. However, as

Adams (1990) pointed out, this could be interpreted as meaning that 'to improve reading achievement, we need to improve both programmes and classroom delivery' (p. 43).

There were other problems in interpreting the data. Many of the projects found no significant differences between methods. In statistics, a 'significant difference' usually means that the researcher can be 95 per cent sure that the difference in results is a real one. Or, put another way, there are only five chances in 100 that the difference is not real. A result of no significant difference is not a strong result; it doesn't rule out the possibility that a difference is there but that the researchers on that occasion did not find it. Another problem was school effects. Thompson and Johnston (1993) commented that schools where phonics is superior may also be schools where teaching is more structured, where teachers are more effective, and where more time is spent teaching reading. Thus, school effect factors might account for any superiority of phonics. Another problem mentioned by Bond and Dykstra (1967) was that there are novelty effects associated with using a new method like phonics as against the traditional basal method. Teachers may be more enthusiastic about methods like phonics, language experience and so on simply because they are different from the existing method used in their schools.

Overall, the First Grade Studies did not find clear-cut results supporting phonics over other methods, although there were two positive findings for phonics. First, many of the phonics versus basal results (not all) showed an advantage for phonics over the mainstream basal method. Second, the language experience approach, which was the only approach with similarities to what is now called 'whole language', was of more benefit to children who started school with good pre-reading skills. It was of less benefit to children without good pre-reading skills.

In 1981 Flesch came back into the debate with a second book, entitled *Why Johnny Still Can't Read*. Chall (1983) also updated her *Great Debate* book. Flesch and Chall still argued that the research literature favoured code-emphasis methods such as phonics over meaning-emphasis methods. Carbo (1988), however, critiqued the adequacy of the database that Chall had used in her analysis of the relative effects of code and meaning emphasis methods. Carbo argued that many of the studies Chall reviewed were flawed. Turner (1989) has reviewed what he regarded as the best designed studies reviewed by Chall and concluded that phonics had a 'weak' advantage over other methods – not enough to get excited about. But, on balance, these reviewers were not saying that phonics was weak; they were saying that much of the research was weak.

### Research Supporting Whole Language

Stahl and Miller (1989) reviewed a number of studies that compared 'language experience' approaches with phonics approaches. In their review, they used language experience as a surrogate for 'whole language' since it shared some of its characteristics, especially the emphasis on children writing and reading their own stories. The term 'whole language' is a post-1960s term, so it was difficult for them to find many whole-language studies. Thus they treated both language experience and whole-language approaches similarly.

The results of their comparisons of studies were positive at the kindergarten level. They found 17 studies supporting language experience as against basal reading methods, two supporting basal methods, and 14 studies where there was no difference. At first grade, however, the results were more neutral: they found nine studies in support of language experience, 13 in support of basals, and 43 where there were no differences.

Stahl and Miller concluded that language experience (whole language) was more effective than basal methods at kindergarten, but at first grade there was no clear difference between the language experience method and the basal method.

These partly positive, partly neutral interpretations were queried by McGee and Lomax (1990) and Schickedanz (1990). They argued that a criticism of the review findings was that whole language was equated with the language experience method, even though they are not identical approaches. To keep it in perspective, however, a key problem for Stahl and Miller was that they were unable to find many studies of whole language compared with other approaches.

Dahl and Freppon (1995) compared the progress of children who received either skills-based instruction or whole-language instruction during their kindergarten and grade one years. Skills-based instruction had a strong emphasis on learning letter–sound relations. Whole-language instruction stressed extended periods of reading and writing. Teachers showed children how to use reading strategies and skills. The children were all from low-income, inner-city classrooms. There were two skills-based schools and two whole-language schools. The researchers followed the progress of 24 children in both the skills-based schools and the whole-language schools. They found that children in the whole-language programmes were superior to children in the skills-based programmes in the quality of their story-writing (narrative register). However, there was no difference between the methods in terms of children's knowledge of sound–letter correspondences as measured by children's attempts at spelling words (e.g. they gave one point for scribbles; three points for semi-phonetic writing, as in PK for 'pink'; and eight points if the majority of the child's spellings were correct conventional spellings).

Dahl and Freppon concluded that neither approach was superior. How credible are these results? If we apply the criticisms we have applied to the First Grade Studies, we would immediately ask about novelty effects in favour of whole language. Some of the qualitative data from the study suggest that the skills-based instruction was uninspiring. Here is a comment about skills-based classrooms: 'Field observations showed that learners sat and stared for periods of time, marked randomly on worksheets, and waited for or asked for help' (p. 64). In contrast, the whole-language learners were observed to be more likely to interact with other peers and help each other. We might also query the relative abilities of the children's teachers. The teachers in the skills-based classrooms may have been less well trained and less motivated. A more enthusiastic group of skills-based teachers might have given different results.

Reutzel and Cooter (1990) compared four first-grade classrooms, each from one of four schools. Two schools used a whole-language approach and two schools used a basal-reader approach. Time spent teaching reading and language in the basal classroom each day was between 120 and 150 minutes; time spent teaching reading and language in the whole-language classrooms each day was 120 minutes. The researchers measured children's reading levels at the beginning and end of first grade. The results showed small but significant differences in reading scores supporting the whole-language approach. Was this a credible finding? Again, we could query whether the teachers in the basal classrooms were matched in terms of teaching ability with teachers in the whole-language classrooms. The researchers noted that the reading achievement differences may have been due to the quality of the teachers. They noted that whole-language teachers were more 'proactive' (p. 256).

It can be argued that a positive finding for whole language is that it does not affect reading progress either up or down. This was the finding of Traw (1996), who looked at standardised reading test scores in two school districts over nearly a decade. The two school districts were middle-class. One district, with 24 primary schools, was Sioux Falls. It was described as 'solid middle-class' (p. 327). Pupils were 95 per cent Caucasian. In 1990, the district changed to a whole-language reading curriculum, with heavy investment in children's literature and a de-emphasis on skills. The other district was West Des Moines, with nine primary schools. It was also described as 'upper middle-class' (p. 327). Pupils were 94 per cent Caucasian. West Des Moines changed to a whole-language curriculum in 1987. The schools in both districts had a policy of using standardised tests every year, so it was possible to see if the introduction of the whole-language method changed the pattern of reading scores. The reading assessments were only done at the fourth-grade level. They showed no clear change as a result of the new whole-language approach. Interviews with teachers supported these findings. Teachers felt that phonics and spelling abilities had not changed, but that children's enthusiasm and enjoyment of reading had improved. These results showed that whole language had not made things worse. More positively, teachers and pupils seemed to enjoy the new approach.

The only query to raise about the Traw (1996) findings is that they applied to children in strongly middle-class schools. Parent support is likely to be very high in such schools. In fact, the study referred to a small delegation of parents who were concerned that the introduction of a whole-language method might mean that their children would not learn phonics skills. As a result, the district agreed to test children's phonics knowledge to put their minds at ease. Children scored well on these tests. It is difficult to know whether parent concerns had an indirect effect on the implementation of the new curriculum. Perhaps teachers unconsciously gave more attention to phonics than is typical within whole-language teaching.

Ezell-Powell (1995) also found no disadvantage for whole language. In Louisiana 187 fourth-grade children in five whole-language and five phonics classrooms were compared and Ezell-Powell found no differences in reading comprehension levels. Also, there were no differences supporting one approach over the other for different levels of reading ability.

Jones (1995) compared a whole language *plus* phonics approach with a basal-reader *plus* phonics approach on the reading development of 97 first-grade children from four different classrooms. She was interested in whether or not whole language would produce better results if it was balanced with some phonics. She found that the basal plus phonics approach was better in terms of improving children's writing; in terms of reading, there was no difference between the basal plus phonics approach and the modified whole-language approach.

**Research Favouring Phonics**

Becker and Gersten (1982) found that the Distar reading method was superior to basal methods. Distar is very much a code-emphasis, phonics method of teaching reading. A potential problem with the findings is that Distar is very structured. Perhaps it was the structure of the method rather than the phonics method itself that produced the superior gains in reading achievement. There was also the question of novelty effect. Did children learn to read more quickly because of the new and different materials rather than because of the method?

Smith (1998) compared the effects of a whole-language approach with a phonics approach on the reading development of 114 preschool children of four years of age in eight different classrooms attending inner-city preschools. The phonics approach was supplemented with phonemic awareness activities. She found that the phonics plus phonemic awareness approach was significantly better than the whole-language approach for word reading, reading comprehension and dictation.

Scarcelli (1995) compared phonics and whole language in terms of effects on reading development of 55 first-grade children attending an urban school. Two classes were taught with phonics; two were taught with whole language. The results showed an advantage for the phonics children in word reading and comprehension for the average and below-average students in these classrooms.

Foorman *et al.* (1998) compared the effects of phonics and whole-language teaching on the reading progress of 285 first-grade children in Houston, Texas. The children in the study, from underprivileged backgrounds, were entitled to receive extra reading instruction. These children had entered school with low levels of reading preparation. Sixty per cent were African-American, 20 per cent were Hispanic. They were taught in small groups, outside the classroom, across 19 different schools. Children were taught with either a direct instruction approach, which was heavily phonics-based, a less direct approach, which used phonemic awareness and onset-rhyme phonics (a phonogram type of approach), or an incidental approach, which was intended to be similar to whole language in emphasis. The phonics approach was Open Court's (1995) *Collections for Young Scholars*. The 66 teachers in the study were trained to implement a particular teaching approach. The whole-language teachers were trained by an experienced whole-language teacher; the phonics teachers were trained by Open Court. Teachers were also regularly observed to ensure that they were teaching their particular method correctly.

The findings were that children who received the direct phonics instruction were able to read words faster than children who received the whole-language, indirect approach. Only 16 per cent of the children in the phonics group did not improve in reading compared to 44 per cent of the onset-rhyme phonics group and 44 per cent of the whole-language group. Children taught with phonics scored close to the national average in terms of decoding ability. This was not the case for the children taught with the 'less-phonics' approach and the whole-language approach. Word-reading skill is a characteristic of good readers. It seemed that the phonics approach had made a strong impact in this area.

The children taught with direct phonics had higher reading comprehension scores, although this advantage was not statistically significant; this showed that comprehension was not compromised in the phonics approach. Sometimes the point is raised that phonics is all about reading words, and not about comprehension. Yet these results showed no negative effects on comprehension.

The children in the whole-language approach in the Texas study had more positive attitudes towards reading than did the children in the direct-phonics approach, even though the whole-language children did not read as well as the phonics children. Yet this may be a reflection of the way in which whole language operates. The philosophy is very positive. Every reader is seen as a good reader, even if they are not. Children in the whole-language group may well have felt more positive about their reading. Chapman and Tunmer (1995) have shown that negative attitudes among poor readers take some time to show up in the whole-language approach.

This is supported by the findings of McKenna *et al.* (1995). They compared grade 1 to 5 children's reading attitudes in whole language and basal classes, yet found no differences in attitudes towards reading. It appears that any advantage in reading attitudes for whole language in the first year of school washes away.

**Australian, New Zealand and Singapore Research on Phonics and Whole Language**

In an Australian study, Tunmer and Nesdale (1985) compared the reading abilities of a group of five-year-olds taught either by a phonics or a whole-language approach. All children were in their first year of school. Thirty-eight children had received whole-language instruction and 25 had received phonics instruction. The results showed that children who received decoding instruction with phonics were significantly better than the other group in reading words and in reading comprehension.

Castle, Riach and Nicholson (1994) reported two studies where five-year-old children were taught phonemic awareness and simple phonics in addition to their classroom whole-language reading and writing instruction. In the first study, 30 children were divided into two groups of 15. One group was taught phonemic awareness and some simple phonics. The other group engaged in 'process writing' where they wrote stories using their own spellings. The children were taught in small groups of five, for 20 minutes at a time, twice a week. The teaching lasted for ten weeks.

The 'process writing' group was encouraged indirectly to learn about letter–sound relationships as part of the process of writing their own stories. For example, they had an alphabet card and were encouraged to use it to help them spell. They were also encouraged to listen for sounds in words as they spelled out the words in their stories. They might, for instance, spell <u>have</u> as <u>hv</u>, or <u>cat</u> as <u>kt</u>). In contrast, children in the experimental group were taught how to segment the phonemes in words (e.g. saying /cat/ slowly, as in /k-a-t. They were also taught how to match alphabet letters to their phonemes, and spell simple words. The findings were that children in the experimental group improved more than the control group in spelling skill.

The second experiment focused on reading. An experimental group of 17 children was taught phonemic awareness and simple phonics, while a matched control group of 17 other new entrants did alternative activities, such as matching pictures for meaning (e.g. which pictures are 'animals'?). A third group of 17 children got no extra instruction at all. The training was also done in small groups, once weekly, 20 minutes per week, for 15 weeks. The findings were that the experimental group was significantly better than the two control groups in pseudo-word reading (i.e. made-up words like 'maz') and in spelling.

Are these results credible? A problem for the reading study was that the gains did not transfer to book reading. Children who were taught with phonemic awareness and simple phonics made gains only in pseudo-word reading. A possible explanation for this is that the ability to read text requires children to be able to read irregularly spelled 'sight' words like 'come', 'of' and 'was'. Words like these occur frequently in children's primers. Until children learn how to identify such words, it is difficult to make the leap from pseudo-word reading to text reading.

In support of this argument, Ng (1997) found that phonemic awareness and simple phonics instruction did have positive effects on children's ability to read text, as long as the text contained regularly spelled words. She taught 24 Singaporean-Chinese preschoolers. They were all learning to speak and read English as a second language, and were from middle-class backgrounds. Children were divided into two groups, with one group receiving phonemic awareness and simple phonics instruction and the other group receiving 'dialogic reading'.

Dialogic reading is where the teacher reads stories to children in an interactive way, asking lots of questions and encouraging children to participate in the reading. Both groups of children were taught daily, for 20 minutes at a time, for six weeks. The findings were that children who received phonemic awareness and simple phonics were better at reading regularly spelled words on a standardised word reading test, and also better at reading a simple passage from the Dr Seuss book, *Hop on Pop*. This result is important. The training in phonemic awareness and phonics produced significant transfer effects to text reading even among three- and four-year-old Chinese children learning to read English as a second language. It may be argued that this is a very simple book, yet it is still a story that many children enjoy. Dr Suess is one of New Zealand children's favourite authors (The Whitcoulls List, 1998).

Further evidence in support of a phonics-type emphasis comes from a New Zealand study by Greaney, Tunmer and Chapman (1997). Thirty six nine-year-old poor readers were given ten-minute lessons for three or four days a week for 11 weeks. Children in the experimental group were taught how to use orthographic rimes (e.g. '-eat') to help them read new words (e.g. meat, heater). Children in the control group were taught to use whole-language reading strategies (e.g. look at initial letters of word, read to end of line and guess).

The findings were that the rime-trained poor readers made significant gains in reading on a standardised test of word reading, which translated into a four-month gain in reading age. The gains did not transfer to a standardised test of passage reading. The reason for this may have been that the whole-language poor readers, when given passages to read, made use of compensatory guessing strategies. This may have obscured the improvement in quality of decoding skills that had occurred for the rime-trained children.

### Cross-National Studies of Phonics and Whole Language

Connelly, Johnston and Thompson (1998) reported a cross-national study of 41 phonics-taught children (five- and six-year-olds) in Scotland with a matched group of 41 whole-language-taught children in New Zealand. The children were matched for age, time in school, vocabulary knowledge, short-term memory and word reading ability. Even though the children were equivalent in word reading ability and in ability to spell real words, the phonics children were superior in spelling of non-words with regular spelling patterns (e.g. 'plam').

A final interesting finding of the study was that the phonics children were close to their age norms for reading comprehension (one month behind), whereas the whole-language children were five months behind.

## Conclusion

The search for the best method of teaching reading has not been easy. The debate about which method is 'best' is still going on (Carroll, 1998; Coddington, 1998; Diegmuller, 1996; Goodman *et al.*, 1988; Kovacs & Hasan, 1998; Leman, 1997; Rothman, 1992). Whole language has been on the reading scene only since the 1970s. There are not many studies that directly compare whole language and phonics.

We reviewed research by Dahl and Freppon (1995) and Reutzel and Cooter (1990), which showed advantages for whole language. Stahl and Miller (1989) found no clear advantage for whole language in 43 different studies. Traw (1996), Ezell-Powell (1995) and Jones (1995) also found no advantage or disadvantage for whole language over phonics. Whole language appears to produce more positive attitudes to reading than does phonics, but it is not clear whether the effect extends beyond the initial years of schooling.

In contrast, phonics (plus phonemic awareness), either by itself or in addition to whole language, seems to have the advantage of getting children off to a quicker start in learning to read. Advantages for phonics were reported in the First Grade Studies, which was a nationwide comparative study of different reading methods (Bond & Dykstra, 1976) by Becker and Gersten (1982), Tunmer and Nesdale (1985), Castle, Riach and Nicholson (1994), Ng (1997), Greaney *et al.* (1997), Scarcelli (1995), Smith (1998), and Foorman *et al.* (1998).

A simple head count of studies reviewed in this chapter shows two cases of whole language being better than phonics, and eight cases where phonics was better than whole language, especially if linked with instruction in phonemic awareness. If phonics does deliver better readers, then we need to consider how to take advantage of the best aspects of this method, to assist those children who are not learning to read, or perhaps who are progressing but could be better than they are.

## References

Adams, M.J. (1990). *Beginning to read. Thinking and learning about print.* Cambridge, MA: MIT Press.

Becker, W. C., & Gersten, R. (1982). A follow-up of follow through: The later effects of the direct instruction model on children in fifth and sixth grades. *American Educational Research Journal, 19*, 75–92.

Bond, G. L., & Dykstra, R. (1967). The cooperative research programme in first-grade reading instruction. *Reading Research Quarterly, 2*, 5–142. (Reprinted in 1997 special issue of Reading Research Quarterly).

Carbo, M. (1988). Debunking the great phonics myth. *Phi Delta Kappan, 70*, 226–240.

Carrol, P. (January, 1998). Phonic approach to reading brings phenomenal results. *New Zealand Herald.*

Castle, J. M., Riach, J., & Nicholson, T. (1994). Getting off to a better start in reading and spelling: the effects of phonemic awareness instruction within a whole-language programme. *Journal of Educational Psychology, 86*, 350–359.

Chall, J. S. (1967/1983). *Learning to read: The great debate.* New York: McGraw Hill.

Chapman, J. W., & Tunmer, W. E. (1995). Development of young children's reading self-concepts: An examination of emerging subcomponents and their relationship with reading achievement. *Journal of Educational Psychology, 87*, 154–167.

Coddington, D. (1998, May 1). Why your employees are illiterate. Educators refuse to acknowledge that our children are struggling to read under the present system. *The National Business Review*, p. 28.

Connelly, V., Johnston, R. S., & Thompson, G. B. (1998). The influence of instructional approaches on reading procedures. In G. B. Thompson, & T. Nicholson (Eds.), *Learning to read: Beyond phonics and whole language* (pp. 103–124). New York: Teachers College Press.

Dahl, K. L., & Freppon, P. A. (1995). A comparison of inner-city children's interpretations of reading and writing instruction in the early grades in skills-based and whole-language classrooms. *Reading Research Quarterly, 30*, 50–74.

Department of Education (1978). *On the way to reading.* Wellington: Author.

Diegmuller, K. (1996, March 20). The best of both worlds. *Education Week.*

Ezell-Powell, S. F. (1995). *The effects of whole language and direct instruction on reading achievement of fourth-grade students.* Unpublished doctoral dissertation, The University of Alabama.

Flesch, R. (1955). *Why Johnny can't read.* New York: Harper & Row.

Flesch, R. (1981). *Why Johnny still can't read.* New York: Harper & Row.

Foorman, B. R., Francis, D. J., Fletcher, J. M., Schatschneider, C., & Mehta, P. (1998). The role of instruction in learning to read: preventing reading failure in at-risk children. *Journal of Educational Psychology.*

Goodman, K. S., Shannon, P., Freeman, Y. S., & Murphy, S. (1988). *A report card on basal readers.* New York: Richard C. Owen.

Greaney, K. T., Tunmer, W. E., & Chapman, J. W. (1997). Effects of rime-based orthographic analogy training on the word recognition skills of children with reading disability. *Journal of Educational Psychology, 89,* 645–651.

Jones, L. R. (1995). The effects of an eclectic approach versus a modified whole language approach on the reading and writing skills of first-grade students. Unpublished doctoral dissertation, The University of Mississippi.

Juel, C. (1988). Learning to read and write: A longitudinal study of 54 children from first through fourth grades. *Journal of Educational Psychology, 80,* 437–447.

Kovacs, K., & Hasan, A. (1998). *Overcoming failure at school.* Paris: OECD Education and training Division.

Leman, N. (1997, November). The reading wars. *The Atlantic Monthly,* pp. 128–134.

McGee, L. M., & Lomax, R. G. (1990). On combining apples and oranges: A response to Stahl and Miller. *Review of Educational Research, 60,* 133–140.

McKenna, M. C., Stratton, B. D., Grindler, M. C., & Jenkins, S. J. (1995). Differential effects of whole language and traditional reading instruction on reading attitudes. *Journal of Reading Behavior, 27,* 19–44.

Ng, G. L. (1997). *'Hop on Pop': Effects of phonemic awareness training on preschoolers learning to read in Singapore.* Unpublished master's thesis, The University of Auckland.

Open Court Reading (1995). *Collections for young scholars.* Peru, IL: SRA/McGraw Hill.

Reutzel, D. R., & Cooter, R. B. (1990). Whole language: Comparative effects on first-grade reading achievement. *Journal of Educational Research, 83*, 252–257.

Rothman, R. (1992, January 8). Studies cast doubt on benefits of using only whole language to teach reading. *Education Week*, p. 12.

Scarcelli, S. M. (1995*). Effects of direct reading instruction on literacy achievement in urban, literature-based classrooms.* Unpublished doctoral dissertation, Old Dominion University.

Schickedanz, J. A. (1990). The jury is still out on the effects of whole language experience approaches for beginning reading: A critique of Stahl and Miller's study. *Review of Educational Research, 60*, 127–131.

Shanahan, T. (August 1999). The National Reading Panel: Using research to create more literate students. *Reading Online* [9 pages]. Available www.readingonline.org

Smith, S. H. (1998). *The effects of a whole language method of instruction and an integrated phonics method of instruction on the reading achievement of inner-city preschool pupils (four-year-olds).* Unpublished doctoral dissertation, The George Washington University.

Stahl, S. A., & Miller, P. D. (1989). Whole language and language experience approaches for beginning reading: A quantitative research synthesis. *Review of Educational Research, 59*, 87–116.

Thompson, G. B., & Johnston, R. S. (1993). The effects of type of instruction on processes of reading acquisition. In G. B. Thompson, W. E. Tunmer & T. Nicholson (Eds.), *Reading acquisition processes.* Clevedon, England: Multilingual Matters.

Traw, R. (1996). Large-scale assessment of skills in a whole language curriculum: Two districts' experiences. *Journal of Educational Research, 89*, 323–339.

Tunmer, W. E., & Nesdale, A. R. (1985). Phonemic segmentation skill and beginning reading. *Journal of Educational Psychology, 77*, 417–427.

Turner, R. L. (1989). The 'great' debate – Can both Carbo and Chall be right? *Phi Delta Kappan,71*, 276–283.

The Whitcoulls List – Kiwi Kids' Top 100 (1998). Auckland: Whitcoulls.

# 5

# THE READING PROCESS

There are at least five competing theories about the reading process, and they can be subdivided into two main theoretical orientations. First, there is a context-driven theoretical position. There is a continuum within this orientation, for example, between the 'psycholinguistic' and 'interactive' theories of reading. Context-driven theory takes the line that the reading process involves the integration of many cues, including graphophonic, syntactic, and semantic and other context features like picture cues. There is a strong emphasis on the power of context, with less faith in print cues.

Second, there is the print-driven theory that reading can involve many cues but that the predominant cue is the print. There is a continuum here as well. At one end of the continuum is phonological coding theory which says that reading involves an indirect processing route from print to sound to meaning. Context is important but only as a back-up cue. The main role of context is for comprehending what has been decoded. Another version of this theory is interactive compensatory theory which is also print-driven. It argues that skilled reading is usually print-driven. The only exception is where the print is difficult to decode. In this situation, the reader has to compensate with context cues. Another print-driven theory is connectionist theory. It gives a primary place to print information, but it lies more toward the middle of the print- and context-driven continuum.

This theory says that all sources of cues operate simultaneously in the process of reading. All print information is decoded and context cues are used as well. All reinforce one another simultaneously.

What are the implications of these different theories for teaching? The context-driven approach is usually associated with meaning-emphasis reading curricula such as whole language, literature-based and language experience approaches. The print-driven orientation is usually associated with reading curricula such as phonics and linguistic reading. But it is not quite as simple as that. Some print-driven and context-driven theorists do not want to take particular sides in terms of teaching. They like to argue that reading theory and reading practice are not necessarily the same. Some reading approaches may not work well. A theory does not vindicate any one approach. The success or failure of a reading method depends on the extent to which it meets the requirements of the theory. There is a difference. For example, print-driven theorists worry that they are portrayed as uninterested in reading for meaning when that is not true. The term 'print-driven' does not exclude meaning, they say, but merely highlights the path to meaning. Likewise, some context-driven theorists do not want to be portrayed as uninterested in accuracy and fluency.

Thus it is wise to avoid branding one theory as supporting meaning and another as supporting the code. It's a matter of emphasis. Some reading theorists do not want to commit themselves to this or that way of teaching. They might even argue that there is no best way of teaching reading, and that we should be looking for new ways. Even so, as we discuss theories, we can still speculate on implications about teaching that could lead from theory to practice.

### The Top-Down View of Skilled Reading

The top-down view of the reading process is that we do not read words so much as 'meanings'. We predict what is on the page, rather than do a letter-by-letter analysis. This is called 'enlightened guessing'. Although the skilled reader can sound out words when necessary, this is not what happens most of the time. Skilled reading is like putting a car into overdrive – sometimes you will need to change down into a lower gear in order to focus on print in some detail, but this is only a temporary change before moving back into top gear again.

## Distinctive feature theory

Is it really possible to read words without looking at and processing all the letters? In the 1970s, a lot of researchers thought so. Frank Smith (1971) thought that reading was not a matter of processing all the letters in words, but involved narrowing alternative meanings through 'prediction'. This was not a random process but a search for 'distinctive features' of letters and words. It seems clear that we recognise letters by their distinctive features, but there is no such agreement about words. The reason letters seem to have distinctive features is that they come in all shapes and sizes. There are capital letters, lowercase letters, cursive, italics and so on. For example, to recognise a capital letter like A, we probably have to rely on distinctive cues. These enable us to recognise the capital A in different forms, such as A, 𝒜, A, and A. In the case of words, this problem is less evident. For example, the word 'cat' will still be spelled c-a-t. As long as we can identify the component letters, we can decipher the word. Also, many words look very similar, such as 'cat' and 'mat'. The thing that distinguishes them is the difference between the letters 'c' and 'm'. In other words, these two words are distinguished by their letters, not by any distinctive shape they have.

Haber *et al.* (1983) looked at whether 24 university students could recognise words by their distinctive shape and length. They presented the students with either blank spaces where the missing word should have been printed, or else with clues as to the length of the word (e.g. xxxx), or the shape of the word (e.g. ⌐￣￣￢). They found that shape and length cues were useful, improving word recognition by up to 20 per cent. But when we look at the success rates, shape and length cues are nowhere near as useful as providing the actual letters of words. Function words (e.g. 'the') are easily guessed (up to 80 per cent accuracy), but content words are not (up to 60 per cent). Even without any shape or length clues at all, it is possible to guess many function (60 per cent) and content (40 per cent) words. It is tempting to argue that these results are positive. Guessing on the basis of word shape and length can, on average, produce 60 per cent correct guesses. But really, if this was the best we could do in reading, we would be dreadfully handicapped. The fact that the same words can be read with almost 100 per cent success when all the letters are provided suggests that skilled readers read words by their letters, not by their distinctive shapes.

Smith (1971) strongly argued in favour of reading words by their distinctive features. He claimed that the distinctive features might be something else beside shape and length; however, researchers since the 1970s have not been able to discover what such features might be (for reviews see Henderson, 1980; Paap *et al*. 1984). One argument against distinctive features is known as the 'ransom note' phenomenon. Researchers have found that changing the shape of words by changing the shapes of component letters does slow down the process of identifying words, but not by much, certainly not by more than ten per cent (Adams, 1990). The following is an example of ransom note writing. Each word has a different shape from its usual shape (we could have many shapes for each word), yet the words are easily readable. If Smith were right, then it would be difficult to read these words since they do not have their regular distinctive shapes:

> HeRe cOMeS a mAn In a TAxI.
> MiSs PoOL's cAr BRoKe dOwN.

Smith (1971) also argued that redundancy made reading easier – by reducing the number of likely alternatives for letters within words (e.g. the consecutive letters in 'stream' can be guessed quite easily once the first few letters are obtained 's...st...str...stre...strea....stream). This is because some letters co-occur more often than others. But even so, this does not prove that we skip letters or do not process them. Pearson and Studt (1973) tried this idea out on children. Each child was given a sentence with a missing word (e.g. 'castle') and had to guess the word. If they guessed incorrectly, the first letter was given (e.g. 'c'). If the child still did not know the word, the second letter was given (e.g. 'ca'), and so on until the word was guessed correctly. Pearson and Studt found that children guessed some words with only some of the initial letters, but most children needed most of the letters in order to be successful. It could be argued that if children need most of the letters of a word in order to read it, then the so-called distinctive features of a word must be the letters themselves.

### Prediction and guessing

Smith (1971) also argued that many words could be predicted from context (e.g. bacon and _____ ; ham on _____ ), so that a full analysis of letters was unnecessary. Some support for the power of context came from a study by Ken Goodman (1965). He went to three classes in an inner-city school in Detroit and assessed children whose ages ranged from six years to eight years. Children were asked first to read a list of words, and then they were given a passage to read in which those same words occurred. Goodman reported that these children were able to read correctly in passages many words they were unable to read when the words were in lists. The improvement varied from class to class, but was between 60 and 80 per cent. These results suggested that context clues could provide a lot of information about the meanings of words, which in turn would reduce the child's need to process all the letters in words. Goodman's results were supportive of Smith's concept of distinctive features.

But Goodman's results have never been satisfactorily replicated. Gough, Alford and Holley-Wilcox (1981) asked one adult to guess words in texts. What they did was select the first 100 words from passages from ten ordinary non-fiction materials (e.g. *The Diary of Che Guevara*). They then asked this skilled, well educated reader to guess the words without looking at them. To give this person a context for the topic, they mentioned the author, title and topic of the reading selection. This person would try to guess the first word. After the guess, the word was read correctly to that person (e.g. the first word might be 'recently'). Then the adult's task was to guess the second word. After the guess, the second word was read (e.g. 'educators'). If the adult requested it, the preceding words would also be repeated, to provide context help before the guess was attempted. The adult then had to guess what word followed 'Recently, educators ...' and so on. The results showed that this adult, on average, could guess up to four in ten function words, but only one in ten content words. The average correct guess was only one in four words. They concluded that context was not a good strategy to rely on since it only accounted for one correct guess in four, and provided three incorrect guesses out of four. Gough (1983) reported similar results from a study using 100 undergraduate students.

Nicholson (1991) replicated the original 1965 study by Goodman. There were some problems with the original study. For one thing, children had the opportunity of practising their reading before they read in context. The practice was the list that was given first. Another problem was that the results were reported only as averages; there was no attempt to look at whether or not there were differences between good and poor readers in their ability to use context.

The replication study was different from the 1965 study. Instead of having children read words in a list first, and then in context, Nicholson had children read words in context first, and then read the same words in a list. It was anticipated that the good readers might get better scores on the lists because they had practised them in context before they saw them on the lists. The principle was that children get better with practice, and that is what happened. The best readers – and even some average readers – read words better in the list, which was an opposite finding to the 1965 study. The poorest readers, however, were better in context even though they also had the opportunity of reading in context before the list. Nicholson concluded that what Goodman had found was only applicable to beginner readers and poor readers; these are the ones who have to rely on context. Good readers, however, do not need this crutch to read words. It's easier and quicker for them to read words directly via their component letters. Guessing is time-consuming, so it seems unlikely that good readers would use this procedure, even though they could do so if they wanted.

Stanovich (1980, 1994) has reviewed many studies that found that poor readers were more likely to be beneficiaries of context clues than were good readers. Stanovich explained this by arguing that good readers did not need to rely on context clues; their skills of reading were such they could read words easily without them. In contrast, poor readers were deficient in the skills of identifying words by their letters, and so had to rely on context as a crutch to help them work out new words.

### Does 'top-down' theory explain learning to read?

What Smith (1971) and Goodman (1965) were saying about context does fit with what beginners and poor readers do. By using context clues, they can be better at reading. By using picture clues and sentence context, they can often guess what a new word might be. This explains why beginners and poor readers find context clues helpful. For example, in the following text the vowels have been deleted. Some would argue that use of context plus a 'sampling' of just the consonants in words is enough to read the text. This seems to be the situation for beginners and poor readers. Yet this strategy seems much less efficient than simply decoding *all* the letters, as in:

Gr\*\*dy c\*t s\*t \*n \* m\*t
by th\* fr\*dg\*
m\*\*w, m\*\*w, m\*\*w

Greedy cat sat
on a mat
by the fridge.
meow, meow, meow!

Why doesn't the good reader use context clues as their main reading strategy? It appears that good readers can guess words in context, but there is a penalty to be paid. Using context as a reading strategy is offset by the time and mental energy that guessing consumes, as well as the potential for error that is involved. So for the good reader, costs outweigh benefits, especially if they can decode the same material just as quickly and more accurately. Stanovich (1980) has argued that cost–benefit deficiencies rule out context as a useful strategy for good readers. But for the poor reader, who lacks decoding skill, there is no such choice. This is why poor readers have to be more reliant on context than good readers.

### The 'bottom-up' view of skilled reading

In the 'bottom-up' model, the assumption is that context is too unreliable and too slow to account for skilled reading. Instead, print information is converted into an iconic form (a kind of picture) in the eyeball, and then mentally recognised as letters. The mind has a set of distinctive features which are used in order to identify the letter forms. In the Gough (1972) model, which is a well known model of skilled reading, the letters in each word are decoded into phonological form (i.e. their sounds) and then the sound form of the word is translated into meaning by consulting our mental dictionary. As words are looked up in the mental dictionary, they are held in working memory until they can be parsed and interpreted. Parsing means working out the grammatical form and interpretation refers to working out the meaning.

Working memory has a limited capacity (Miller, 1956). It can only hold about seven items of information at a time (e.g. a telephone number). This is why working memory has to process information in short chunks, such as phrases and clauses. When interpreted, the meanings of sentences are then fitted into an overall meaning of the text as a whole. Information has to be processed quickly and then sent on. Where is it sent to? Gough (1972) called it 'The place where sentences go when they are understood', or TPWSGWTAU, which is a humorous way of describing the mysterious nature of how we store our general knowledge in the mind. The storage process is still somewhat of a mystery. We know a lot more about how we parse the grammar of sentences than how we store the meanings of those same sentences (for a review, see Rayner & Pollatsek, 1989).

### Criticisms of the bottom-up model

Has this model stood the test of time? Yes and no. Gough (1985) has admitted that the model was wrong in many ways, but it was right about some things. It was right about context. Currently most researchers don't agree with the idea that we guess words, or read them by shapes or distinctive features: the current belief is that we process all the letters in words.

The model was also mostly right about the idea that we do a mental 'sounding out' of words. This may not be the case for all words, and it is probably not the case for frequently occurring words like 'the'; we see them so often that we form a visual storage of their letter forms in our minds (Ehri, 1992). This is called the direct access route to the mental dictionary – no sounding out is involved. But many words are not frequent and may be processed by an indirect route that involves applying letter–sound rules to sound them out. These are words that we meet infrequently. They may only crop up once in every million or so printed words. How do we process these infrequent words? This question is extremely difficult, and is still debated (Adams, 1990; Just & Carpenter, 1987; Rayner & Pollatsek, 1989; Seidenberg, 1993).

### Do we sound out words or not?

There is some evidence that we do engage in phonological recoding of the printed forms of words; that is, we mentally sound them out. You can try it yourself. Count how many times you see the letter F in the following sentence:

FINISHED FILES ARE THE RESULT OF YEARS OF SCIENTIFIC

STUDY COMBINED WITH THE EXPERIENCE OF YEARS.

Did you count three, four, five or six? The answer is six. Read (1983) found that most adults get the wrong answer. Most say that there are three Fs. They do not count the F in OF when asked to count the number of Fs in the sentence. Read argued that the F is missed because the reader, while looking for Fs, is working from a phonological representation of each word (the F in OF is pronounced as /V/) instead of looking just at its printed form. This happens when we mentally (and very quickly) convert printed words into phonological forms. That is, it happens if we use an indirect route to process the words.

Another unusual finding about phonological processing comes from a study by Van Orden (1987), who tested adults' ability to decide about the meanings of words that are ambiguous. The ambiguous words were homophones (e.g. meet, meat; hare, hair; rows, rose). Homophones are spelled differently, but they sound the same. Adults were shown lists of homophones and had to decide what their meanings were. For example, they would be shown the word 'meet' and asked if this was a kind of food. It was found that words like 'meet' were confusing. Adults were slower in making decisions because 'meet' sounds like 'meat' which is a kind of food. This researcher also did work with pseudo-homophones (e.g. sute). It was found that adults still found it difficult to make decisions. For example, everyone knows that 'sute' is not a piece of clothing, but there is still something in your head which says that it sounds like 'suit'. And this may be what confuses adults who do this task. (Here are some more examples. Is 'hare' a part of the human body? Is 'rows' a kind of flower?) These results suggest that many words are re-coded into sound before their meanings are accessed.

Research on proofreading (Foss & Hakes, 1978) shows that spelling errors which retain the sound of the word (e.g. 'werk' for 'work') are more likely to go undetected than errors that change the sound of the word (e.g. 'wark' for 'work'). Again, this suggests that words are phonologically re-coded during lexical access.

### Do we sound out words and store sight words as well?

Ehri (1992) suggests that beginning readers need to have the ability to sound out words. This is the indirect route that gets them started reading words on their own. But as they read and re-read many words, beginning readers start to build an orthographic representation of the word in memory as well. These words are then stored as 'sight' words (see also Thompson, 1999). These visual entries are just like entries in a regular dictionary, but they are linked directly to the spoken form of the word. Thus, over time, many words get stored visually. Why? The reason is that their letter forms become familiar to the reader. Of course, these forms depend on the ability to sound out words. A reader who is not proficient at decoding words phonologically is likely to make many mistakes, and will store visual forms incorrectly. This is the problem facing many poor readers. They have poor sight word knowledge because their decoding skills are so poor. Thus, they are unable to store words accurately as sight words, and they are unable properly to decode words. They lose out on both fronts.

Are context clues useful at all within the bottom-up model? The model does not give context a major role in identifying words. It is argued that decoding is the better and faster way to identify words. However, the model recognises that beginning readers can make good use of context as a back-up to their emerging phonological recoding abilities (Gough & Hillinger, 1980; Tunmer & Hoover, 1992). For example, the child may initially misread a word as 'izland' but then use context to correct the mistake to 'island'.

The bottom-up model also accepts that contextual information is very important for comprehension of what is read. Context helps the reader to disambiguate words. For example, take the sentence, 'She saw several spiders, roaches and bugs'. Does 'bugs' refer to insects or spy devices? Context also helps with ambiguous phrases and sentences. For example, notice how your mind gets a bit confused by the word 'by' in this sentence, 'The criminal was interrogated by the lawyer by the window'. Here is another sentence where context is needed to work out who 'she' refers to: 'Although she spoke softly, the speaker could hear the little girl's question'. These are called 'garden path' sentences. The reader is quickly processing meaning, but takes the wrong path and has to back up and re-read the sentence. This is where context comes into its own.

**The Connectionist Theory of Skilled Reading**

We've discussed indirect and direct routes for word recognition. Another possibility is that both routes are used at the same time. This is the basis of connectionist theory, in which there are orthographic, phonological, meaning and context processors, all operating simultaneously and all doing a complete job on the data. If one processor is not working properly, then the others compensate for this weakness. Adams (1990) argues that the orthographic processor (i.e. visual memory for words) wouldn't be able do all the work on its own, since most words in a text occur infrequently. Thus, word recognition relies on cooperation among all these different processors simultaneously.

Adams (1990) notes that many words occur very infrequently and may not have a visual representation in the mind, mainly because the reader has never seen the word before. How many words are like this? Croft (1997) has studied the frequency of occurrence of words used in New Zealand children's writing. A mere 100 words make up 60 per cent of the words children write, and 300 words account for 75 per cent of the words children write. This means that some words are very likely to be stored as sight words.

But what of the other 25 per cent that are not in the list of 300? Carroll, Davies and Richman (1971) counted the frequency of occurrence of 86,000 different words. They selected the words from commonly used materials children were asked to read in school. Like Croft (1997), they found that some words cropped up all the time. A mere 6,000 of the 86,000 words made up 90 per cent of all the words that children read in their school primers. The remaining 80,000 words made up just 10 per cent of the text material. These are probably the words we are likely to have to read by sounding out (i.e. phonological recoding). We could try to work them out through context clues, but as mentioned earlier, context clues are only 25 per cent accurate. Adams (1990) suggests that in order to efficiently process both commonly and rarely occurring words, we must use orthographic, phonological and context processors all at once. This is the connectionist answer.

Connectionist theory differs from bottom-up theory in that it involves parallel processing. It is saying that word recognition involves direct and indirect routes working cooperatively and in parallel using bottom-up processes along with top-down contextual and linguistic knowledge.

Is connectionist theory closer to top-down or to bottom-up theory? On the continuum of bottom-up to top-down, it is closer to the bottom-up view in that it argues for a complete processing of the print. The context/

meaning processors focus on meaning, the orthographic processors search memory for a visual representation of the word as a whole, and the phonological processors re-code the visual form to its spoken form. This is all done at the same time, with each processor cooperating to identify the word with no short-cuts and no sampling of the print.

This notion of a complete processing of the text fits with research which shows that good readers do not sample or skip words. They process almost every word. Also, it fits with research that even the richest context does not speed up processing time very much – only about 10 per cent (Rayner & Pollatsek, 1989). Also, it fits with research showing that good readers are sensitive to even slight misspellings of predictable words (Strange, 1979), which indicates that skilled readers process all the letters in words. It also fits with research on sentence processing which shows that we process sentences very quickly, making decisions about sentence meaning even before we have finished processing them. Context clues come into action quickly, immediately after we identify words in the text.

### Phonological Processors and Learning to Read

If the phonological processor is so important in word recognition, then we can argue that phonemic awareness must also be an important ingredient in learning to read. Children have to be taught that each word they speak is actually made up of a series of little sounds. For example, the spoken word 'cat' consists of three phonemes: /k-a-t/. It may be that phonemic awareness is a result of learning to read, that is, while children learn to read, they will naturally acquire awareness that words are made of phonemes. But the fact that poor readers often show weakness in phonemic awareness skills suggests that phonemic awareness is needed in order to learn to read (Nicholson, 1997). Also, phonemic awareness is a skill that many children find difficult to acquire even while they are at school, which may explain why many children need extra reading tuition in programmes such as Reading Recovery (at least 20 per cent of New Zealand children go through this programme). For many pupils, phonemic awareness may be best acquired by direct instruction (Nicholson, 1999), but it is possible that children can acquire it indirectly though language games (e.g. 'I Spy') or through familiarity with rhyme and alliteration in books. For example:

*Rhyme*
'General Border gave the order,
Major Scott brought the shot,
Captain Bammer brought the rammer'
(from Drummer Hoff, Emberley, 1967)

'She grazes on grass, and she likes to say 'moo!'
I don't think that is what a llama would do.'
(from Is Your Mama a Llama?, Guarino, 1997)

*Alliteration*
How many trucks can a tow truck tow
if a tow truck tows tow trucks?
(from How Many Trucks can a Tow Truck Tow?, Pomerantz, 1987)

As Foss and Hakes (1978) point out, the fact that letter–sound rules in English are complicated is one explanation for reading failure. But reading failure also occurs in languages that are much more regular than English (e.g. German), so the cause must be more than the complexity of the spelling system. The problems children have in acquiring phonemic awareness is a better explanation, in that these problems occur across many languages (Nicholson, 1997).

Can phonemic awareness training help? Phonemic awareness training programmes have been tried in a number of countries, including New Zealand (Castle *et al.*, 1994) and also Singapore, with Chinese-speaking preschoolers learning to read English (Ng, 1997). Training in phonemic awareness and in simple phonological recoding has been found to facilitate initial reading and spelling development. If phonological awareness is such an important part of learning to read, then it follows that it is an important part of the process of becoming a skilled reader as well. But more of this later ...

## References

Adams, M.J. (1990). *Beginning to read: Thinking and learning about print.* Cambridge, MA: MIT Press.

Carroll, J., Davies, P., & Richman, B. (1971). *The American heritage word frequency book.* Boston: Houghton Mifflin.

Castle, J.M., Riach, J., & Nicholson, T. (1994). Getting off to a better start in reading and spelling: The effects of phonemic awareness instruction within a whole-language program. *Journal of Educational Psychology*, *86*, 350–359.

Croft, C. (1997). Write to spell in primary classrooms. *Set: research information for teachers*. Item 11.

Ehri, L.C. (1992). Reconceptualizing the development of sight word reading and its relationship to recoding. In P.B. Gough, L.C. Ehri, & R. Treiman (Eds.), *Reading acquisition* (pp. 107–143). Hillsdale, NJ: Erlbaum.

Emberley, B. (1967). *Drummer Hoff*. Englewood Cliffs, NJ: Prentice Hall.

Foss, D., & Hakes, D. (1978). *Psycholinguistics*. Englewood Cliffs, NJ: Prentice Hall.

Goodman, K.S. (1965). A linguistic study of cues and miscues in reading. *Elementary English*, *42*, 639–643.

Gough, P.B. (1972). One second of reading. In J.F. Kavanagh & I.G. Mattingly (Eds.), *Language by ear and by eye* (pp. 331–358). Cambridge, MA: MIT Press.

Gough, P.B. (1983). Context, form and interaction. In K. Rayner (Ed.), *Eye movements in reading: Perceptual and language processes* (pp. 203–211). New York: Academic Press.

Gough, P.B. (1985). One second of reading: Postscript. In H. Singer & R.B. Ruddell (Eds.), *Theoretical models and processes of reading* (3rd ed., pp. 687–688). Newark, DE: International Reading Association.

Gough, P.B., Alford, J.A., & Holley-Wilcox, P. (1981). Words and contexts. In O.L. Tzeng & H. Singer (Eds.), *Perception of print: reading research in experimental psychology* (pp. 85–102). Hillsdale, NJ: Erlbaum.

Gough, P.B., & Hillinger, M. (1980). Learning to read: An unnatural act. *Bulletin of the Orton Society*, *30*, 179–186.

Guarino, D. (1989). *Is your mama a llama?* New York: Scholastic.

Guarino, D. (1997). *Is your mama a llama?* New York: Scholastic.

Haber, L.R., Haber, R.N., & Furlin, K.R. (1983). Word length and word shape as sources of information in reading. *Reading Research Quarterly*, *18*, 165–189.

Henderson, L. (1980). Wholistic models of feature analysis in word recognition: A critical examination. In P.A. Kolers, M.E. Wrolstad &

H. Bouma (Eds.), *Processing of visible language* (Vol. 2, pp. 207–218). New York: Plenum Press.

Just, M.A., & Carpenter, P.A. (1987). *The psychology of reading and language comprehension*. Boston, MA: Allyn & Bacon.

Miller, G.A. (1956). The magical number seven, plus or minus two: Some limits on our capacity for processing information. *Psychological Review, 63*, 81–97.

Ng, G.L. (1997). *'Hop on Pop': Effects of phonemic awareness training on preschoolers learning to read in Singapore*. Unpublished master's thesis, The University of Auckland.

Nicholson, T. (1991). Do children read words better in context or in lists? A classic study revisited. *Journal of Educational Psychology, 83*, 444–450.

Nicholson, T. (1997). Closing the gap on reading failure: Social background, phonemic awareness, and learning to read. In B.A. Blachman (Ed.), *Foundations of reading acquisition and dyslexia: Implications for early intervention* (pp. 381–407). Mahwah, NJ: Erlbaum.

Nicholson, T. (1999). *At the cutting edge: Learning to read and spell for success*, (2nd ed.) Wellington, New Zealand: New Zealand Council for Educational Research.

Paap, K.R., Newsome, S.L., & Noel, R.W. (1984). Word shape's in poor shape for the race to the lexicon. *Journal of Experimental Psychology, 10*, 413–428.

Pearson, P.D., & Studt, A. (1975). Effects of word frequency and contextual richness on children's word identification abilities. *Journal of Educational Psychology, 67*, 89–95.

Pomerantz, C. (1987). *How many trucks can a tow truck tow?* New York: Random House.

Rayner, K., & Pollatsek, A. (1989). *Psychology of reading*. Hillsdale, NJ: Erlbaum.

Read, J.D. (1983). Detection of Fs in a single statement: The role of phonetic recoding. *Memory and Cognition*, 11, 152–160.

Seidenberg, M.S. (1993). Connectionist models and cognitive theory. *Psychological Science, 4*, 228–236.

Smith, F. (1971). *Understanding reading*. New York: Holt, Rinehart & Winston.

Stanovich, K.E. (1980). Toward an interactive-compensatory model of individual differences in the development of reading fluency. *Reading Research Quarterly, 16*, 32–71.

Stanovich, K.E. (1994). Romance and reality. *The Reading Teacher, 47*, 280–291.

Strange, M. (1979). The effects of orthographic anomalies upon reading behavior. *Journal of Reading Behavior, 11*, 153–161.

Thompson, G.B. (1999). The processes of learning to identify words. In G.B. Thompson & T. Nicholson (Eds.), *Learning to read: Beyond phonics and whole language* (pp. 25–54). New York: Teachers College Press.

Tunmer, W.E., & Hoover, W.A. (1992). Cognitive and linguistic factors in learning to read. In P.B. Gough, L.C. Ehri & R. Treiman (Eds.), *Reading acquisition* (pp. 175–214). Hillsdale, NJ: Erlbaum.

Van Orden, G.C. (1987). A ROWS is a ROSE: Spelling, sound and reading. *Memory and Cognition, 15*, 181–198.

# 6

# EMERGENT LITERACY –
# WHAT IS IT?

## Emergent Literacy: Definitions

Sulzby and Teale (1991: 728) define emergent literacy as follows: 'Emergent literacy is concerned with the earliest phases of literacy development, the period between birth and the time when children read and write conventionally'. Emergent literacy skills include behaviours such as knowing that, in English, words are read left to right, that stories have a beginning and an end, that words are made of letters, that letter names can be used for spelling, and so on.

## Is Learning To Read Like Learning To Talk?

When looked at this way, the emergence of literacy appears to be similar to the emergence of talk. Children appear to teach themselves to talk. For example (Torrance & Olson, 1985): 'Remember when we brang things to the teacher and I fell down and mine got broke?' (p. 270).

Children's talk in the first few of years of their lives is often not grammatically correct, yet they gradually seem to acquire the correct rules of language without any explicit teaching. Some theorists (e.g. Goodman & Goodman, 1979) argue that learning to read is a similar process to learning to talk. In the right environment, children will naturally teach themselves to read just as they taught themselves to talk.

This idea is plausible, but there is a lot of research against it. There are too many things that indicate clear differences between learning to read and learning to talk. One important difference between talking and reading is that humans have evolved a special ability to produce and comprehend speech. There are special parts of the brain that are designed for speech. There is no special part of the brain that is designed for reading. Nearly all children learn to speak quite well by three years of age. Yet a proportion of children, perhaps 20 per cent, do not learn to read well even after several years of conscientious instruction from teachers.

Liberman (1989) has explained why many children find it a lot harder to read than to talk. He argued that the reason why learning to read is hard is because speech is easy. When we read a printed page, we are seeing speech written down. For example, the spoken word /bag/ is written 'bag'. But when we hear the spoken word, we do not hear it as separate sounds, like beads on a string. We hear it as one sound. We have an evolved system to work out spoken words. But the child who wants to read is faced with the task of working out how to map letters on the page to their spoken form. This is a counter-intuitive task. Children hear a word as one sound, but they must become aware that spoken words consist of smaller phonological units called phonemes. Children have to relate these abstract phonemes, some of which can't even be pronounced (e.g. /b/ can only be said as /beh/, with an extra /eh/). Arguing against Goodman and Goodman's theory that reading is natural, Liberman defends his theory that reading is difficult. By comparison, he feels, listening is easy, simply because humans have evolved to be able to speak. They have not evolved to read.

In support of the idea that learning to read is different from learning to talk is a study by Crain-Thoreson and Dale (1992). They studied 25 children who were early talkers to find out if they became early readers. The researchers found that although these children remained verbally precocious, only one out of 25 was a precocious reader. They found that factors much more important for learning to read were those which had something to do with reading, such as exposure to instruction in letters of the alphabet, and story-reading with parents.

Many researchers are in agreement with Liberman (1989) that learning to read is not like learning to talk. Learning to read is an unnatural task (Gough & Hillinger, 1980). It is agreed that instruction is needed for almost every child. The debate is about how explicit the instruction should be.

As we have seen, another reason why learning to read can't be natural is that very few children spontaneously learn to read. If learning to read happened just like learning to talk, children from print-rich environments would be reading before they started school. Since this is not the case, it appears that learning to read is a different process to learning to talk.

**Should Parents Read To Their Children?**

Although reading stories to preschool children will not teach them to read, story-reading is certainly not a waste of time. Whitehurst *et al.* (1988, 1994) have found that 'interactive' storybook reading by parents did improve young children's spoken vocabulary but not their reading skills. Ng (1997) also found that interactive reading did not enable preschool children to read; that teaching phonemic awareness and simple phonics did. But vocabulary is part of reading. Children need to understand what they read, and reading books to children appears to help with this. What is 'interactive' reading? It involves the parent asking questions in a way that encourages the child to participate. Ineffective questions are yes–no type (e.g. 'Did you see the duck in the picture?') Also ineffective are 'what' questions (e.g. 'What's that?') because the child's response is restricted to one word. Effective questions encourage the child to say more (e.g. 'There's Eeyore. What's happening to him?', or 'Tell me what's happening on that page'). When the child answers the parent's question, the feedback to the child also has to be extremely informative, so that the child gets clear explanations about new words and concepts (Whitehurst, undated). The parent should expand on what the child says (e.g. 'Yes, that's a snake. Snake skin is all smooth and dry. Snakes help humans because they eat rats. Some snakes can poison you, but there are no snakes where we live'). The parent is also encouraged to comment on unfamiliar words while reading to the child. For example, the parent might come to a place in the book where she reads about an 'owl'. She might say, 'Do you know what an owl is? It's a bird. And it goes hoo-hoo'.

Other researchers have found that interactive explanation of words does help children acquire new vocabulary. Nicholson and Whyte (1992) found that getting older children to think explicitly about words in the context of a sentence from a story improved their understanding, even without telling them exactly what words meant. They read the story 'Farmer Palmer's Wagon Ride' (Steig, 1974) to 57 eight-year-olds who varied considerably in reading ability. For more able readers, using context clues alone enabled them to learn 20 per cent of unfamiliar words in a story. For less able readers, questioning in context produced a nine per cent improvement. For example, the researchers asked questions such as, 'What do you think the word 'harmonica' means? I'll re-read what the story says. Can you say harmonica in your own sentence for me?' If the Whitehurst *et al.* (1994) idea of full explanation of word meanings had been added to this implicit questioning, children's understanding of new words may have improved much further.

Does storybook reading help children learn to read? It would be great if reading to children helped them to learn to read. We have already noted that story-reading to children helps to improve listening vocabulary, so you might also expect it to help children with reading. Many people believe story-reading does help. When I have asked my students 'What is the most important thing parents can do to help their children learn to read?' almost all of them have replied that the best thing is for parents to read books to their children. This is a very popular belief.

But as we have seen so far, the supporting evidence is not as strong as the evidence against this theory. In support of reading to children, Wells (1985) studied 32 English preschoolers and found that children who were read to by their parents were more likely to be better readers by the time they had finished their second year of school. But it is hard to claim a definite cause and effect here. For one thing, the children in the study were from middle-class families, and their parents were well educated. Such parents are often highly ambitious for their children. So it could be that parents helped them in other ways as well, such as learning letters and reading words. This may have been the real cause of their later success. Thus, although these children benefited from listening to stories, the process may not have been just due to the reading.

On a positive note, reading stories to children can give them a better vocabulary and will teach them strategies for discussing books, which may in turn assist them to know what to say when the teacher asks them questions about books while reading stories to the class. Children who have heard lots of stories acquire knowledge of how stories are written (e.g. that there are characters, a plot, and usually a happy ending). They also learn skills of interaction with an adult (e.g. asking questions, taking turns). These experiences are of great help in school.

Mason (1992) has reviewed several studies that support the relation between reading books to preschool children and their learning to read. However, Scarborough and Dobrich (1994) reviewed research on this topic over a 30-year period and found only a small relationship between reading aloud to preschoolers and whether or not they learned to read more easily. In some ways, it is understandable that reading aloud to a child might not facilitate reading; the child might not be able to realise that all those squiggles on the page have something to do with reading. There is no reason why they should make the discovery – most of the time, all they are doing is listening to a good story. Yet there are preschool children who *do* learn to read. Why is that some do and some don't?

### Children Who Are Early Readers

Research indicates that precocious readers and their home environments are not typical. Anbar (1986) reported on six children who learned to read before they got to school. She found that each of the six children went through similar stages. First, there was a period of time where they became familiar with books. The children turned pages, their parents read to them daily, they played with magnetic letters and alphabet blocks. Second, they went through a stage where they learned to recognise letters and some sight words. Third, they showed interest in the sounds of letters using ABC books, invented sound games and alphabet letters. Fourth, they started to use their letter–sound knowledge to 'make words' using plastic letters, blocks or cards. Fifth, they got interested in sounding out new words, as long as the words contained only a few letters. Then they started reading for themselves. When Anbar interviewed the children's parents, she found that they read stories every day, helped with learning the alphabet, with spelling, with sound games and with 'making words'. As Anbar (p. 75) put it:

> Parents eagerly helped their children with spelling attempts and encouraged efforts in 'making words'. They daily read books to and with the child, often pointing at each word, and with much patience

and enthusiasm listened to the children read aloud to them. They also enjoyed making rhymes with words. "What rhymes with Mommy?" one of the mothers used to ask. (Her son's favourite response would be "salami") (p. 75).

Anbar's study showed that these parents willingly put countless hours into their children's preschool reading development. They seemed to have a massive armoury of books, but they also had alphabet letters, flashcards, dictionaries, workbooks, computer games, and so on. In only one case did a parent deliberately 'hothouse' her child; that is, deliberately teach the child to read. Why did these parents sacrifice so much time? Anbar suggested that these parents had their own 'personal' reasons. Here are some things she noticed. Victor's parents did a lot of reading work with him because he was asthmatic. It kept him calm. Sean's father did not have much education himself and wanted his boy to do better. He really enjoyed helping him learn to read. Mark's father and mother were very keen that their son did not fail in reading (as Mark's uncle had) and did not drop out of school (as Mark's own sister had). Marna's parents were very busy people, and frequently had to use a babysitter a lot. They read lots of stories to her to make up for their absences, and also because they were fearful that Marna might develop learning difficulties due to the mother's late pregnancy. Betty's mother had resigned from her teacher career to bring up her daughter. Her early reading development was a vindication that she'd done the right thing. One child, Janice, was explicitly taught to read by her mother, whose cultural background taught that it was the 'duty' of a mother to teach her children to read. Conclusion? These precocious readers did not just appear naturally. For all sorts of reasons, their mums and dads had taken keen interest in their reading development.

Another reason for precocious readers may be that some children play a role in their own success. Some are quick to see what reading is about and are more likely to request books, ask for pencil and paper, and so on. Some parents may not deliberately teach their children to read so much as respond to their interest in reading. In the special cases of 'spontaneous' readers, it is hard to work out cause and effect. It may be a bit of both.

Clark (1976) reported on 32 children who could all read fluently when they started school. She found that many of their parents had a keen personal interest in their children's progress. In one family, this was their first child after several attempts and the child was very important to them. In another family the parents were not well educated, but they wanted their child to do better than them. Few of these parents worked while their children were preschoolers. Parents were very absorbed in their children's activities. Several parents also mentioned that it was the child, not them, who was most intent on reading activities (an example of children themselves creating the conditions for their own success).

**What Do Preschool Children Know About the Alphabet?**

Most children start school unable to read or write, but all children vary in terms of their pre-reading skills such as ability to recognise the letters of the alphabet. Nicholson (1996) surveyed 88 five-year-olds from low-income, mostly Māori and Pacific Islands backgrounds who were starting school. These children could recognise an average of 10 alphabet letters out of 26. In contrast, a group of 25 mostly Pakeha five-year-olds from middle-income backgrounds could recognise an average of 20 alphabet letters out of 26.

Worden and Boettcher (1990) assessed the alphabet skills of 180 middle-class English-speaking children, whose ages ranged from three to eight years. The researchers found that children learned uppercase letters more quickly than they did lowercase, possibly because uppercase letters have a simpler structure and are more distinctive. For example, B and D are easy to tell apart, but b and d are more difficult to distinguish. Only orientation separates them. Children also learned the names of letters much more quickly than their sounds. They found that three-year-olds could name four uppercase letters, four-year-olds could name 14 uppercase letters, five-year-olds could name 22 uppercase letters. By age six, when American children start school, they could identify nearly all letters. All children in the survey were less able to identify lowercase letters, although the difference was only three or four letters. Children found it easier to name letters than to write them. They were also worse at giving sounds for letters. Five-year-olds could only give half as many sounds for letters (eight out of 26) as they could give the names of letters (22 out of 26). Children were not fully able to give sounds for letters until seven years of age.

### Is Knowing the Alphabet a Good Prognosis for Learning to Read?

There is a strong relationship between being able to name the letters of the alphabet and learning to read (Bond & Dykstra, 1967; Clay, 1966, 1993). It is a very good predictor, along with phonemic awareness. It is not a guarantee of learning to read. Like phonemic awareness, it is a key to the door. Why is it useful? The reason is that being able to identify the letters takes a mental load off the child who is learning to read. It's one part of the puzzle that they have already worked out, so they can devote their minds to other parts. Ehri (1983) also suggests that the names of the letters contain some of the letter sounds (e.g. the /f/ in 'ef'). Thus, children may be able to work out intuitively many of the letter sounds that are necessary in order to read words. Letter knowledge is not a guarantee, but it is one part of the foundation (along with phonemic awareness) needed for children to build their reading skills.

### When Should Children be Taught to Read?

Children are taught to read at different ages around the world. In England, Australia and New Zealand they begin formal schooling at five years of age, whereas in America it is six years of age and in many parts of Europe it is seven years of age. When is the best time to teach a child to read? Coltheart (1979) argues that there is no evidence to show that any one age is privileged. The age of starting school instruction depends on the relative importance our culture gives to reading, as against other things a child might be doing such as music, art or sport. Although opinions vary about the best age to teach reading, Coltheart reviewed research on reading 'readiness' and concluded that it did not stand up to criticism. The best known study of when to begin reading was that of Morphett and Washburne (1931) in America. They surveyed 141 children in Winnetka, Illinois, giving them both reading tests and intelligence tests. They found that children did not seem to make reasonable reading progress until their cognitive development was at about six and a half years. This translated into the everyday idea that a child with normal intelligence was not going to be ready for reading until six and a half years of age.

But there were several problems with this study. First, there was no comparison with places where children began their formal schooling at earlier ages than six years. In America children begin school at six, but in England, Australia and New Zealand, many children begin school at five years of age. This is called the 'base rates fallacy'. Bracey (1997) described the problem as one in which the researcher finds an interesting pattern of results in the research sample and then generalises it to the wider population. In the case of learning to read, Morphett and Washburne (1931) based their conclusions on a sample of children learning to read at six years of age. To avoid the base rates fallacy, the study should have included children starting school at ages five and seven as well. Would they have found that five-year-olds do not start learning to read until they are six and a half years? Would they have found that seven-year-olds would already be reading, since they were older than six and a half years? I doubt it. Coltheart (1979) concluded that whether or not a child learns to read depends not so much on mental or chronological age as on the kind of instruction they receive, the ability of the teacher and the size of the class, as well as on the ability and motivation of the individual child.

### What are the Long-Term Effects of Learning to Read Early?

Coltheart (1979) also reviewed studies on this topic and again found problems with them. Where researchers had found long-term benefits for children who had learned to read before they started school, there were technical problems with their data. Some researchers have followed children's reading progress over two and three years and have found that the initial gains fall away. A possible explanation is that the school curriculum does not take advantage of the fact that some children have learned to read early. Teachers spend more time with the low-ability readers than they do with the high-ability ones. Durkin (1974, cited in Coltheart, 1979: 26) quoted one teacher as saying: 'They [the highest achievers] seem to get everything pretty well. I like to spend more time with the slower ones'. Henson (1993) surveyed 77 middle-primary teachers. He summarised their comments as: 'A large number of teachers expressed concern that they were not giving these pupils [very able readers] enough attention'. He quoted one teacher: 'They're masters of their own destinies'. Thus, it seems that the reading advantage of early readers is eventually whittled away. But on the positive side it is better to start school ahead than to start school behind. Juel (1988) found that children who got off to a slow start in learning to read were still poor readers when re-tested four years later. Likewise, those who got off to a quick start were outstanding readers when re-tested four years on.

## Can Babies Learn to Read?

Learning to read should be easy. There are television shows such as *Sesame Street* and *The Magic Box* that give lots of attention to the ABCs. Supermarkets sell children's books, magnetic letters, crayons, pencils, and so on. You can even find companies on the Internet claiming that parents can teach babies to read, that even one-year-olds can read. They advertise books and flashcards to use with infants. One company quotes an amazed parent who wrote to tell them that her 16-month old child could read the word 'clap'.

There is no harm in playing reading games with infants, especially if they enjoy the activities. Yet we really should be cautious about claims that little babies can be taught to read. The vast majority of children start school unable to read, even though many parents spend countless hours reading to their children, playing with alphabet blocks, and so on. The reason is that learning to read requires a considerable amount of mental development. It takes several years for children to develop such learning abilities.

Preschool children can often recognise signs in the street, such as McDonald's and Pizza Hut. But this is probably only because of their distinctive features, for example, the 'golden arches' on McDonald's signs. Preschool children may know that books tell a story, and even that books contain 'words'. Some researchers call this Stage 1 of learning to read, where the child is still unaware of the alphabetic principle but is drawn to a distinctive cue, such as the visual distinctiveness of the letter pattern (e.g. the 'tail' on the word <u>dog</u>), or the visual context surrounding the word (e.g. the distinctive colours and shape of the McDonald's sign). But most four- and five-year-olds have not yet figured out the alphabetic principle; that is, that there is a set of letter–sound rules, and these rules enable us to read the print on the page. This is Stage 2, called cipher reading, which is the really important stage in learning to read (Gough & Hillinger,

1980). This does not mean that very young children can't learn to read, but to do so they will need to be able to relate letters to phonemes, a very difficult task for a toddler.

You may be thinking, this can't be right. I've read magazine articles about babies who can read. According to one television documentary in the 1970s, 'spontaneous reading' is not uncommon (Rose, 1975). But this is not true. Spontaneous reading is very uncommon. Durkin (1966) surveyed 10,000 five-year-olds and found that only two per cent could read 18 or more words on a list. The list was made up of familiar words like 'mother', 'look' and 'funny'.

### How Important are 'Books in Homes'?

Some parents can't afford books. For example, the following written note is from a parent who participated in an evaluation study I once carried out:

> Yes I have two children who need books bad. They are very backwood [sic] in their readying [sic] at school. How do I get the right books for them. I am give you my name and address would you let me know about the books for my children I hope so.
>
> (Nicholson, 1980: 21)

In case you are wondering, I did write back to that parent and sent her a list of books. I wish I could have done more. For such parents, the Alan Duff 'Books in Homes' project, which aims to provide high-quality children's books to those from low-income homes, seems very worthwhile (see 'Books for every child', 1994).

But having books is not a guarantee that a child will learn to read. In a newspaper article on the Books in Homes project (Young, 1998), it was reported that 'A Ministry of Education evaluation last year found that children's reading skills had risen markedly. Among five-year-olds and six-year-olds in the evaluation, reading skills had improved by 35 per cent' (p. 27). This was the result that had been given to the media. But this result could be misunderstood. The evaluation (Elley, 1997) concluded that children in the project 'improved their reading by 35 per cent more than they would have without the programme' (p. 25). This seems a remarkable improvement, but let's look at the evaluation in more detail.

The Books in Homes project started in 1992 with one school. The aim was to give books to school children from homes where there are few or no books. In 1998, the scheme operated in 135 schools, mostly in low-income areas. It had 60 commercial sponsors as well as funding from the government, and had provided 380,000 books to schools. The books were chosen by the children themselves, with help from their teachers and parents. Children receive about four books each year. They are allowed to keep the books.

The project had other features, including role model visits from famous sporting and television personalities. The role models talked to children about the importance of reading. There was also a 'caught being good' programme. If children did something helpful during the week, their names went into a draw and they had the possibility of winning a book.

The project is available to low-decile schools, which are schools in low-income areas. Children in these schools are mostly of Māori (50 per cent) and Pacific Islands (25 per cent) ethnicity. Schools can join the project for three years. Schools contribute one-third of the cost of the books in year one, and half of the cost in years two and three. Sponsors make up the balance of the costs.

The study found that the Books in Homes project was really popular with children. When they asked children whether the books they were given had helped them with reading, 70 per cent of the children said the books had helped 'a lot'.

What the Books in Homes results showed was that pupils who received the books were reading, a year later, 35 per cent better than would 'normally' be expected for them. But what is a 'normal' expectation for these children? Other research (Nicholson, Ell & McIntosh, 1999) shows that, in general, children read below average for their age in low-decile schools. The pupils in the Books in Homes project gained 35 per cent more than normal. Yet it may well be the case that these children were making fewer gains than did average readers in other schools in the same period of time. In order to catch up, these pupils will require far more significant interventions.

On a positive note, pupils in the study liked having their own books. These were children who had few or no books of their own. If we assess the worth of the project in terms of doing something worthwhile for children who have very few of the advantages of middle-class children, the project was a success.

### Are there Cultural Factors that Influence Preschool Children's Learning?

Children who begin their schooling in New Zealand come from diverse cultural backgrounds. Every year, about 60,000 five-year-olds start school. The majority of children will be from European ('Pakeha') backgrounds, but approximately 20 per cent will be Māori, five per cent will be Pacific Islands, and three per cent will be Asian or Indian. It has been argued that Māori and Pacific Islands children are disadvantaged in a school system that favours the Pakeha New Zealand culture. In regard to Māori children, an article by a former school inspector illustrates how these children may be disadvantaged by the school system (Ennes, 1987):

> A Maori five-year-old new entrant enters a rather frightening new world when he/she is ushered into the hurly burly of his/her first classroom. The majority of teachers are middle-class and monocultural, know little of 'things Māori', consider Pakeha [European New Zealand] culture to be superior to Maori culture, speak only English and do not consider the Māori language to be very important. Many have low expectations for Māori pupils and hold 'deficit' views of Māori children's competence in the English language, intelligence and home environment' (p. 22).

Penetito (1988) has argued that there are 'Māori Education Policies' that are bottom-up, coming from the iwi – that is, the tribe. In contrast, there are 'Policies for Māori Education' that are top-down and come from the government and the teaching profession. In the top-down approach, 'taha Māori' is seen as a way of 'improving or enhancing the self-image or identity of Māori young people', but with a long-term goal of 'assimilation and conformity' (p. 101). The bottom-up approach, however, starts from Māori initiatives, focuses on the iwi, and provides 'an infrastructure where the life chances of young Māori people are enhanced' (p. 101). When looked at this way, Māori children are caught up in a battle about who has power in the education system, who has control. Penetito (1988) wrote:

> Over the years the field of Māori Education has been plagued with experts who knew the answers before most people on the ground even knew what the questions were. The last five years has shown a definite

shift in the debate on Māori education. Māori people caused it (and so they should have) and now they are waiting to see whether the shift has been to their advantage or not' (p. 102).

At the centre of the argument seems to be a distrust about whether a Pakeha-dominated educational system can best serve Māori interests, and whether or not there is sufficient respect for Māori interests. Penetito (1988) suggests that racism may be a factor:

> Few would admit to being racist, and fewer still would want to see racism perpetuated, if it could be proven it existed. Yet there is a growing body of evidence to suggest that the public education system of New Zealand started with racism at its core, and that it is still alive and well today (p. 98).

## Conclusion

When is a child ready for reading? There does not seem to be a decisive answer to this question. A lot will depend on whether or not the child shows interest in reading. Some children show interest earlier than others, and parents respond to this interest. Also, much depends on how children are instructed. It appears, for example, that learning the alphabet and acquiring phonemic awareness are critical foundations in building reading skill. It also seems to be the case that New Zealand schools do a better job of teaching these skills to Pakeha pupils, and are not as effective at teaching Maori and Pacific Islands children.

Reading stories to children and 'interacting' with them (i.e. asking lots of questions) seems to build spoken vocabulary and helps children understand how books work (e.g. that books are read left to right, from the first page to the last). Children also learn to talk about stories with their parents. They gain discussion and turn-taking skills which are useful when the teacher talks to them in class. Reading stories to young children may indirectly teach them to sit quietly and give sustained attention to the print, and to be cooperative. These abilities are important when they go to school, when the teacher will expect pupils to sit still while she reads a story to them and to work cooperatively with other children when they do reading tasks in small groups.

## References

Adams, M.J. (1990). *Beginning to read: Thinking and learning about print.* Cambridge, MA: MIT Press.

Anbar, A. (1986). Reading acquisition of preschool children without systematic instruction. *Early Childhood Research Quarterly,* 1, 69–83.

Bond, G. L., & Dykstra, R. (1967). The cooperative research program in first-grade reading instruction. *Reading Research Quarterly,* 2, 5–142.

Books for every child is author's mission (1994, August 14). *Sunday Star-Times,* p. A5.

Bourdieu, P. (1977). Cultural reproduction and social reproduction. In J. Karabel & J. Halsey (Eds.), *Power and ideology in education.* Oxford, England: Oxford University Press.

Bracey, K. (1997, September). The base rates fallacy – Or Bracey goofs in June. *Phi Delta Kappa,* 79, 88.

Clark, M.M. (1976*). Young fluent readers: What can they tell us?* London: Heinemann.

Clay, M. M. (1993). *An observation survey of early literacy development.* Auckland, New Zealand: Heinemann.

Coltheart, M. (1979). When can children learn to read – and when should they be taught? In T. G. Waller & G. E. Mackinnon (Eds.), *Reading research: Advances in theory and practice* (Vol. 1, pp. 1–30). New York: Academic Press.

Crain-Thoreson, C. & Dale, P. S. (1992). Do early talkers become early readers? Linguistic precocity, preschool language, and emergent literacy. *Developmental Psychology,* 28, 421–429.

Durkin, D. (1966). *Children who read early.* New York: Teachers College Press.

Ehri, L. C. (1983). A critique of five studies related to letter–name knowledge and learning to read. In L. M. Gentile, M. L. Kamil & J. S. Blanchard (Eds.), *Reading research revisited* (pp. 143–153). Columbus, OH: Merrill.

Elley, W. B. (1997). *An evaluation of Alan Duff's 'Books in Homes' programme.* Final report. Wellington: Ministry of Education.

Ennes, J. (1987, June/July). Why do our schools fail the majority of Maori children? *Tu Tangata: A Maori Perspective on New Zealand,* pp. 21–25.

Feitelson, D., & Goldstein, Z. (1986). Patterns of book ownership and reading to young children in Israeli school-oriented and nonschool-oriented families. *The Reading Teacher, 39*, 924–930.

Goodman, K. S., & Goodman, Y. M. (1979). Learning to read is natural. In L. B. Resnick & P. A. Weaver (Eds.), *Theory and practice of early reading* (Vol. 1, pp. 137–154). Hillsdale, NJ: Erlbaum

Gough, P.B., & Hillinger, M. (1980). Learning to read: An unnatural act. *Bulletin of the Orton Society, 30*, 179–196.

Henson, N. (1991). *Reading in the middle and upper primary school.* Wellington, New Zealand: Ministry of Education.

Hughes, D., & Lauder, H. (1991). Human capital theory and the wastage of talent in New Zealand. *New Zealand Journal of Educational Studies, 26*, 5–20.

Hundreds of school children missing. (1996, 13 March). *East and Bays Courier*, p. 17.

Juel, C. (1988). Learning to read and write: A longitudinal study of fifty-four children from first through fourth grade. *Journal of Educational Psychology, 80*, 437–447.

Juel, C. (1994). *Learning to read in one elementary school.* New York: Springer-Verlag.

Liberman, A. M. (1989). Reading is hard just because listening is easy. In Euler, C. V., Lundberg, I., & Lennerstrand, G. (Eds.). *Brain and reading* (pp. 197–205). London: Macmillan.

Mason, J.M. (1992). Reading stories to preliterate children: A proposed connection to reading. In P.B. Gough, L.C. Ehri & R. Treiman (Eds.), *Reading acquisition* (pp. 215–241). Hillsdale, NJ: Erlbaum.

Mason, J.M., & Allen, J. (1986). A review of emergent literacy with implications for research and practice in reading. *Review of Research in Education, 13*, 3–48.

Morphett, M. V., & Washburne, C. (1931). When should children begin to read? *Elementary School Journal, 31*, 496–503.

Ng, G. L. (1997). *'Hop on Pop': Effects of phonemic awareness training on preschoolers learning to read in Singapore.* Unpublished master's thesis, The University of Auckland, New Zealand.

Nicholson, T. (1980). *An evaluation study of the radio series 'On The Way To Reading'.* Unpublished report, The University of Waikato, Hamilton, New Zealand.

Nicholson, T. (1996). Can the poor get richer? A study of the effects of phonemic awareness and letter–sound correspondence instruction on the reading and writing development of children from low-income backgrounds. Unpublished manuscript, The University of Auckland.

Nicholson, T., Ell, F., & McIntosh, S. (1999). The rich get richer and the poor get poorer. A Longitudinal study of children's literacy development through years 1–4. Paper presented to Australian Association of Special Education, Sydney, September.

Nicholson, T., & Whyte, B. (1992). Matthew effects in learning new words while listening to stories. In C.K. Kinzer & D.J. Leu (Eds.), *Literacy research, theory and practice: Views from many perspectives* (pp. 499–503). Chicago: National Reading Conference.

Penetito, W.T. (1988). Maori education for a just society. In Richardson, Sir I., Ballin, A., Bruce, M., Cook, L., Durie, M. & Noonan, R. (Eds.), *Social perspectives: Report of the Royal Commission on Social Policy* (Vol. 4, pp. 91–114). Wellington: Royal Commission on Social Policy.

Rose, S. (Producer) (1975). *How do you read?* (Film). London: BBC 'Horizon'.

Scarborough, H., & Dobrich, W. (1994). On the efficiency of reading to preschoolers. *Development Review, 14*, 245–302.

Steig, W. (1974). *Farmer Palmer's wagon ride.* New York: Atheneum.

Sulzby, E., & Teale, W. (1991). Emergent literacy. In R. Barr, M.L. Kamil, P.B. Mosenthal & P.D. Pearson (Eds.), Handbook of reading research (Vol. 2, pp. 727–757). White Plains, NY, Longman.

Torrance, N. & Olson, D.R. (1985). Oral and literate competencies in the early school years. In D.R. Olson, N. Torrance & A. Hildyard (Eds.), *Literacy, Language and learning: The nature and consequences of reading and writing* (pp.256–284). Cambridge: Cambridge University Press.

Wells, G. (1985). Preschool literacy-related activities and success in school. In D.R. Olson, N. Torrance & A. Hildyard (Eds.), *Literacy Language and Learning* (pp. 229–225). Cambridge: Cambridge University Press.

Whitehurst, G. J. (undated). *The Stony Brook emergent literacy curriculum.* Stony Brook, NY: Author.

Whitehurst, G. J., Epstein, J. N., Angell, A. L., Payne, A. C., Crone, D. A., & Fischel, J. E. (1994). Outcomes of an emergent literacy program in Head Start. *Journal of Educational Psychology, 86*, 542–555.

Whitehurst, G. J., Falco, F. L., Lonigan, C. J., Fischel, J. E. , DeBaryshe, Valdez-Menchaca, M. C., & Caulfield, M. (1988). Accelerating language development through picture book reading. *Developmental Psychology, 24*, 552–559.

Worden, P. E., & Boettcher, W. (1990). Young children's acquisition of alphabet knowledge. *Journal of Reading Behavior, 22*, 277–295.

Young, A. (23 October 1998). Books in Homes. *New Zealand Herald*, p. 37.

# 7

## First Steps in Learning to Read at School

'What are all those funny squiggles on the page?' That must be the question many beginning readers ask themselves. For example, see if you can read the following word: Καλισπερα

It is the modern Greek word for 'good afternoon', pronounced 'kalispera'. For most beginning readers, the print on the page is just like this – impenetrable (see illustration on the following page). How are they to translate the alphabetic characters into a form they can recognise as a spoken word? If you were in the position of a child just starting to learn to read, what would you do? The straight and narrow path is to learn all the letters of the alphabet, and the sounds they represent. For example, the Greek symbol 'p' is their version of our letter 'r'. The letter 'p' is pronounced as /r/. Thus, the beginner Greek reader has to learn that 'p' is pronounced /r/. You could take this hard way (i.e. some work is required) and learn all the letter sounds; then you could sound out the words on the page.

But this is not what beginners do. Why not? It's a hard task. Learning the sounds of the letters will take quite a few hours of study. So instead, the beginner naturally looks for easier clues, such as a distinctive feature which will trigger memory for the word. This is how children are sometimes able to 'read' well known signs and labels. They can sometimes read the 'Vegemite' label at the supermarket, or they can

*This sign says "Beware of the dog" – in Greek. If you were a beginner reader, you might get a fright if you opened the gate.*

read the 'McDonald's' sign while the family is out for a Sunday drive (see illustration opposite). At first it seems as if they are really reading, but they are not. Instead, they look for some part of the label or something around it that is really distinctive (Gough, Juel, & Griffith, 1992).

These strategies have been known about for a long time. Durrell (1956) for example, wrote about a child who was unable to read a word in a story, even though she could read the same word in isolation on a card. When she was asked why it was easier to read the word when printed on a card, she mentioned that the card had a smudge on it. The smudge was the cue which triggered her memory for the word.

Is there research to show that children use such cues? Goodall (1984) studied the sign- and label-reading of 20 Australian preschoolers. The children were from middle-class homes. Goodall found that many of the children could recognise traffic signs and labels on supermarket products. For example, 100 per cent of the children correctly read 'Band-Aid', 'Milk', 'Vegemite', 'Australia Post' and 'Telephone'; 95 per cent correctly read 'McDonald's' and 'Golden Fleece'; 90 per cent correctly read 'Statebank' and 'Coca-Cola'. In scoring a response as correct, the child either had to say the exact word or else a word that had the same meaning, for example, 'letter box' instead of 'Australia Post'.

But did they really read the words, or were they relying on other cues beside the print? Were they using distinctive cues such as the 'golden arches' that surround the word 'McDonald's' on the signs outside their stores? Goodall found that these other cues were much more important than the print. When only the printed words themselves were shown (i.e. 'Coca-Cola' on its own, not on the bottle), children had much more trouble reading

*McDonald's, Newmarket, Auckland. Notice the distinctive M.*

them. They still did well on 'McDonald's' (95 per cent) and 'Coca-Cola' (85 per cent) because the letters in these words are printed in distinctive colours and fonts. But they had trouble reading words like Golden Fleece (0 per cent), 'Band-Aid' (5 per cent), 'Australia Post' (10 per cent) and 'Telephone' (10 per cent) that are printed in regular capital letters. These data suggest that children start reading by using the easiest, most salient cues, and that these cues usually have nothing to do with the print at all.

Similar results were obtained by Masonheimer *et al.* (1984). From a sample of 228 preschoolers (between 3 and 5 years of age) they selected 102 who were experts at reading signs. They could read at least eight out of ten signs and labels like 'Pepsi' and 'McDonald's'. They wanted to see if preschool children's many experiences in a print-rich environment caused them to rely on non-print cues such a colour or special writing.

When the signs and labels were printed in regular letters without the distinctive colours and shapes that surround them on the labels, only six of the 102 children could read the labels in regular printing. The other 96 children did very badly on this task, reading only 23 per cent of the signs and labels correctly. To make sure of these results, Masonheimer *et al.* (1984) asked the 96 non-readers to read labels where one of the letters had been altered. For example, they changed 'Pepsi' to 'Xepsi' on the label. They found that the non-readers did not notice that the first letter was incorrect even when prompted to look for errors. Ehri (1987) noted that the non-readers in the study were partly successful at naming the letters of the alphabet (62 per cent correct) whereas the six readers in the sample were almost completely successful (98 per cent correct). These findings indicate that children do not naturally learn about reading by attending to words in the environment around them. Children who are successful sign- and label-readers are not likely to be readers.

In another study Gough (1993) taught 32 preschoolers (five-year-olds) to read four words presented to them on flashcards. Half the group learned words that looked similar to one another (bag, bat, rag, rat), while the rest of the group learned words that looked different to one another (box, leg, sun, rat). Also, for each child, one card had a thumbprint on it. The children were taught the words by simply reading the flashcards again and again until they could say all the words.

Gough reasoned that if children used a simple strategy of looking for a distinctive cue, then they would learn the different-looking words more easily than the similar ones. This is because the cues for each word in the different group are more distinctive. For example, with b̲o̲x̲, they could choose b̲, o̲ or x̲ to remember the word, and there would be no problem, because none of the other three words have those letters. But with the similar words, the child could easily confuse the same cue for two different words, for example, there is a b̲ in b̲a̲g̲ but there is also a b̲ in b̲a̲t̲. Unless the child picks a different cue for these two words, such as the g in b̲a̲g̲ and the t̲ in b̲a̲t̲, then he or she is likely to get some of the words mixed up. It was found that the different-looking words were a lot easier to learn than the words which looked very similar.

What about the thumbprint? What was that there for? Gough reasoned that the thumbprint was a highly distinctive cue, like the golden arches on 'McDonald's' signs. Children would use this cue to remember the word that was also on the flashcard. The results showed that the word with the thumbprint on the card was learned first. These preschool children took the easiest cue they could to remember the word. To show just how much the children relied on this thumbprint cue, they were shown a different word, but with a thumbprint on the card. Nearly all of the children thought the new word was the original 'thumbprint' word.

What sorts of distinctive cues will children use? The cues can vary from one word to the next. Gough, Juel and Griffith (1992) suggest five different cues:

- a single letter cue, such as the <u>d</u> in <u>dog</u>
- a double letter cue, such as the <u>ee</u> in <u>feet</u>
- a cue which suggests the meaning of the word, such as the 'humps' on the letter <u>m</u> in <u>camel</u> or the 'eyes' [<u>oo</u>] in <u>look</u> or the 'tail' on the letter <u>g</u> in <u>dog</u>
- a cue such as length (<u>ant</u> is short; <u>crocodile</u> is long)
- a letter which has the same sound as the word, such as the <u>b</u> in <u>bee</u>.

But how is this relevant to real reading of text? Gough, Juel and Roper-Schneider (1983) asked 63 first-grade children to read a passage about the adventures of a mouse. They found that children in the study who could not yet read would rely on memory for words they had seen before rather than sound-out the word. For example, children might read <u>grey mouse</u> as <u>good mouse</u>, because <u>grey</u> looks like the word <u>good,</u> which they have seen before in another primer.

## Other Early Reading Strategies

Gibbs (1987) read the story *Paru* to five-year-old beginners and then asked them to read the story on their own. He found that the beginners relied on picture clues and their memories for the story. For example:

*Text* (with picture of wet dog shaking off the water).
'I see you bathed Paru,' said Aunty Mina.
'That's good.'
Arf! Arf! barked Paru as he shook water all over Aunty Mina.
*Child*

I glad you had a bath, and a woof woof, and he went all over Aunty Mina.

Gibbons (1981) found that some beginners are better than this. They have pre-reading skills, such as the ability to identify most of the letters of the alphabet. Also, through lots of home experiences in reading stories with their parents, they have learned that the story has to be read a certain way, and that the story has to stay the same, and that even minor changes are not allowed. Gibbons compared the re-readings of children who had been read to many times with children who had been read to hardly at all. She found marked differences in re-readings. The four-year-olds who had been read to very little had difficulty in retelling a story; but the four-year-olds who had been read to many times were much more sophisticated. Here is an example from a child who had been read to many times:

*Text*
'I am taking a walk,' said the duckling.
*Child*
I am taking a walk, said the chick, I mean duckling.

This child was relying on what she remembered of the story after it was read to her. She was aware that there was a story to be told and that the text could only be read one way. Children who have not had experiences of being read to may not see this. They may have trouble picking up what the story is about. Here is an example of a five-year-old beginner who was given a book not seen before (Gibbs, 1981):

*Text*
Look! Here comes a man in a taxi.
'He'll do,' says the ghost.
The taxi stops and the man jumps out.
'Boo,' says the ghost.
*Child* (reading the pictures):
There's a tree, a taxi, the lady and the man, tree with branches, words for the story, wheels, path, leaves and the bricks.

In the above example, the 'words for the story' are seen in the same way as the pictures on the page. They are there, just like the pictures of the taxi and the bricks on the wall, but the child is unable to recognise them. Even the pictures are not perfect cues for the text. For example, the child thought the picture of the ghost was a picture of a tree. This was a child who had not yet learned that the book tells a story.

### Can Children Learn to Read by Being Read To?

Gibbs and Nicholson (1999) found no evidence of this. Sixty-four beginning readers, from homes in a low-income small town in New Zealand, were given the opportunity to listen to simple, predictable books that were read to them via an audiotape recorder and headphones. Children listened to stories and were encouraged to read along, with a tone-cue to turn the page when needed. The study compared the effects of just listening to stories with being able to read along, turning the pages of the book along with the pace of the audiotape. Some children in the study simply read the books on their own, while others listened to the audiotaped readings. The children listened to 12 stories. Some of the stories were repeated many times, so that in all they had up to eight opportunities to listen to each story.

It was hoped that these simulated home-reading experiences of listening to stories might enable children to acquire some pre-reading skills in a natural way without explicit instruction. The results were disappointing. Children who listened to the audiotapes made considerable gains in ability to retell stories very accurately. But when asked to read a list of commonly occurring words in the stories and when asked to read new stories at the same level of difficulty, they were no better than children who had not had stories read to them. They had learned the art of telling the story as it was told to them, but they had not learned to read.

Why is it that children can't learn to read by having books read to them? It seems that listening to talking books is like being driven to a destination in a taxi. Someone else is doing the driving for you so there is no need to pay attention. The child who is being read to does not have to confront the alphabetic principle, since someone else is doing it for them.

This does not mean that reading to children is unimportant. Whitehurst *et al.* (1988) found that reading picture books to two- and three-year-olds improved their language development by increasing their vocabulary. But the reason this happened is that they used a reading technique called 'dialogic reading', where the parent was taught to ask open-ended questions to the child while reading and to encourage the child to think about words. The parents were also trained to give complete explanations of what words meant when the story contained words the child did not know. So, reading books to children can have value – the key is what parents do while reading the book. If the child is allowed to sit back and enjoy, that's fine, but not very much will be learned. If the child is to learn some new things, the parent has to be a source of information and also someone who encourages the child to engage with the words and the print. Otherwise, being read to will not provide the kinds of experiences necessary to learn to read.

### Necessary, But Not Sufficient: Phonemic Awareness

The non-reader may be a child who is read to by parents on a daily basis. A non-reader may also be an expert label and sign reader. Such a child will be drawn to look for distinctive cues to remember words. This child may be able to write his or her name, but it will be learned by rote rather than recognised as a series of letter sounds.

If a child wants to acquire the alphabetic principle, he or she has to become aware of phonemes. The path to phonemic awareness starts with a general awareness that spoken language has a structure to it. Children have to go through stages of understanding where they realise that spoken language is made up of sentences, that sentences are made of words, and that spoken words are made up of phonemes.

This general awareness of the properties of language is called 'metalinguistic awareness' (Tunmer *et al.* 1988). The child needs to realise that books represent spoken language, but in visible form. What is written on the page corresponds to spoken language. Words and sentences are made visible in writing. When we write sentences, we write them in words. When we write words, we use letters. These letters represent phonemes. When we write, we separate the words with spaces, we use punctuation to show the ends of sentences and so on. The child has to understand all these things.

Children who are aware that there are such things as 'words' and that the letters in words are little 'sounds' have figured out an important principle, that we use letters to make spoken words visible in writing. This understanding will not happen unless that child has metalinguistic awareness, which means knowing that spoken utterances can be broken into words, that spoken words can be broken into sounds, and that utterances have to follow certain grammatical rules which specify when words or utterances are correct or incorrect.

Metalinguistic awareness emerges late, in the middle-childhood period between five and 12 years of age, although it can appear earlier. For example, here is a remark from a three-year-old girl (Limber, 1973, cited in Hakes, 1980): 'When I was a little girl I could go "geek-geek" like that. But now I can go "this is a chair"' (p. 164). The child seems to have some awareness of the properties of language. She knows that utterances must make sense. There are four types of metalinguistic awareness: word awareness, syntactic awareness, pragmatic awareness and phonemic awareness (Tunmer & Bowey, 1984).

Awareness of grammatical acceptability is called *syntactic awareness*. For example, four-year-olds have been found to say that 'apple the soap' is wrong (which it is), but that 'horn the blow' is correct (de Villiers & de Villiers, 1972). This is because, at that age, they think of an utterance in terms of whether or not it makes sense. While they might agree with you that 'apple the soap' does not make sense, they will say that 'horn the blow' is correct because they can make sense of it when the words are reversed. In contrast, the syntactically aware child analyses a sentence in terms of whether or not it is grammatically correct. For example (Hakes, 1980): 'Adult: "The little boy didn't have some cookies in his lunch. Is that okay or silly?" Child: "That's a little silly. You have to say 'any cookies', or perhaps 'many cookies'"' (p. 163).

Awareness of how to use language appropriately is called *pragmatic awareness*. It means being aware that utterances should be adequate, comprehensible and appropriate for the audience, otherwise they will not be understood. In the example below, five- and even seven-year-olds had trouble deciding whether the utterance was adequate and comprehensible, even though the word 'she' made the message impossible to understand (Bearison & Levey, 1977): 'Jane got a bicycle for Xmas, and Mary got a new coat. What did she get for Xmas, a bicycle or a new coat?'. In terms of 'message comprehensibility', preschoolers sometimes respond to 'silly' sentences without seeming to be aware that they are nonsense. For example (Finn, 1976): 'Adult: "Are there more wugs or glugs?" Child: "There are more wugs." Adult: "Why?" Child: "Because they're taller"'. Pragmatic awareness is important for learning to read. The pragmatically aware child demands from the print that it is adequate and comprehensible. Such a child is aware that the print is meant to convey a sensible message, that printed information is not just a chaos of squiggles on the page.

A third form of linguistic awareness is *word awareness*. This involves knowing that 'word' is a term we use for talking about language. The word-aware child knows that 'words' are arbitrary labels and that a 'word' can have more than one meaning. Many preschool children have trouble answering the question, 'Tell me a word – any word you know' (Francis, 1973). Beginner readers can be confused about the term 'word'. One child was reported as saying that 'words are made up of words' (Reid, 1966). I noticed this myself on a recent occasion, when I said to a five-year-old pupil, "I'd like you to read some words for me". The child replied, "What's a word?" Word awareness is important for learning to read. The word-aware child begins school knowing what letters and words are. When the teacher says, 'Point to the *letter* M' or 'Tell me what that *word* says', the word-aware child knows what the teacher is talking about. In contrast, the word-unaware child may think that an adult reading to them is just that person talking, even though the adult may have a book in his or her hands (Gough & Hillinger, 1980). Such a child is also likely not to understand what the teacher means when using terms like *word* and *letter*.

Clay's (1967) longitudinal study of five-year-old New Zealand school beginners found that children moved from fluent reading of primers, which they had memorised, to a stage of word-by-word reading where the child's reading became staccato as he or she overemphasised the breaks between words. This is the 'voice pointing' or 'reading the spaces stage' (p. 16). After that, as the child became more skilled at reading, voice pointing was replaced by phrase reading as the child began to read more naturally.

Adams (1990) explains that children are not initially aware of what a word is. They have the idea that all words should be three to five letters in length, and that longer words consist of more than one word. This is why some teachers visually show how words are separated by spaces. They might write a sentence on a strip of paper. And then cut up the sentence, word by word (Clay, 1993). Another technique is to use flash-cards. You can string them one after the other to make a sentence (e.g. I love my mum) and switch the cards around (e.g. my mum love I) so that the child can see that sentences are just words in different combinations.

The fourth and most important form of metalinguistic awareness is *phonological awareness* ['phono-' means 'sound'; 'logos' means 'word'], which is being aware that spoken words are made up of phonemes. Many preschoolers can't decide whether the sound of a word is short or long. Rozin *et al.* (1974) were able to show that preschool children don't relate the number of sounds in a word to the length of its printed form. They showed preschool children two printed words – mow and motorcycle. They said to each preschooler, 'One of these printed words is 'mow' and one is 'motorcycle'. Can you point to the word that is 'mow'? They found that only four in ten preschool children chose the correct word, only one child in ten children in their sample who were from low-income backgrounds was correct. Why did this happen? The reason is that preschool children think about a word in terms of its meaning. While they lack phonemic awareness, they lack the knowledge that some words have more phonemes in them than do other words, whether its meaning is long or short.

As we noted earlier, preschool children may have arbitrary ideas about what 'word' means, for example that a word consists of several words, or that a word needs only three or four letters to be a word. For example, Papandropoulou and Sinclair (1974) asked preschool children to decide which spoken word was longer – 'train' or 'dandelion'. Children thought that 'train' was long, and that 'dandelion' was short, which was true about their meanings, but not about their sounds.

Why is phonemic awareness important? It has classroom value in that it makes the task of learning the sounds of the alphabet easier. The child who lacks phonemeic awareness may know what the teacher is talking about when instruction turns to letter–sound correspondences such as 'The sound of the letter *m* is /mmmm/. And *m* is the first sound in *mouse*'. When the teacher talks like this, the phonemically aware child can switch on, while other children, who lack this skill, will not understand. The phonemically aware child will know what to do when the teacher says 'Watch my mouth as I say the phonemes *s ... a ... m*. What word did I say? Yes, *Sam*. Now, you can write your name, *Sam*. What you do is you look for the letters on your alphabet card that have the same sounds as in your name'. Classroom talk like this is a lot easier to understand if a child has phonemic awareness. The child can benefit from instruction.

### Learning the Alphabet

Learning the alphabet has never been easy, but it may be a lot easier if children already have phonemic awareness. Over the centuries there have been many resources printed to help children learn their ABCs. The letters of the alphabet are 26 abstract symbols that are not related to anything in a child's real life. This is why many children are given alphabet books. The idea is to make the task easier for them by providing illustrations to associate to the letters. An alphabet chart is shown on page 190. Children are often given a chart like this in school to help them with their writing. Teachers can informally check a child's knowledge of the alphabet by randomly pointing to letters and asking the child to tell them the names of the letters and their sounds.

Adams (1990) and Ehri (1987) suggest that a good way to learn the letters is to learn their names. Children can be introduced to the alphabet song at an early age. The song is based on the tune 'Twinkle Twinkle Little Star'. Once children can sing all the names of the letters, they can begin to associate each printed letter to its name. Over the centuries many techniques have been used to help children link letters to their names. Parents have made alphabet cookies, shops sell alphabet soup, and there are numerous alphabet books. There are also television programmes which teach the alphabet, such as *Sesame Street* and *The Magic Box*.

Why learn the names of letters rather than their sounds? Adams (1990) argues that the letter names are a base for further learning. It's also a traditional way to start. There must be some merit in learning the names, given that it's been done for thousands of years. It's easy to see the advantages. The child and the parent (and the teacher) have a set of labels for talking about letters. The parent can play games like 'Find me the letter k', and so on. The teacher can use repetition to teach children how to spell very frequent words that are not easy to sound out, like 'the'. The teacher can say or sing out the spelling, 'Let's spell the. It's 'tee aitch ee', and so on.

Worden and Boettcher (1990) surveyed 188 children whose ages ranged from 2.5 to 7.5 years. They found a sequence of alphabet skills. Children learned uppercase letters before lowercase, they learned letter names before letter sounds, and they learned to identify letters better than they could write them by hand. Should we therefore teach uppercase letters first? The problem is that primers and picture books for children are all printed in lowercase (Adams, 1990). So children really need to start with lowercase, although many reading textbook authors suggest that children start with both (see Lesiak, 1997). This seems to be commonly done. Children's alphabet cards, for example, have lowercase and uppercase letters on them (e.g. Butterflies, 1993). It may be easier to start with lowercase and uppercase letters which are very similar (e.g. Pp, Ss, Cc, Kk).

## When Should Children Learn to Write the Alphabet?

Children are usually taught to write letters early. One possible advantage is that this helps to direct their attention to the distinctive features of letters. Demonstrating how to write the letters may also be important. For example, writing the letter b (vertical line, then the circle) involves a different approach to that of the letter d (circle, then the vertical line). Keeping these writing formats distinct may help children to avoid confusion.

In old primers (e.g. Whitcombe & Tombs, undated), children were taught to visualise the letter d as a person with a drum tied in front, and the letter b as a person with a bag on his or her back. There is no evidence that these strategies were at all helpful. Orientation is a difficult problem for children in identifying letters like b, d, m, w and so on. Perhaps the only visual association that I've seen work is the one where the child is taught that b and d are opposite ends of a bed. The child physically forms a bed shape using both hands. The idea is to remember that the first sound in 'bed' is /b/. The child looks at the beginning of the 'bed' shaped by their hands, which gives a visual clue as to which way to write the letter b. Copying letters onto paper, tracing their shape in the air with the fingers, tracing sandpaper alphabet letters, and leaping from one square to another while playing alphabet hopscotch are all commonplace activities in schools as children find ways to distinguish the shapes and orientations of the 26 alphabet letters.

## Can Letter Names Help Reveal Their Sounds?

Ehri (1987) has argued that letter names give cues as to the sounds of the letters. She feels this is the first stage of being able to decipher

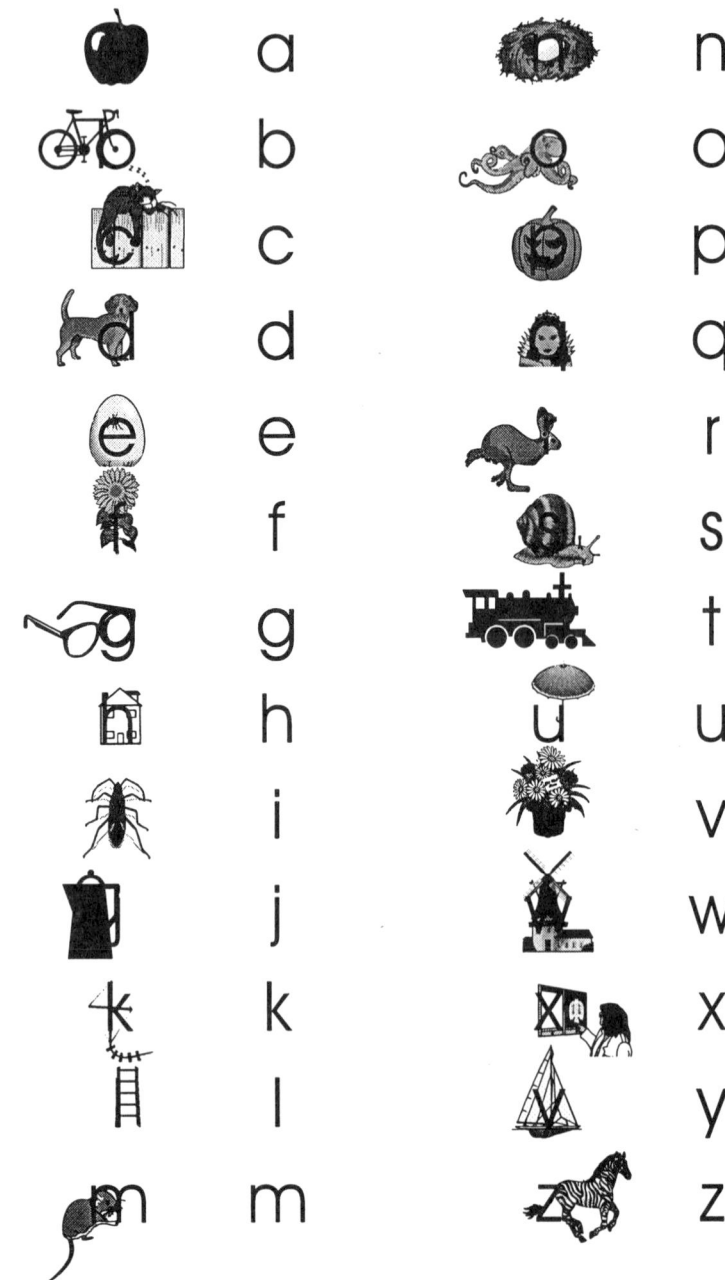

words, which she calls 'phonetic cue reading' (p. 14). This is where the child uses the name of letters to assist in reading and spelling words. Put another way, children use letter names to link to phonemes (e.g. <u>bee</u> is spelled with the letter <u>B</u>; <u>elephant</u> is spelled <u>LFT</u>). The phonetic cue stage is intermediate between the non-reader stage of using distinctive associations (e.g. initial letter) and word length and the final stage of reading and writing words according to their phonemic construction. This intermediate stage of phonetic cue reading may be a good place to start teaching the sounds of letters. For example, teachers can begin with letter sounds that are almost the same as the letter names (e.g. <u>s</u>, <u>r</u>, <u>m</u>).

Mathews (1966) wrote that the Greeks used to name their slaves after the letters of the alphabet to help their children associate the letters with something real. Bormuth (1982) noted that the Phoenician letters were names after real things. For example, the letter A was called 'aleph', which was their word for 'ox'. In the middle east, the letter A is still called 'aleph'. Nowadays, the best we can do to teach the sounds of letters is to use pictures that start with the sound of the letter. The pictures become key words. Alphabet cards capitalise on the association between picture and letter sound. So do most (not all) alphabet books. Ehri, Deffner and Wilce (1984) found that children learned to relate letters to sounds faster if the letter and key word pictures were integrated (e.g. a picture of the letter <u>h</u> looking like a little house, with smoke coming out a chimney on the hump of the <u>h</u>). Opposite is an example of an alphabet chart that integrates the letters with key-word illustrations. Note that the chart focuses on the sounds of the letters. Children will need to be told that letters have names *and* sounds, and that some letters can have two sounds (i.e. the five vowels, as well as <u>c</u> and <u>g</u>).

### Handwriting

In English, the written forms of the letters of the alphabet are not always taught in the same way. For example, in New Zealand, children must use the sequences of strokes that are recommended by the Ministry of Education (undated). In Australia, the forms of letters used in schools vary from state to state.

The use of lined paper when learning to write the letters of the alphabet is an issue. Opinions vary (Lesiak, 1997), but it seems that lined paper can be useful if the spaces between the lines are generous (e.g. 25 millimetres). Is it alright for children to use adult-size pencils? The answer appears to be yes. Use a plain lead adult-size pencil (Askov & Peck, 1982; Ministry of Education, undated). The ballpoint pen can come later, after children are able to write the letter forms.

It appears that handwriting errors occur when the child practises without supervision, when no immediate feedback is given, and when children copy by rote rather than thinking about the quality of their efforts compared with what they are copying. It appears to be more effective if children copy just the troublesome letters instead of repeatedly copying all the letters.

## Conclusion

Children begin their reading development struggling to find distinctive cues to help them remember words (e.g. the 'tail' on dog). They do not learn to read simply by being read to; they rely on memory for the text. They learn the text by heart so they can read it just as well without the book even being present. They will rely on picture clues and context clues. The non-reader can leave this stage by using phonetic cues, where the name of the letter helps to read or spell a word (e.g. the b in bee.) The next stage is to learn how to decipher words by blending the letter sounds to make a word that can be recognised as a spoken word. When this happens, the child has made the very important move from being a cue reader to a cipher reader. To help make this happen it means: (a) learning the alphabet song, (b) learning to identify the letters of the alphabet according to their names, (c) learning the most common sound of each letter, (d) learning to write the letters, and (e) learning to do all these things for both uppercase and lowercase letters. This is a big task but a very important one. It is another key to the door.

## References

Adams, M. J. (1990). *Beginning to read. Thinking and learning about print.* Cambridge, MA: MIT Press.

Askov, E., & Peck, M. (1982). Handwriting. In H. Mitzel, J. Best & W.

Rabinowitz (Eds.), *Encyclopedia of educational research* (pp. 764–769). New York: The Free Press

Bearison, D.J., & Levey, L.M. (1977). Children's comprehension of referential communication: Decoding ambiguous messages. *Child Development*, *48*, 716–720.

Bormuth, M. (1982). *The roots of phonics: A historical introduction*. Baltimore, MD: York Press.

Butterflies (1993). *Alphabet card*. Auckland, New Zealand: Author.

Clay, M. M. (1967). The reading behaviour of five-year-old children: A research report. *New Zealand Journal of Educational Studies, 2*, 11–31.

Clay, M.M. (1993). *Reading Recovery*. Auckland: Heinemann.

De Villiers, P.A., & De Villiers, J.G. (1972). Early judgements of semantic and syntactic acceptability by children. *Journal of Psycholinguistic Research, 1*, 299–310.

Durrell, D. D. (1956). *Improving reading instruction*. New York: Harcourt Brace & World.

Ehri, L. C. (1987). Learning to read and spell words. *Journal of Reading Behavior, 19*, 5–31.

Ehri, L. C., Deffner, N. D., & Wilce, L. S. (1984). Pictorial mnemonics for phonics. *Journal of Educational Psychology, 76*, 880–893.

Finn, G.P. (1976). Ask a silly question: But get a serious answer. Unpublished paper, University of St. Andrews, Scotland.

Foss, D., & Hakes, D. (1978). Psycholinguistics: An introduction to the psychology of language. Englewood Cliffs, NJ: Prentice Hall.

Francis, H. (1973). Children's experience of reading and notions of units in language. *British Journal of Educational Psychology, 43*, 17–23.

Gibbons, J. (1981). *The effects of book experience on the responses of four-year-olds to texts*. Unpublished master's thesis, The University of Waikato, Hamilton, New Zealand.

Gibbs, C. (1981). *The effect of repeated tellings of stories on young children's telling about the pictures in the stories*. Unpublished manuscript, The University of Waikato, Hamilton, New Zealand.

Gibbs, C. (1987). What do beginners say when they 'read'? *Australian Journal of Reading, 10*, 158–170.

Gibbs, C. J., & Nicholson, T. (1999). When you've heard it all before and still can't read. *Effective School Practices, 17*, 78–84.

Goodall, M. (1984). Can four-year-olds 'read' words in the environment?

*The Reading Teacher, 37*, 478–482.

Gough, P. B. (1993). The beginning of decoding. *Reading and Writing, 5*, 181–192.

Gough, P. B., & Hillinger, M. L. (1980). Learning to read: An unnatural act. *Bulletin of the Orton Society, 30*, 179–186.

Gough, P.B., Juel, C., & Griffith, P.L. (1992). Reading, spelling, and the orthographic cipher. In P.B. Gough, L.C. Ehri & R. Treiman (Eds.), *Reading acquisition* (pp. 35–48). Hillsdale, NJ: Erlbaum.

Gough, P. B., Juel, C., & Roper-Schneider, D. (1983). Code and cipher: A two-stage conception of initial reading acquisition. In J.A. Niles & L. A. Harris (Eds.), *Searches for meaning in reading/language processing and instruction* (pp. 207–211). Rochester, NY: National Reading Conference.

Groff, P. (1984). Resolving the letter name controversy. *The Reading Teacher, 37*, 384–388.

Hakes, D. (1980). The development of metalinguistic abilities: What develops? In S.A. Kuczaj (Ed.), *Language Acquisition: Language, cognition and culture* (pp. 163–210). Hillsdale, NJ: Erlbaum.

Juel, C. (1988). Learning to read and write: A longitudinal study of 54 children from first through fourth grades. *Journal of Educational Psychology 80*, 437–447.

Juel, C., Griffith, P.L., & Gough, P.B. (1986). Acquisition of literacy: A longitudinal study of children in first and second grade. *Journal of Educational Psychology 78*, 243–255.

Lesiak, J. L. (1997). Research based answers to questions about emergent literacy in kindergarten. *Psychology in the Schools, 34*, 133–166.

Masonheimer, P. E., Drum, P. A., & Ehri, L. C. (1984). Does environmental print identification lead children into word reading? *Journal of Reading Behavior, 16*, 257–271.

Mathews, M. (1966). *Learning to read: Historically considered.* Chicago, IL: The University of Chicago Press.

Ministry of Education (Undated). *Teaching handwriting.* Wellington, New Zealand: Author.

Papandropoulou, I., & Sinclair, H. (1974). What is a word? Experimental study of children's ideas on grammar. *Human Development, 17*, 241–258.

Pratt, C., & Nesdale, R. (1984). Pragmatic awareness in children. In

W.E. Tunmer, C. Pratt, & M.L. Herriman (Eds.), *Metalinguistic awareness in children: Theory, research and implications* (pp. 105–125). Berlin: Springer Verlag.

Reid, J.F. (1966). Learning to think about reading. *Educational Research*, *9*, 56–62.

Rozin, P., Bressnan, B., & Taft, M. (1974). Do children understand the basic relationship between speech and writing? The mow–motorcycle test. *Journal of Reading Behavior, 6*, 327–334.

Tunmer, W.E., & Bowey, J. (1984). Metalinguistic awareness and reading acquisition. In W. E. Tunmer, C. Pratt & M. L. Herriman (Eds.), *Metalinguistic Awareness in Children* (pp. 144–168). Berlin: Springer Verlag.

Tunmer, W.E., Herriman, M.L., & Nesdale, A.R. (1988). Metalinguistic abilities and beginning reading. *Reading Research Quarterly, 23*, 134–158.

Whitcombe & Tombs (undated). *The teaching of reading to infants: A guide to the method of the Progressive Primer Serie*s. Christchurch, New Zealand: Author.

Whitehurst, G. J., Falco, F. L., Lonigan, C. J., Fischel, J. E., DeBaryshe, B. D., Valdez–Menchaca, M. C., & Caulfield, M. (1988). Accelerating language development through picture book reading. *Developmental Psychology, 24*, 552–559.

Worden, P. E., & Boettcher, W. (1990). Young children's acquisition of alphabet knowledge. *Journal of Reading Behavior, 22*, 277–295.

# 8

# PHONEMIC AWARENESS AND READING

Most children start school with very good spoken language skills. They understand thousands of different words and can understand almost any sentence you put to them. Yet hardly any of them can read. Within a year of school, most will be able to read simple texts, while some will still be struggling with the reading task. One major stumbling block for the struggling beginner is phonemic awareness.

### What is Phonemic Awareness?

Phonemic awareness is an awareness that spoken words can be deconstructed into their component phonemes ('phone' means 'sound' in Greek). A phoneme is a minimal sound unit that can change the meaning of a word. For example, /k/ and /r/ are phonemes that can change a spoken word like /at/ into /kat/ or /rat/. Phonemic awareness is not all-or-nothing. A child can have a little bit of phonemic awareness if he or she is able to break a word into its onset and rime (e.g. /k/ - /at/) or if the child can tell you that /f/ is the first sound in, say, /fish/. Some researchers might say that the child who can do this has some awareness of the phonological structure of a word, but does not have full phonemic awareness (Share, 1995). Phonological awareness means knowing about sounds in words at a broader level, for example knowing how to break a word into syllables, or how to break the syllable into its onset and its rime. A syllable is a speech unit that contains a vowel (e.g. 'fish' is one syllable; 'fish ing' is two syllables. The onset of a syllable is the beginning consonant(s) and the rime of the syllable (rime is a technical term) is the remainder, including the vowel and optional consonants. Thus, the onset of 'cat' is /k/ and the rime is /-at/. The child who has complete phonemic awareness, however, has the ability to segment a spoken word completely (e.g. the sounds in /fish/ are /f/-/i/-/sh/.)

### Is Phonemic Awareness Like Phonics?

Phonics is a method of teaching how to associate letters to sounds, so as to sound out words in reading. It assumes phonemic awareness but does not necessarily teach it. In contrast, phonemic awareness instruction involves teaching how to analyse sounds within spoken words, not written ones. The easiest way to distinguish phonemic awareness from phonics is to ask yourself, is this activity just focusing on spoken language, or am I teaching alphabet letters as well? If you are teaching about how letters correspond to phonemes, then you aren't teaching phonemic awareness. You are teaching phonics. When teaching phonemic awareness the teacher will use spoken words, or illustrations, but will not use letters. In practice, though, it is hard to resist combining phonemic awareness instruction and phonics. In fact, teaching children how to relate letters to phonemes seems to be more effective than teaching phonemic awareness on its own (Bradley & Bryant, 1983).

### Is Phonemic Awareness Like Phonetics?

Phonetic analysis is a way of describing how speech sounds are made; it is not phonemic awareness and it is not phonics. Phonetics is the study of speech sounds: how they are produced, and how to classify them. What is the difference? In phonetics, the interest is in the phone, that is, the way the phoneme is expressed. For example, the same phoneme can be expressed in a slightly different way in different words because of phonemes that precede or follow it. The /p/ in pin is different phonetically to the /p/ in 'spin' or 'nip'. You can easily tell this by holding your hand to your mouth when saying these words. There is a puff of air when you say 'pin', less so when you say 'spin', and not at all when you say 'nip'. Another example is the sound of /b/ when you say 'bunny' or 'big' or 'beautiful'. The /b/ phoneme is slightly different phonetically in each spoken word, although we hear each /b/ as the same phoneme. A phonetician is interested in such small variation (called allophonic variation). But phonemic awareness is not concerned with that. In teaching phonemic awareness we want the child to break free of phonetic sensitivity and realise that sounds like the /b/ in bunny and bounce are phonemically the same. Thus, phonemic awareness is the ability to think about the sounds of words separately from their spellings and from the slight phonetic variations that occur within the structure of phonemes.

### Testing For Phonological Awareness

Tests of phonological awareness usually involve looking at pictures of objects or listening to spoken words. The assessment of phonological awareness can include awareness of syllable components of words (e.g. 'Can you say bunny without the 'ny'?') and awareness of the onset-rime structure of syllables (e.g. 'I'll say the sounds in Mike. M-ike. Now, can you say the sounds in shop?'). A phonological awareness test might assess children's knowledge of syllables, onset-rime, and phonemes. But a phonemic awareness test will focus on awareness of specific phonemes in words.

Gough, Larson and Yopp (1993) concluded that phonemic awareness does not just happen overnight. Instead, it dawns gradually across the word. The stages appear to be:

- can blend phonemes (e.g. m-a-t)
- can isolate the last phoneme (e.g. /m/ in 'thumb')
- can isolate the first phoneme (e.g. /f/ in 'fish')
- can delete a phoneme (e.g. 'spot' without /s/ is 'pot').

Thus, some tests of phonemic awareness will be easier than others. Gough, Larson and Yopp argue that it is easier for a child to say what is left if we take the last sound (/t/) off meat (answer is 'me') than it is to say what is left if we take the (/m/) off meat (answer is 'eat'.) This is because it is mentally harder to take off a beginning phoneme than an ending one. Also , it's easier for a child to verify to you that 'cat' and 'hat' rhyme than it is for the same child to think of a word that rhymes with 'cat'. Why? The reason is that the 'cat-hat' task gives the child a 50 per cent chance of being right. To think of another word that rhymes with 'cat' is much harder. The key skill of phonemic awareness is that the child has to ignore the meaning of a word and focus on its form. The child has to think about sounds in words, not meanings of words. This can be difficult. For example, a five-year-old who can only think of the meaning in a word is likely to say that the sounds in 'cat' are 'meow' or the sounds in 'dog' are 'woof'.

## A Short History of Phonemic Awareness Research

Research on phonological awareness and reading is quite recent (Leong, 1991). Researchers in Moscow in the 1960s were aware that preschool children lacked phonological awareness. Elkonin wrote about 'glass theory' (1971: 139). He had decided that for beginner readers language was like a clear glass window through which the child looked at the world. If children could be taught that the glass was there, then they would have phonemic awareness. Elkonin wanted to put a smudge on that window in the mind of the child, to create an awareness that words could be analysed in terms of their sounds.

Also in the 1960s, United States researchers Alvin and Isabelle Liberman were also tackling the phonological awareness problem. Liberman (1968, cited in Bertelson & de Gelder, 1993: 394) wrote that if phonemes 'are real, they are not necessarily real at a high level of awareness. That is to say, it does not follow from anything I have said that the man in the street can tell you about phonemes, or that he can even tell you how many phonemes there are in particular utterances'. According to Mann (1991), Isabelle Liberman in 1970 presented a paper in which she also linked phonological awareness with the task of learning to read. Looking back, it seems clear that the Russian researchers had an intuitive understanding that phonemic awareness was a problem for school beginners. But the American researchers had a better understanding of why it was a problem. They had done the speech research that showed how phonemes in spoken words were *not* like eggs lined up in an egg carton, one after the other (Liberman, 1996). They had found that phonemes do not exist separately in the speech stream. Instead, information about particular phonemes was often found in phonemes that preceded and followed them. To pursue the egg metaphor, phonemes in spoken words are more like an omelette than a linear series of sounds. This is called parallel transmission – phonemes overlap one another. This is why it is difficult mentally to split phonemes off from spoken words. We can learn to do it, but it doesn't come naturally. Some phonemes can be said in isolation (e.g. /m/ and /s/), but others are not like this. For example, the phoneme /b/ in 'bag' is not able to be isolated and pronounced on its own. If we say /b/ on its own, we say /beh/, which is two phonemes. Thus, children have quite a difficult task in learning about phonemes.

### Research since the 1960s

In England, Bruce (1964) found that many children had difficulty with deletion of phonemes. For example, when asked to say what word would be left if the 's' were taken from the middle of 'nest', one child said, 'I can't actually do it. You see, I can't say the last letter without the middle'.

Liberman *et al.* (1974) in the United States found that only 20 per cent of five-year-olds could tap the number of phonemes in words like ice (2 phonemes) and spy (3 phonemes).

Bradley & Bryant (1978) in England found that older, poor readers were significantly worse than younger, average readers in picking one word out of four that did not follow the same phonological pattern (e.g. 'weed', 'peel', 'need', 'deed', where 'peel' is the odd one out).

Juel *et al.* (1986), in the United States, found that American children who later became poor readers had entered first grade with little or no phonemic awareness. In contrast, children who became good readers had entered first grade with much higher levels of phonemic awareness.

### Teaching phonemic awareness

Elkonin (1973) taught preschoolers to segment spoken words. The child would name a picture (e.g. 'gusi' is Russian for goose), then say the word sound by sound (e.g. 'g-u-s-i'), at the same time putting down a cardboard chip (different colour for consonants and vowels) for each sound. Children in kindergarten and first grade were able to learn how to analyse sounds in words in ten to 12 lessons.

Bradley and Bryant (1983) reported that five-year-old children who received phonological awareness training along with the use of letters of the alphabet to create simple words (e.g. and, sand), made significant gains in reading and spelling over a two-year period of instruction.

Lundberg, Frost and Petersen (1988) were able to produce significant gains in the phonological awareness skills of preschool children before they began formal schooling. This training programme has since been published (Adams *et al.*, 1998). They followed these children through their first two years of school and found the training contributed to reading progress though not until the second year. Note that teaching phonemic awareness is usually done verbally, without using letters of the alphabet. The focus is on teaching children to 'hear' sounds in words, not to relate sounds to letters.

### What Predicts Reading Progress?

Bryant *et al.* (1989) found that English children's knowledge of traditional English nursery rhymes at three years of age strongly predicted their reading ability at six years of age. Layton *et al.* (1996) reported that pre-reading English children in nursery school (four-year-olds) responded better to rhyme activities (e.g. 'What is wrong with Jack and Jill / Went up the road?') than to training involving word onsets. A difficulty with training of onsets is the concept of 'beginning sound'. Another idea is to use 'I spy' games to teach preschoolers about beginning sounds, for example, 'I spy with my little eye, something beginning with /f/', where the first phoneme is pronounced as /f/, not as /ef/ (which is the name of the letter f).

### Can Phonemic Awareness Instruction be Included in Whole-Language Teaching?

Castle, Riach and Nicholson (1994) found that phonemic awareness training added to a whole-language reading programme had a positive effect on five-year-old children's reading and spelling progress. Children receiving phonological awareness training engaged in activities which focused specifically on phonemes. Castle (1998) gives examples of the training, such as slowed pronunciation of words (e.g. What word is mmmm-ou-sss?), segmenting of the initial phoneme (e.g. What is the first sound in bbbbb-bear?), rhyme (e.g. Which pictures rhyme? – show pictures of log, dog and sun), phoneme deletion and substitution (e.g. Say cat. Now instead of 'cuh', let's start it off with 'm'. What is the mystery word?) and complete phonemic segmentation (e.g. using the Elkonin [1973] method, where the child places counters in square boxes below the picture of an object, one counter for each sound in the word).

### Are There Problems With Phonemic Awareness Research?

A problem with much of the research is that phonological training has also been accompanied by reading instruction, which makes it difficult to know whether it is the phonological awareness training or reading instruction that makes the difference.

Ehri (1996) thinks that learning to read probably teaches children phonological awareness. The invisible nature of phonemes is made visible in print. Read (1978) also argues that the emergence of phonemic awareness while learning to read is 'highly suspicious' (p. 73), in that teaching reading probably facilitates phonemic awareness. The results of the Castle *et al.* (1994) study showed that some control group children did acquire phonemic awareness without explicit instruction. The control group made gains, even though they did not receive special phonemic awareness teaching.

However, research such as that carried out by Lundberg *et al.* (1988) and Juel (1988) supports the alternative view that phonological awareness is an important prerequisite in learning to read. It helps children get off to a better start in reading and spelling. Juel found that the children in her study who did not learn to read well were the ones who started school with very low levels of phonemic awareness.

Another problem is the level of phonological awareness the teacher aims for. Do we have to aim for complete segmentation ability (e.g. where the child can explicitly segment all of the sounds in cat)? Gough *et al.* (1993) argue in favour of full segmentation skill, since this will make it easier for the child to infer letter–sound relationships.

### Implications

The key to the door of reading appears to be skills in phonemic awareness. The goal to aim for is the ability to segment all the phonemes in a word (e.g. /cat/ = /k/-/a/-/t/). But this is not going to happen overnight. Some researchers have a systematic procedure for teaching about phonemes. Byrne and Fielding-Barnsley's (1991) 'Sound Foundations' teaches children to isolate, both at the beginning and end of spoken words, six consonants (s, m, p, l, t, g), a consonant digraph (sh), and two vowels (a, e). They use posters and other illustrated materials to do this teaching. But an informal way of teaching the task would be to go through the various consonant vowels and digraphs until most of them have been covered. Keeping a checklist of the ones covered each day would be helpful. It is also a good idea to start associating phonemes to the alphabet letters as soon as possible.

Here is an example with the sound /s/. Link the sound to the letter s. The next day, move to a new sound and its corresponding letter.

- Play 'line-up'. Show the child a picture of little animals lining up at the bus stop (or something similar). Talk about the line-up. Who is first in the line? Second? Third? Explain that when we say a word, we can line up the sounds and say them. Give an example of the word 'see'. We can say it sound-by-sound. The first sound in the word is /s/. The second sound in the word is /ee/. Revise the concepts of first in line /s/, second in line /ee/ and so on.

- Put some picture cards on the desk. Play the 'I Spy' game: I spy with my little eye something that starts with the sound /s/. Yes, it's snake. Look at that! Can you say it slowly with me? s-nake .... That's great. What is the *first* sound in snake? /S/. Yes, that's right. Can you put your teeth together and hiss like a snake? Can you tell me the last sound in snake? Yes, it's a /k/ sound. Can you say snake slowly? s-n-ay-k. Yes, that's right. Can you show me which one of these pictures starts with that /k/ sound?

- Put some alphabet cards on the desk. 'Can you find me the letter of the alphabet that has the /s/ sound? Yes, that's great. It's the letter "s". Can you say the /s/ sound again and again? Yes, s s s s s.'

### Beyond Phonemic Awareness to Phonics

As children become familiar with phoneme segmentation, alphabet cards or blocks can be introduced. Fun Fit (Dykes, 1993) consists of 12 sets of mixed alphabet cards. There are 15 cards in a set, with ten consonants and six vowels. It is not necessary to have all sets on the desk at any one time. Just use one set. You can also make your own sets. Simple phonics teaching can begin with words like at, mat, sat, and so on.

Once children can read simple three-letter words, they can be given lists of words with contrasting phonogram patterns. These are sometimes referred to as 'word families'. The aim is to teach as many 'rhymes' as possible (e.g. -at, -ot, -ig, etc.). Adams (1990) points out that just 30 or so phonograph patterns can generate 500 different words.

Calfee and Patrick (1995) have a detailed chart of the main phonics patterns that a child has to learn. One of these patterns is the difference between the 'short' and 'long' sounds of vowels. A common way of signalling that a vowel 'short' sound has changed to a 'long' sound is the 'silent e' pattern. Nicholson (1997) sets out similar activities. (See also the Appendix in Chapter 3.)

### Reading and Writing for Success. How Does this Happen?

What is it that enables some children to become successful readers and writers? Juel, Griffith and Gough (1986) and Juel (1994) argue that a key element in successful reading and writing is a strong foundation of phonemic awareness skills (e.g. being able to segment the sounds in words, as in c-a-t). Awareness that spoken words consist of sound segments smaller than the syllable is not well understood by many children. Children who start school knowing how to manipulate sounds in words have an advantage. Ehri (1998) argues that a good knowledge of the alphabet is also very important in learning to read. It is a solid foundation for learning letter–sound correspondences. Ehri argues that if children have a good understanding of the names of letters, they can use this knowledge to assist them in writing words using phonemes within letter names (e.g. the letter names 'gee', 'ar' and 'ef' are used for spelling 'giraffe' as GRF; 'el', 'ef' and 'tee' are used to spell 'elephant' as LFT).

## New Zealand Case Studies of Early Readers

Nicholson *et al.* (1998) conducted interviews with the parents of two early readers. The two children were identified during the screening process of a larger study (Nicholson, 1996). The screening involved assessing the reading and writing skills of 113 five-year-old children. Of these children, 88 attended schools in low-income suburbs of Auckland, while the remaining 25 were from a school in a high-income suburb. All these children had been at school for only a few months. Although the vast majority of children in the study were unable to read, having just begun school, there were two children who could read well above average for their age (for a more detailed description see Nicholson, 1999). One child was from a low-income suburb, and the other was from a middle-class suburb.

Angelika (not her real name) had travelled with her parents to New Zealand when they immigrated from Germany. At that time, she was two years old. She attended school in a high-income suburb. At the time of assessment in March she was five years and four months in age. This was about two months into the school year. Her receptive vocabulary knowledge was at a seven-year-old level. Her alphabet knowledge was near perfect, with 26 upper- and 24 lower-case letters correct, for a total of 50 out of 52 (96 per cent). The mean score for her group on the alphabet test was 41 out of 52 (79 per cent). She also had a good level of phonemic awareness, scoring 25 out of 42 (60 per cent correct). The average phonemic awareness score for her middle-income school group was nine correct out of 42 (21 per cent). On a pseudo-word reading task, she read three out of 30 words correctly (ten per cent). The average for her group was zero. On a New Zealand test of word reading she was at a beginning seven-year-old level. On a test of passage-reading three months later, her oral reading and reading comprehension were at an eight-year-old level. Nearly eight months later, in late October, when she was exactly six years old, her receptive vocabulary was at a mid-eight-year level and her phonemic awareness score was 32 out of 42 (76 per cent correct). The average phonemic awareness score for her group was 24 out of 42 (57 per cent). Her pseudoword reading had improved to nine out of 30 (30 per cent). The average for her group was three out of 30 (ten per cent). Her word reading accuracy was at a beginning eight-year-old level. Her passage oral reading was at a high eight-year-old level. Her passage comprehension was at a beginning ten-year-old level.

Niwa (not his real name) came from a family that had Chinese, Samoan and Māori background. He was able to speak Samoan, Māori and English, and attended school in a low-income suburb of Auckland. He was assessed at the beginning of the school year, but unlike Angelika was not assessed later in the school year. At time of assessment in April, Niwa was five years and four months. He was in his third month of school. His receptive vocabulary score was at a beginning seven-year-old level. He identified 25 upper- and 25 lower-case letters of the alphabet, giving a score of 50 out of 52 (96 per cent) , whereas the mean for his low-income sample group was 20 out of 52 (38 per cent). He scored 35 out of 42 on the phonemic awareness test (83 per cent). The mean score for his group was three out of 42 (seven per cent). He read 29 out of 30 pseudo-words correctly (97 per cent). The mean for the group was zero. On a test of word reading, he was reading at a beginning eight-year-old level. On a test of passage reading, his oral reading was at a mid-eight-year-old level, and his reading comprehension was at a beginning seven-year-old level. Niwa's reading skills were unusual in that children from minority groups or from poor home backgrounds often do not do well in school. Here was a boy from a minority culture background, living in a low-income suburb of Auckland, who could read at a level several years above his chronological age. Yet, as his father put it, 'He's still learning to tie his shoelaces'.

**Problems With Case Studies**

Niwa and Angelika both started school with above-average vocabulary knowledge, letter knowledge and phonemic awareness; however, we can't be sure if their superior alphabet and phonemic awareness knowledge was a cause or a consequence of their early reading. The problem in interpreting these case studies is that both children could already read when they started school, so it is difficult to know to what extent these high levels of alphabet knowledge and phonemic awareness were a result of their reading.

On the positive side, these two case studies are well detailed, with assessment information about phonemic awareness and alphabet knowledge. This is in contrast to other case studies, such as Smith's (1976) description of his son, Matthew. In his case study of Matthew, at age 3.5 years, very little information was given about his pre-reading skills. Instead, we were given examples of Matthew's responses to environmental signs. In a supermarket setting he misread a brand name packet as 'corn flakes'. In a department store, he correctly read the word 'Cards' in the card section, but in the footwear section, he misread the word 'Footwear'. He said, 'It either says eff-off or shoes' (p. 298). He was able to read a 'stop' sign correctly. When asked how he did this, he said that it was because it was spelled 'p-o-t-s' (p. 298). When asked to read a street sign, he gave the name of the street he lived in, which was nothing like the sign he was asked to read. In the case study of Matthew, it was by no means clear what pre-reading skills he had. The fact that he spelled 'stop' backwards suggests that he did not recognise the word by sounding it out, though he knew that reading the word 'stop' involved its letters. He also showed that he had knowledge of the names of the alphabet. When he came to 'Footwear', he showed that he recognised the name of the first letter F (Matthew said 'ef'). He may have remembered that 'off' was spelled off, and recognised the letters F and o in 'Footwear'. It is very difficult to know whether these responses were those of a child who would read successfully or not. There was no indication that he had phonemic awareness.

### Longitudinal Studies

In order to establish if phonemic awareness and alphabet knowledge are a consequence of reading and writing success, it is necessary to carry out either a longitudinal study or a training study. A good example of a longitudinal study is Juel (1988, 1994). In this study, children were assessed every year from first grade to fourth grade. There were 129 children in the first year of the study, although only 54 children were still in the study at fourth grade. The high dropout rate was due to the fact that many of the children attending the school had parents who were in the military. In the United States, children of military parents tend to move around from place to place. The school was situated in a low-middle-class area of Austin, Texas. The school made use of two different commercial reading schemes. Children in the study were taught with either a graded set of reading materials that had a phonics emphasis, or one that had a meaning emphasis. In addition, all children in the study received a 20-minute phonics lesson every day. The phonics lessons were required by the school district.

Juel, Griffith and Gough (1986) assessed these children in first and second grades on a range of reading and writing measures. They assessed knowledge of the alphabet, phonemic awareness, ability to decode pseudo-words (e.g. 'tiv') as well as oral reading, reading comprehension and writing. Verbal intelligence and listening comprehension were measured. Juel (1988) repeated the same assessments in third and fourth grades. She reported that children who started school with high levels of phonemic awareness were much more likely to make progress in reading and writing. Juel (1994) documented six case studies which illustrated this finding. Three of the children became successful readers and writers and three fell behind. What was interesting about these case studies is that they were well detailed, with children being given a number of assessments on starting school, which were repeated in subsequent years.

## Children Who Succeeded in Reading and Writing

In the Juel (1994) case studies, three children were successful in literacy – Jenny, Leon and Marcela. Jenny (not her real name) was European, from a single-parent home. She was friendly, but shy. When she started first grade, she was assessed as having above average intelligence and oral language. She was unable to read any words but knew every letter of the alphabet, both lower and uppercase (100 per cent). She scored very highly on the phonemic awareness test, correctly answering 32 out of 42 of the items (76 per cent). At the end of grade one she could read 14 out of 50 pseudo-words (28 per cent), which was below the average scores of better readers in her class. In second grade, she continued to make progress, and by the end of the year was reading at beginning fourth-grade level. At the end of third grade her oral reading and reading comprehension were both at mid to high fifth-grade level. She could decode 45 out of 50 pseudo-words (90 per cent). At the end of fourth grade her reading comprehension was at high sixth-grade level.

Leon was African-American. He had an energetic personality. 'Leon is a handful,' said his first-grade teacher. When he started first grade, he was assessed as having average intelligence and oral language. He was unable to read any words but knew 41 out of the 52 lower and uppercase letters (79 per cent). At the beginning of first grade, he only correctly answered 19 per cent (eight out of 42) of the items on the phonemic awareness test, but at the end of first grade he could correctly answer 76 per cent (32 out of 42) of the phonemic awareness test items. At end of first grade he could read 27 out of 50 pseudo-words (54 per cent), which was above average even for the better readers in his class. In second grade he continued to make progress, and by the end of the year was reading at mid third-grade level. At the end of third grade his oral reading was at seventh-grade level and his reading comprehension was at fourth-grade level. He could decode 45 out of 50 pseudo-words (90 per cent). At the end of fourth-grade his oral reading was at seventh-grade level and his reading comprehension was at mid fifth-grade level.

Marcela was Hispanic. Her mother and father could not speak English. When she started first grade she was assessed as having very low oral language skills. She was at the bottom of the scale on the language test. At the beginning of first grade she was unable to read any words but knew 42 out of the 52 lower and uppercase letters (81 per cent), and she answered correctly 32 out of 42 (76 per cent) of the items on the phonemic awareness test. After only two months of school she could read 18 out of 50 pseudo-words (36 per cent). At end of first grade she could read 44 out of 50 pseudo-words (88 per cent). That was outstanding in terms of the class average. At the end of first grade her reading comprehension was at third-grade level. She could probably have done better except that her English language knowledge was still below average for her age.

By the end of second grade she was reading at fourth-grade level. In third grade she became an avid reader. She visited the public library each week. All this extra reading must have helped to improve her English vocabulary, because at the end of third grade her reading comprehension was at mid fifth-grade level. Her English language comprehension was at mid fourth-grade level. In fourth grade she was reading books three nights a week. Her oral reading ability was at mid seventh-grade level, and her reading comprehension was at sixth-grade level. Her English language understanding was at mid fifth-grade level.

What was common to all three of these successful readers and writers was that although they could not read when they started school, they had very good letter knowledge and either had very good phonemic awareness at school entry or else acquired this knowledge very quickly. These skills appear to have helped them to learn to decode. Although decoding is not all there is to reading, it appears that these skills can have a positive effect on language skills and reading comprehension. Marcela, for example, started school with poor language skills, but her above-average decoding skills enabled her to become a keen reader of books, which in turn assisted her English language skills. She became a regular reader of books, which provided her with opportunities to learn many new words.

**Children Who Fell Behind**

Juel (1994) also documented the cases of three children who fell behind – Javier, Grace, and Anna. Javier was from a home where English and Hispanic were spoken. At the beginning of first grade he had low scores on English language ability. He was one of nine children. He started school knowing 41 out of 52 letters (79 per cent). His score on the phonemic awareness test was zero. It was still zero at the end of first grade. The same zero pattern of results occurred for reading of pseudo-words. In his second year of school, he repeated first grade. At the start of the repeated year he scored 16 out of 42 on the phonemic awareness test. At the end of the repeated year he could read a few pseudo-words. In his third year of school he moved to second grade, but was still reading below average for that grade. In his fourth year of school he moved to third grade, but even at the end of third grade he had not achieved second-grade reading level. When he was asked whether he liked reading, he said 'I hate reading'.

Grace was a bubbly, outgoing African-American pupil. In an interview she said that no one read to her at home. She started school able to identify 39 out of 52 alphabet letters (75 per cent). She scored zero on the phonemic awareness test at the beginning of first grade, scored 17 out of 42 (40 per cent) at mid-year, and 28 out of 42 (67 per cent) at the end of the year. She could read 15 out of 50 pseudo-words (30 per cent) by the end of the year. At the end of second grade, she was unable to read beginning second-grade material. At the end of third grade, she was reading at early second-grade level. At the end of fourth grade, she was unable to cope with beginning third-grade material. When asked whether she liked reading, Grace said that she did, 'because it is a good way to learn'. Juel (1994) described Grace as a fighter, with strong spirit.

Anna was from an Hispanic background. Her parents spoke Spanish and English at home. She was able to speak English at school. She was quiet and shy. Her parents did not read to her at home, but they bought her comics and books. At the start of first grade she could identify 34 out of 52 letters of the alphabet (65 per cent). Three months later she could identify all 52 letters. At the start of the year her phonemic awareness was zero. At the end of the year she scored 23 out of 42 (55 per cent). At the end of first grade she could read 12 out of 50 pseudo-words (24 per cent). At the end of second grade she was unable to cope with beginning second-grade material. At the end of third grade she could read beginning third-grade material. At the end of fourth grade she was reading at mid third-grade level. When asked whether she liked reading, Anna said she hated reading and hated school.

What was common about all three children who fell behind in reading and writing was that they started school with very low levels of phonemic awareness (Javier, Grace and Anna all scored zero at the beginning of first grade; Javier still scored zero, Grace scored 67 per cent and Anna scored 55 per cent at the end of first grade). In contrast, the three children who were successful readers and writers started school with higher levels of phonemic awareness (Jenny and Marcella each scored 76 per cent at the beginning of first grade and Leon scored 19 per cent at the beginning of first grade but 76 per cent at the end).

The children who became successful readers and writers started school with higher levels (100 per cent, 79 per cent and 81 per cent) of alphabet knowledge than did the children who fell behind (79 per cent, 75 per cent, and 65 per cent). Among the children who did not succeed, Javier and Grace started with reasonably high alphabet scores (79 per cent and 75 per cent). Anna's entry score of 65 per cent for alphabet knowledge rose to 100 per cent a few months after starting school. The differences in alphabet knowledge were not as great as for phonemic awareness. The three children who succeeded started school with scores of 76 per cent, 19 per cent and 76 per cent. The children who did not succeed started school with phonemic awareness scores of zero, zero and zero. The children who advanced in reading and writing also showed better ability to read pseudo-words at the end of first grade

(28 per cent, 54 per cent, and 88 per cent) than did the three children who fell behind (zero, 30 per cent and 24). This gives support to the view that phonemic awareness and decoding skills are very important in getting off to a good start in learning to read and write.

### What School Factors are Related to Getting Ahead or Falling Behind?

Juel (1994) was concerned that for some children a series of negative Matthew effects set in very soon after they start school. The term 'Matthew effect' derives from the book of Matthew, Chapter 25, verse 29: 'To everyone who has, will be given more, and they will have more than enough [positive effects]; but from those who have not, even what they have will be taken away [negative effects]. In Juel's study in the United States, where instruction starts at age six, she found a near 90 per cent probability (a correlation of .88) that a child who was a poor reader after the first year of school would still be a poor reader four years later. In New Zealand, where children start school at age five, Clay (1979) reported the same dismal probability, arguing that where a child was placed in relation to classmates at the end of the first year of school was about where the child would be at age seven or eight. In Sweden, where instruction starts at age seven, Lundberg (1984) found that 40 out of 46 low-achieving readers in first grade were still poor readers in sixth grade. That was a .87 probability.

Juel (1994) argued that for the children who fell behind in her longitudinal study, early teaching of phonemic awareness and linking of letters to phonemes was necessary very early in first grade. She recommended lots of reading of stories and discussion of vocabulary to improve language depth of knowledge and teaching children a 'sense of story' to help them with writing. Juel (1994) argued that children should only be given reading materials that they can read with 90 per cent accuracy or better. The poor readers in her study were given books that were too hard for them. She argued that phonics instruction had to be linked to text reading, so children could see how to apply phonics rules to read. Teachers had to focus on developing children's decoding skills. Finally, she argued that there has to be intervention for children who are not moving forward, by mid first-grade at the very least. As she put it, 'To prevent the cycle of failure, early intervention in first grade is mandatory' (p. 126).

Juel (1994) believed that bombarding well-prepared beginners with worksheets and reading readiness activities was mostly a waste of time when these children already had good pre-reading skills such as phonemic awareness and knowledge of the alphabet. She also suggested that good readers are not challenged enough with reading. They are given books that are too easy for them. An awareness of how good some children are at reading, and finding books appropriate to their level, is important.

## Is Getting Ahead a Result of Phonemic Awareness?

Coles (1998) has suggested that phonemic awareness is not so much a cause of reading and writing success but a marker of social support. It may be that children with high levels of phonemic awareness come from homes where there are many books, where there is a rich language environment, and where they encounter many experiences with written language through having books read to them. Phonemic awareness is a result of social opportunities and written language experiences.

If this is the case, then, it could be argued that the best way to create successful readers and writers is to provide at school the kinds of opportunities that some children receive at home, such as interacting with books and so on. As a result of these experiences children would pick up phonemic awareness skills, making phonemic awareness instruction unnecessary.

However, there is no strong evidence to show that this does occur. Scarborough and Dobrich (1994) reviewed research on the effects of reading storybooks to preschoolers and found only a modest relationship between storybook reading to preschoolers and whether or not they learned to read more easily. The mean correlation was .28. Nicholson (1997) reported similar findings. In a sample of 57 children (mean age of seven years) from low socio-economic backgrounds, the correlation between number of books at home and reading was low, r = -.22, whereas the correlation between phonemic awareness and reading was much higher, r = .55. The correlation between invented spelling ability (which requires phonemic awareness) and reading was also high, r = .68.

In support of these correlational results is a study by Stuart *et al.* (1998) who conducted an interview survey of 61 parents of children from Year 0 (new entrants), Year 1 and Year 2 classes in a North London primary school. The parents were divided into two social class groups.

The middle-class parents spent more time reading to their children than did the low-income parents, but time spent reading to children did not correlate significantly with reading progress. Anderson and Matthews (1996) reported a study of the emergent literacy development of 15 kindergarten children from low-income homes. Storybook reading was emphasised in class and children took storybooks home at least once each week. At the end of the school year only one of the 15 children was showing print-oriented behaviours. This study was conducted for a one-year period, similar to that of Sulzby (1985), yet in the Sulzby study, which involved middle-class children, 17 of 24 children showed print-oriented behaviours. It was concluded that there may be a middle-class bias in the Sulzby study, in that not all children acquire pre-reading skills as a result of having books read to them.

Gibbs and Nicholson (1999) reported a study of 64 five-year-olds in a low-income mining town in New Zealand. In their first term of school they were assigned either to an experimental group who listened to a 'talking book', every day for five weeks, or to a control group who looked at the same books but did not get the 'talking book' audio support. The results showed that pupils who listened to the 'talking books' were able to read them more accurately and had better recall of ideas in the books than did pupils who did not read along with the audiotaped books. The children had memorised the 'talking book' stories. But this advantage did not transfer to new, unseen stories, which the 'talking book' children were unable to read. The experimental group children had not gained in reading skills as compared with the control group. It could be objected that 'talking books' are not like the natural interactive reading situation between parent and child, but other researchers have found similar results. Interactive reading seems to have positive effects for vocabulary development, but not for reading (for a review, see Pressley, 1998).

## Conclusions

It seems that parents can get their children off to a better start in school if they help them to acquire some phonemic awareness skills. But there is a down-side to this conclusion: parents should not be so intent on teaching these skills that home becomes just another classroom. Parent pressure is a turn-off for some children. Some children are very sensitive and can get very anxious if they think they are not meeting their parents' expectations. As one newspaper article put it (in a humorous way), parent help does *not* mean 'standing over your child with an electric cattle prod while she tries to spell chrysanthemum' (Berrington, 1997). Children enjoy learning, but not if it becomes scary for them. For example, I remember an interview with a child who said that his father listened to him read (which is good) but that his father gave him a smack if he got a word wrong (which is *not* good). Although parents sometimes feel that they are to blame for their children's not being able to read, it is wise to remember that learning to read and write is something that parents and schools can both work together on. Parents are there for love and support. They are also there to help their children get the best instruction. If things aren't going well, they have to check what is happening at school. They can't do it all by themselves.

If some children start school not knowing the alphabet and without phonemic awareness, then it is a signal to teachers that these children may be at risk. Some will get ahead with normal instruction and will acquire these skills pretty much on their own. But it seems likely that most children in this category will benefit from explicit instruction in these pre-reading skills. It seems the skills are best taught not in isolation, but by showing how they can be useful for reading of words and text. When children do start reading, it seems very important that they be reading at high levels of accuracy, 95 per cent correct or better. Children who get behind are often given materials that are too hard for them. Also, these children are not given enough instruction in how to decode words.

Children from low-income backgrounds often start school with low levels of pre-reading skills. They need sustained and intensive instruction, much more so than middle-class children. Intervention at preschool levels may be necessary in order to enhance their pre-reading skills, so that when they enter primary school they have much better phonemic awareness skills and knowledge of the alphabet than is presently the case.

## References

Adams, M.J., Floorman, B.R., Lundberg, I., & Beeler, T. (1998). *Phonemic awareness in young children: A classroom curriculum.* Baltimore, MD: Paul H. Brookes.

Anderson, J., & Matthews, R. (1996). Re-examining emergent storybook reading: A sociocultural perspective. Paper presented at meeting of American Educational Research Association, New York.

Berrington, L. (1997, January 8). Parents – Do I have to be a genius? *Guardian* (England), p. 8.

Bertelson, P., & de Gelder, B. (1993). The emergence of phonological awareness: Comparative approaches. In I.G. Mattingly & M. Studdert-Kennedy (Eds.) *Modularity and the motor theory of speech perception* (pp. 393–412). Hillsdale, NJ: Erlbaum.

Bradley, L., & Bryant, P. E. (1978). Difficulties in auditory organisation as a possible cause of reading backwardness. *Nature* , *271*, 746–747.

Bradley, L., & Bryant, P. E. (1983). Categorizing sounds and learning to read – A causal connection, *Nature, 301*, 419–421.

Bredlin, L. (1996, July 28). House and home – The danger of too much, too young. *Sunday Telegraph* (England), p. 24.

Bruce, D. J. (1964). The analysis of word sounds by young children. *British Journal of Educational Psychology, 34*, 158–170.

Bryant, P., Bradley, L., Maclean, M., & Crossland, J. (1989). Nursery rhymes, phonological skills and reading. *Journal of Child Language 16*, 407–428.

Byrne, B., & Fielding-Barnsley, R. (1991). Evaluation of a program to teach phonemic awareness to young children. *Journal of Educational Psychology, 83*, 451–455.

Byrne, B., & Fielding-Barnsley, L. (1991). *Sound foundations*. Artarmon, N.S.W., Australia: Peter Leyden.

Castle, J.M. (1998). Learning and teaching phonological awareness. In G. B. Thompson & T. Nicholson (Eds.), *Learning to read: Beyond phonics and whole language* (pp. 55–73). New York: Teachers College Press.

Clay, M.M. (1979). *The patterning of complex behaviour*. Auckland: Heinemann.

Coles, G. (1998). *Reading lessons. The debate over literacy*. New York: Hill and Wang.

Dykes, B. (1993). *Fun fit*. Kalbar, Queensland, Australia: Nutshell Products.

Ehri, L.C. (1996). Researching how children learn to read: Controversies in science are not like controversies in practice. In G.G. Brannigan (Ed.), *The enlightened educator* (pp. 179–206). New York: McGraw Hill.

Elkonin, D.B. (1971). Development of Speech. In A.V. Zaporozhets & D.B. Elkonin (Eds.), *The psychology of preschool children* (pp. 111–185). Cambridge, MA: MIT Press.

Elkonin, D.B. (1973). USSR. In J. Downing (Ed.) *Comparative reading: Cross-national studies of behavior and processes in reading and writing* (pp. 551–580). New York: Macmillan.

Gibbs, C. J., & Nicholson, T. (1999). When you've heard it all before and still can't read. *Effective School Practices, 17.*

Gough, P.B., Larson, K., & Yopp, H. (1993). The structure of phonemic awareness. Paper presented to the International Society for the Study of Behavioral Development, Recife, Brazil.

Juel, C. (1988). Learning to read and write: A longitudinal study of fifty-four children from first through fourth grade. *Journal of Educational Psychology, 80,* 437–447.

Juel, C. (1994). *Learning to read and write in one elementary school.* New York: Springer Verlag.

Juel, C., Griffith, P. L., & Gough, P. B. (1986). Acquisition of literacy: A longitudinal study of children in first and second grade. *Journal of Educational Psychology, 78,* 243–255.

Layton, L., Deeny, K., Tall, G., & Upton, G. (1996). Researching and promoting phonological awareness in the nursery class. *Journal of Research in Reading 19,* 1–13.

Leong, C.K. (1991). From phonemic awareness to phonological processing to language access in children developing reading proficiency. In D. J. Sawyer & B. J. Fox (Eds.), *Phonological awareness in reading* (pp. 217–254). New York: Springer-Verlag.

Liberman, A. M. (1996). *Speech: A special code.* Cambridge, MA: MIT Press.

Liberman, A. M. (In Press). The reading researcher and the reading teacher need the right theory of speech. *Scientific Studies of Reading.*

Liberman, A.M. (1997). When theories of speech meet the real world. *Applied Psycholinguistics.*

Liberman, I., Shankweiler, D., Fischer, W.F., & Carter, B. (1974). Explicit syllable and phoneme segmentation in the young child. *Journal of Experimental Child Psychology 18,* 201–212.

Lundberg, I. (1984, August). Learning to read. *School Research Newsletter.* National Board of Education of Sweden.

Lundberg, I., Frost, J., & Petersen, O. P. (1988). Effects of an extensive program for stimulating phonological awareness in preschool children. *Reading Research Quarterly 23*, 267–284.

Mann, V. (1991). Phonological awareness and early reading ability: One perspective. In D. J. Sawyer & B. J. Fox (Eds.), *Phonological awareness in reading* (pp. 191–216) New York: Springer-Verlag.

Nicholson, T. (1997). *Does phonemic awareness training improve the literacy skills of children from low-socioeconomic backgrounds?* Unpublished manuscript, School of Education, The University of Auckland.

Nicholson, T. (1998). *At the cutting edge: Learning to read and spell.* Wellington: New Zealand Council for Educational Research.

Nicholson, T. (1999). *At the cutting edge: Research on learning to read and spell* (2nd ed.). Wellington: New Zealand Council for Educational Research.

Nicholson, T., Lam, R., Van Kuyk, T., Brown, G.T., & Lemke, S. A. (1998). *Case studies of two precocious readers*. Unpublished data.

Pressley, M. (1998). *Reading instruction that works. The case for balanced teaching*. New York: Guilford Press.

Read, C. (1978). Children's awareness of language, with emphasis on sound systems. In A. Sinclair, R. J. Jarvella & W. J. Levelt (Eds.), *The Child's Conception of Language* (pp. 65–82). Berlin, Germany: Springer-Verlag.

Scarborough, H. S., & Dobrich, W. (1994). On the efficacy of reading to preschoolers. *Developmental Review, 14*, 245–302.

Share, D. L. (1995). Phonological recoding and self-teaching: *sine qua non* of reading acquisition. *Cognition, 55*, 151–218.

Smith, F. (1976). Learning to read by reading. *Language Arts, 53*, 297–299, 322.

Stuart, M., Dixon, M., Masterson, J., & Quinlan, P. (1998). Learning to read at home and at school. *British Journal of Educational Psychology, 68*, 3–14.

Sulzby, E. (1985). Children's emergent reading of favorite storybooks: A developmental study. *Reading Research Quarterly, 20*, 458–481.

# 9

# READING AND SPELLING

## Spelling: A Cinderella Subject?

In New Zealand, the teaching of spelling might be seen as a Cinderella subject – as a poor stepchild. In many classrooms, spelling is not taught as a separate subject. Instead, the child is encouraged to approximate correct spellings through the process of writing. Teachers, when reading writing, are expected to build on children's spelling skills when opportunities arise, taking advantage of the 'teachable moment' (Ministry of Education, 1996: 69) to model for the child the process of transforming good approximations into correct spellings.

Children are encouraged to monitor their spelling by keeping a 'spelling notebook' (Ministry of Education, 1996: 116) that contains words they use in their writing, including words they want to write but find hard to spell. Children are expected to show some accuracy in spelling. They are encouraged to approximate the spellings of words they don't know how to spell and to correct misspelled words. They are expected to develop a 'spelling conscience' (p. 62); that is, the habit of looking for possible misspelled words in their writing and then correcting them by looking them up in a dictionary. The Report of the Literacy Task Force (Ministry of Education, 1999) suggests that a successful nine-year-old writer 'consistently makes informed attempts at spelling' (p. 34).

In the past, formal spelling instruction has been regarded as less effective than an informal approach of learning to spell through writing and keeping a personal spelling list. A classic study in the United States by Rice (1897), published over 100 years ago, has often been cited as evidence to support keeping formal spelling instruction to a minimum. In a national survey of many thousands of classrooms, Rice found no clear differences in spelling achievement, although there were many different ways of teaching spelling and the amount of time spent teaching spelling varied widely from one school to the next. Rice felt that the main factor in becoming a good speller was time, or maturation. As pupils got older, they got better at spelling. Since the amount of time devoted to spelling instruction did not seem to make a difference in spelling achievement, Rice recommended that teachers keep spelling lists and drills to about 15 minutes each day.

There are other reasons why traditional spelling instruction, including lists of words created by the teacher, have been seen as unproductive. It can be argued that the words in the lists to be learned may be unrelated to the words children actually use in their own writing. In the 1940s and 1950s, many New Zealand teachers used a spelling list, such as *The essential spelling list* (Schonell, 1932). This was a list of 3,200 'everyday' words; that is, words used most often in children's reading and writing. The words in the list were grouped from those easiest to spell (e.g. 'man', 'get', 'mud', 'nut') to those hardest to spell (e.g. 'courageous', 'skilful', 'siege'). Arvidson (1960) argued that although this was a logical way of learning words, the problem was that the words that children most needed to write (e.g. 'good', 'because', 'come', 'said') were not the ones that were learned first on the list.

In the 1960s, a new approach to spelling was introduced. Children were encouraged to build their own personal spelling lists. To help them do this, the New Zealand Council for Educational Research produced the *Alphabetical Spelling List* (Arvidson, 1968). The list was published in two books. Book 1 was a list of 1,200 words grouped into levels 1–3. Book 2 was a list of 2,700 words, grouped into levels 4–7. Level 1 was the beginning level; level seven was advanced. The words were grouped according to whether children needed them in their writing, not according to whether they were easy to spell. When children needed a word for writing or if they made a mistake in their writing and needed to correct it, they looked it up in their *Alphabetical Spelling*

*List*. If it was a word that they should know how to spell at that age (i.e. it was at the right 'level' for their class), they entered it into their personal list, usually an exercise book (Arvidson, 1960). By age 12 or 13, children were expected to have worked their way through the seven levels.

But how effective would this new method be? Freyberg (1964) reported a large study of nine-, ten-, and 11-year-old children in New Zealand, in which he compared the effects of the two different methods of teaching spelling. At the time, the 'new' Arvidson (1960) method was in the process of being introduced to schools, but it had not reached all schools. Freyberg saw an opportunity to compare the new method with the traditional method. He pre-tested 838 nine-year-olds in 14 schools. During this pre-test phase of the study, all the schools were still using the traditional list method where teachers selected words from the *Essential Spelling List* (Schonell, 1932). Two years later 12 of the 14 schools had switched to the new method of personal spelling lists, which was the *Alphabetic Spelling List* prepared by Arvidson (1960), but the remaining two schools were still using the *Essential Spelling List* approach.

Freyberg post-tested children in the 12 schools that had switched to the new method. He compared children's results on a dictation and essay writing test to scores from the same 12 schools some two years previously. The results showed that the change to the personal spelling list approach led to slightly more errors on the dictation test than had been the case two years previously, but there was very little change in the number of errors made in children's essay writing. However, children wrote shorter essays than they had done two years previously. Also, poorer spellers made more errors on the dictation test than they had done two years previously, while good spellers were about the same. The fact that the scores of above-average spellers on the dictation test had changed very little over the two-year period indicated that the new spelling approach was just as effective as the traditional approach. The below-average spellers in the study, however, achieved better results in the dictation test two years previously when they were taught with teacher lists. On the writing task, below-average spellers also wrote shorter essays than above-average spellers no matter what approach was used.

Why should this happen? The explanation given by Freyberg was that good spellers seem aware of the value of accurate spelling and get into the habit of checking their work They write more, they use more words, and they practise and cross-check more spellings. In contrast, the poor speller writes less and thus gets less practice in checking spellings. In their writing, they also tended to write only the words they knew how to spell, and so did not extend their spelling knowledge.

It was recommended that above-average spellers could teach themselves to spell, using their own personal lists. But below-average spellers, and perhaps younger spellers, needed to combine personal lists with teacher-provided list instruction to extend their spelling skills.

Since the 1960s, research on spelling has taken a different turn. There has been considerable work on the role of phonemic awareness in spelling, as revealed in children's 'invented spellings'. Researchers such as Read (1986) and Treiman (1993) have shown that beginning spellers use their awareness of sounds spoken, along with their knowledge of the names of letters, to invent the spellings according to the way words are pronounced (e.g. 'pepl' for 'people'). These findings have convinced many researchers that the way to start learning is not with lists, but with invented spelling.

Is this it? No more lists? This question will be considered later, concluding that there is a place for both ways of teaching children to spell. The point is also made that learning to spell has positive spin-offs for reading as well.

### What is Spelling?

Perfetti (1997) defines spelling as 'the encoding of linguistic forms into written forms' (p. 22). In terms of spelling in English, we can be more specific – that spelling involves writing alphabetic characters that correspond to the sequence of phonemes in spoken words. This is not quite right as a definition; what if the spellings are incorrect (e.g. 'wos' for 'was')? The definition needs the qualification that the string of alphabetic characters should match those that are society's agreed spellings as revealed in a dictionary. This is because many sounds lack a one-to-one correspondence with letters. Some sounds can be represented by several letters or clusters of letters. Most of the consonants represent just one or two sounds, but the vowels are much more variable (e.g. the sound /oo/, as in 'boot', 'soup', and 'truth').

Another qualification is that this kind of sound–letter spelling only applies to an alphabetic writing system like English. In a logographic system, the written symbol represents a meaningful unit, a morpheme; in a syllabic system, the written symbol represents a syllable. The ability to spell requires both cipher knowledge and lexical knowledge (Juel, 1994). Cipher knowledge means knowing letter sound correspondences. This knowledge can vary from simple (e.g. b͟ = /b/) to complex (e.g. knowing that -ation is pronounced /ayshen/. Lexical knowledge involves knowing the unusual spellings of certain sounds (e.g. that /uh/ in c͟ome is spelled with and o͟; /oh/ in w͟as͟ is spelled with an a͟).

### How Do We Learn To Spell?

Treiman (1994) comments that the traditional way of learning to spell was by rote memorisation – children were given lists of words and had to remember their spellings. Learning to spell was a matter of storing sequences of letters in their correct order in visual memory. This idea does not fit with recent work on children's invented spellings. Treiman reviews research to show that beginning spellers use a combination of spelling by sound and spelling by memory. She says that in the beginning stages the sounds of words are the factors most important in children's spellings. They spell words according to the sounds they hear in them. Not all the sounds in spoken words are salient to the beginning speller, so some sounds are not spelled. When children spell the sounds they hear, they initially rely very much on the names of letters. For example, the letter c͟ has the letter name /see/. Children use that letter to spell the /s/ sound. And so on.

To illustrate children's invented spellings, Treiman (1994) gives the example of a sentence written by a child, 'We kend the haos for the prte. We at kack.' This translates as 'We cleaned the house for the party. We ate cake.' Treiman points out some interesting features. This child was using letter names to represent sounds in words (e.g. at͟ makes use of the letter name /ay/ in a͟). But the child is also aware of lexical spellings. He or she knows, for example, that the /k/ sound at the end of 'cake' should be spelled ck. This reflects the child's knowledge of spelling–sound relationships seen in print and stored in memory. Treiman concludes that learning to spell is continuous. Children do not start with invented spellings and then learn the correct spellings later; children, from the start, are combining both kinds of knowledge to spell words.

This makes sense. Children are exposed to a lot of orthographic spelling patterns in their reading and writing from the beginning. They read words like to, was and so on. Seeing words like back in print or on simple dictionary cards may trigger in memory a rule that says spell /k/ as ck when it is at the end of a word. Treiman thinks this is what happens. Beginning spellers, for example, do not spell 'cake' as ckack. Certainly children will never become good spellers if they continue to 'invent' spellings. They have to go beyond this, adding lexical knowledge. How else will they learn to spell words like 'know' and 'knight'? Roald Dahl, in his autobigraphy (Dahl, 1984) wrote that he learned to spell 'knight' the hard way. He mistakenly spelled 'Tuesday knight' with a k. The principal yelled at him, 'k-n-i-g-h-t is a knight in shining armour you idiot! Tuesday night is n-i-g-h-t'.

### Spelling test: How good is your spelling?

There are many tricky words that require lexical knowledge. Ask someone to say these words and see how well you spell them:

| | |
|---|---|
| accommodation | descend |
| battalion | interrupt |
| broccoli | privilege |
| campaign | receiving |
| conscience | temporary |

### Is spelling similar to reading?

If you are a good reader, does that mean you will be a good speller? The two processes are similar but not the same. Take the word green. Reading it is not the same as spelling it. When spelling, the /e/ sound can be spelled as either ee or ea or ei. We have to store in memory the fact that the /e/ in green is spelled as ee. This is lexical knowledge.

But there must be a great deal of common ground in reading and spelling. Ehri (1987) reported that correlations between reading and spelling abilities were positive, ranging from .66 to .90. These correlations indicate that reading and spelling are related. A good reader is likely to be a good speller. This is not always going to be the case. The correlations are high but not perfect. Frith (1980) reported that some children are good readers, yet not good spellers (about 12 per cent). It would be rare (impossible?), however, to find children who are poor readers, yet good spellers. Good readers are highly likely to be good spellers.

### What is spelling ability composed of?

Gough and Walsh (1991) argue that the ability to spell irregular words depends on children's depth of knowledge of regular letter–sound rules. They found that children who had good 'cipher knowledge' (i.e. could read and spell regular words) were also better at learning to read and spell exception words. They concluded that children's ability to learn to spell irregular words (like come) depends on their strengths in being able to spell regular words (like jump). This seems important. It suggests that teaching children letter–sound rules will also help them with the spellings of irregular words.

### Invented Spelling and Cue Spelling

Younger children use their knowledge of letter names to spell sounds in words. For example, car is spelled as cr. Why? The name of the letter r is /ar/. Another term for this is temporary spelling. Many researchers see this kind of writing as exhibiting phonemic awareness. This is because the child is aware that the spoken word is composed of sounds (phonemes). The child then uses his or her knowledge of letter names to link to his or her awareness of phonemes within words.

Some researchers think there is a stage of spelling prior to this, where the child relies on irrelevant visual cues in order to remember how a word is spelled (see examples of early 'invented spelling' attempts in Figure 6.1 on p. 228). It is called cue spelling (Gough, Juel & Griffith, 1992). For example, they may associate the spelling of the word camel with the apparent 'hump' which is part of the shape of the letter m. As they put it, the child 'will record the m, but the rest of the spelling will be nothing but luck' (p. 43). Another sign of a child in this early stage of non-spelling is when the child writes a different word altogether. Gough, Juel and Roper-Schneider (1983: 211) commented

**Figure 6.1: Examples of 'emergent' writing skills of five-year-olds.**

I went to the movies

I went to my Nan's house

as follows: 'To watch a child with pencil poised respond to with by saying, 'I think I'll just write play' (which she did), or a child who writes mom for mother, or one who has no idea of how to begin to spell cat, is to see a cue speller in action'.

They found (p. 308) examples of reliance on memory for one or two letters in children's spellings of rain. Some of the errors had at least one of the letters in rain (e.g. weir, ramt, Rup). But other errors were different words altogether (e.g. yes). One child even drew raindrops.

Why did these errors occur? Presumably the cue speller does not yet understand the rules of the cipher, that is, sound–letter correspondences. Cue spelling is a stage prior to invented spelling, or cipher spelling. Cue spellers rely on the strategy of selective association to help them remember. They are not trying to spell out the sounds of the word. This is why they are likely to make strange errors, such as writing a different word altogether. There is quite a difference between this kind of spelling and that of the child who knows that letters in words correspond to sounds in words. I remember a child saying to me once that he hoped he didn't spell uncle as nana. Cue stage?

Once children have learned the names of letters, if they have awareness of the phonemic structure of words then they are able to invent phonetic spellings. They may begin with the first and last sounds represented (hearing middle sounds is harder). For example, they may spell 'giraffe' as GF (Ehri, 1987). As children acquire stronger phonemic segmenting ability and learn more about how to relate letters to sounds, their spellings become more complete. For example, they may spell 'giraffe' as 'GERAF', or 'crocodile' as CROKADIEL.

Invented spelling relies on cipher knowledge. Children's spellings at this stage have some or all of the phonemes in words but they are not correctly spelled. They are still coming to grips with irregular spellings of some words and they have yet to store these exceptions in memory.

The evidence suggests that invented spelling is not at all like cue spelling. It is the beginning of real spelling. Spellings are very phonetic. Some of the features of these spellings, shown below in capitals, are (Chomsky, 1979):

- Long vowels are represented by the letter name (e.g. BOT for 'boat', KAM for 'came').
- short vowels are represented by the letter name that has the closest

sound (e.g. BAD for 'bed', GIT for 'got', WOTR for 'water').

- R and L are treated as syllables, with no vowels attached (e.g. GRL for 'girl', KLR for 'colour').
- M and N are omitted before consonants (e.g. WOT for 'won't', AGRE for 'angry').
- letters sometimes have their full name (e.g. YL for 'while', THAQ for 'thank you', NHR for 'nature') where the child has used the letter Y because its name is pronounced 'wye', and the letter H because its name ('haitch') has a 'ch' sound.
- CHR and JR to stand for initial letters 'tr' and 'dr' (e.g. CHRAN for 'train' and JRIV for 'drive') because children are sensitive to the fact that we pronounce the tr in 'train' as 'ch' and we pronounce the dr in 'drive' as 'j'.
- H is used to stand for the 'sh' sound (e.g. FEHEG for 'fishing'), presumably because the 'ch' in the letter name 'haitch' is close to a 'sh' sound.

Some of the early messages of invented spellers show these strategies in action. For example (Chomsky, 1979):

- R U DF (are you deaf?)
- FES SOWEMEG EN WOODR (fish swimming in water)
- MOMME I WOOD LIK YOU TOO GET UP (mummy, I would like you to get up)
- I WIL KOMM DAOON STERS (I will come down stairs).

Treiman (1993) analysed the spellings of 43 first-grade (6-year-old) children over a one-year period. They spelled 6,000 words during the year. She analysed the mistakes children made and found that children were more likely to spell a word incorrectly if it had several possible ways of being spelled (e.g. the /k/ sound can be spelled as c, k or ck). She also found that children produced spellings which were legal in terms of our spelling system. For example, the /ay/ in haystack was misspelled a̲. But in our spelling, a̲ can be used for the /ay/ sound. So it is legal. Some errors were orthographically illegal, for example where cheese was spelled as ce̲z. Here the c̲ does not usually represent /ch/. Treiman figured that the child had remembered some of the word's spelling, but had forgotten the h. Treiman also found that children were likely to omit letters if they were the second sound in a consonant cluster, like the t in star.

## Spelling and Grapho-phonemic Awareness

Ehri and Wilce (1987) taught children how to spell syllables with regular spellings. Another group simply learned letter–sound correspondences. The results showed that the children who were trained to spell the syllables were better at spelling other new one-syllable words. The results indicated that the most direct way of teaching children to spell is to teach them how to spell whole words rather than just teaching letter sounds or just teaching phonemic awareness.

Ehri (1998) argues that many words have irregular spellings and that children have to acquire grapho-phonemic awareness in order to spell them. There are letters, such as the 'silent e', which stand for no phoneme at all. There are also sounds which are ambiguous in terms of phonemes. Is /er/ two phonemes or one? Is the /l/ in /little/ one phoneme or two? Why is /l/ written as le and not el? These are things the beginning speller must learn. Phonemic awareness teaching is only one side of the story. She also argues that learning the spellings of words affects how many sounds children think there are in words. She found that fourth-grade children who learned to spell the words rich and pitch had different segmentation patterns for the words. They segmented /pitch/ into four phonemes, but /rich/ only into three. This indicated that learning how to spell words makes children more conscious of their phonemic composition. She concluded that phonemic awareness is learned as children learn to spell words.

## Learning to Spell Correctly

At a later stage children become less bound to the rule of one letter for one sound. For example, they may use the same -'ed' suffix at the end of words like 'stepped' where the '-ed' is pronounced 't', or words like 'hugged' where '-ed' is pronounced 'd', or words like 'ragged' where '-ed' is pronounced 'ed'. Children have learned that the past tense in these words is always spelled 'ed' even though it may not be pronounced that way (Ehri, 1987).

But how do children remember the spellings of irregularly spelled but common words such as <u>come</u> and <u>could</u>? This is lexical knowledge. Ehri (1987) suggests that children best learn these words through reading and through specific spelling instruction. For example, she found that focusing on specific spellings of words by using flashcards was more effective than reading the same words in sentences. Likewise, Croft (1997) suggests lots of practice activities such as personal spelling lists and word study as a way of increasing spelling skills. Ehri (1987) suggests teaching children to over-pronounce some words in order to remember their spellings (e.g. pronouncing 'chocolate' as 'choc-o-late' or 'know' as 'k-now'). Lots of close study of words can act as a mnemonic to help remember spellings. Mnemonics such as '*i* before *e*, except after *c*' when the sound is 'ee' can help with words like <u>thief</u> and <u>receive</u>. A mnemonic for the word <u>necessary</u> is 'it is ne<u>cess</u>ary to have one cream and two sugars in your coffee', and another – 'there is a lion in <u>battalion</u>!' Spellings can influence children's pronunciations. If children know how to spell <u>February</u> they are more likely to pronounce it as 'February', not 'Febyuary'. These spelling strategies help children move toward the last stage of spelling development, when they are able to spell words correctly.

### Is Invented Spelling the Best Way to Become a Good Speller?

It's a good start, but will not necessarily guarantee good spelling. One argument against invented spellings is that this approach doesn't give the child enough direct knowledge of how to spell. It does not teach the child about the sound–letter correspondences that are different to those the child invents. For example, the /ch/ sound is spelled <u>ch</u>, but the child may continue to use invented spellings such as WAH for 'watch' (using the /ch/ sound in the letter name 'haitch'). Or the child may spell <u>sat</u> with a <u>c</u>, or spell <u>jump</u> as gump, using the /j/ sound from the name of the letter g. Or, the child may not get to learn about r-controlled vowel spellings, that is, that the sound /ar/ is spelled <u>ar</u>. The point here is that learning correct spellings of words requires more skills than those of invented spelling.

But there is research to support invented spelling as a way to teach beginners to spell. Clarke (1998) compared children who were taught either to invent spellings or to write with conventional spellings. In the study there were 102 middle-class first-grade children. One difference between the methods of teaching spelling was the length of children's stories. The invented spelling group wrote longer stories than the conventional spelling group (40 word stories as against 13 word stories). The conventional spelling group made fewer mistakes (six per cent against 34 per cent) but the invented spelling group seemed to make better progress as spellers. They made more spelling mistakes in their personal writing, but then they wrote more words so the chances of making mistakes were greater. They scored better than the conventional group on a test of word reading, though this advantage was only detected among children who began first grade with very little knowledge of letters.

Garcia (1997) compared invented spelling with a commercial high-frequency word list programme. The invented spelling children produced longer stories, used more advanced vocabulary and more complex grammar. The invented spelling children were more likely to re-read their writing, draw and colour in their work and ask their friends for help than were the children in the word list programme. There were no differences in the accuracy of spelling between the two groups. There was also no transfer from spelling instruction to reading skills.

Healy (1991) studied a group of 96 first grade children. The control group received traditional phonics and spelling with little writing. The experimental group received phonics and were also encouraged to use phonetic spelling. The results showed that the phonetic spelling children had a higher quantity and quality of writing than did children who received traditional spelling instruction. There was no indication that either spelling programme affected reading.

## Conclusion

Spelling and reading have much in common, yet they are not the same. Some research shows that spelling skills do not necessarily transfer to reading. It appears that children need to be taught both reading and spelling. It is tempting, for example, to think that teaching invented spelling will enable children to learn the phonics rules of reading. But this assumption may be wrong (see Thompson & Fletcher-Flinn, 1993).

The simple view of reading (Juel, 1994) indicates that spelling and word reading draw on similar kinds of knowledge. They both draw on the cipher, which is a large set of letter–sound rules, yet they also draw on lexical knowledge which is one's memory of specific spellings of words, especially irregular spellings. Cipher spelling seems to be what happens in invented spelling – children spell words the way they sound. But to become good spellers, children have to remember the spellings that are exceptions to the rules.

How best to teach spelling is still not clear. Invented spelling has many advantages. Children write more and are more creative in their writing. Yet they may pay a price in not learning the correct spellings of many words. This is where the traditional teaching of high-frequency words can help children quickly learn the correct spellings of irregular words like <u>was</u>. The child who gets the opportunity to spell <u>was</u> with traditional methods is less likely to write a sentence like, 'If I wos a dog'. It appears that below-average spellers can benefit from the more traditional technique of teaching words in lists, as well as from invented spelling. The conclusion is that above-average spellers may be able to teach themselves to spell. Yet struggling spellers may need a combination of both new and traditional ways of teaching spelling.

### References

Adams, M. J. (1990). *Beginning to read*, Cambridge, MA: MIT Press.

Arvidson, G.L. (1960). *Learning to spell*, Wellington: New Zealand Council for Educational Research.

Arvidson, G.L. (1968). *Alphabetical Spelling List. Books 1 and 2*, Wellington: New Zealand Council for Educational Research.

Chomsky, C. (1979). Approaching reading through invented spelling, in L. B. Resnick & P. A. Weaver (Eds.), *Theory and practice of early reading* (Vol. 2, pp. 43–65). Hillsdale, NJ: Erlbaum.

Clarke, L. (1988). Invented spelling versus traditional spelling in first-graders' writings: Effects on learning to spell and read. *Research in the teaching of english, 22*, 281–309.

Croft, C. (1997). Write to spell in primary classrooms, *Set: Research information for teachers*, Article 11.

Dahl, R. (1984). *Boy. Tales of childhood*, London: Puffin.

Ehri, L. C. (1987). Learning to read and spell words, *Journal of Reading Behavior, 19*, 5–31.

Ehri, L.C. (1997). Learning to read and learning to spell are one and the same, almost. In C.A. Perfetti, L. Rieben & M. Fayol (Eds.),

*Learning to spell. Research, theory and practice across languages* (pp. 237–270). Mahwah, NJ: Lawrence Erlbaum.

Ehri, L. C. (1998). Research on learning to read and spell: A personal–historical perspective, *Scientific Studies of Reading, 2,* 97–114.

Ehri, L.C., & Wilce, L.S. (1987). Does learning to spell help beginners learn to read words? *Reading Research Quarterly, 22,* 47–65.

Freyberg, P. (1964). A comparison of two approaches to the teaching of spelling, *The British Journal of Educational psychology, 34, 178–186.*

Frith, U. (1980). Unexpected spelling problems. In U. Frith (Ed.), *Cognitive processes in spelling* (pp. 495–515). London: Academic Press.

Garcia, C. A. (1997). The effects of two types of spelling instruction on first-grade reading, writing, and spelling achievement. Unpublished doctoral thesis, Oakland University.

Gough, P. B., Juel, C., & Griffith, P. L. (1992). Reading, spelling, and the orthographic cipher. In P. B. Gough, L. C. Ehri & R. Treiman (Eds.), *Reading acquisition* (pp. 35–48), Hillsdale, NJ: Erlbaum.

Gough, P. B., Juel, C., & Roper-Schneider (1983). Code and cipher: A two-stage conception of initial reading acquisition. In J. A. Niles & L. A. Harris (Eds.), *Searches for meaning in reading/language processing and instruction* (pp. 207–211). Rochester, NY: National Reading Conference.

Gough, P. B., & Walsh, M. A. (1991). Chinese, Phoenicians, and the orthographic cipher of English. In S. A. Brady & D. P. Shankweiler (Eds.), *Phonological processes in literacy: A tribute to Isabelle I. Liberman,* (pp. 199–209). Hillsdale, NJ: Erlbaum.

Healy, N. A. (1991). First-graders writing with invented or traditional spelling: Effects on the development of decoding ability and writing skill. Unpublished doctoral thesis, University of Minnesota, Minnesota.

Juel, C. (1994). *Learning to read in one elementary school.* New York: Springer–Verlag.

Landry, M. L. (1995). The spelling strategies of middle school children. Unpublished doctoral dissertation, The University of New Brunswick, Canada.

Ministry of Education (1996). *Dancing with the pen.* Wellington: Learning Media.

Perfetti, C.A. (1997). The psycholinguistics of spelling and reading. In C.A. Perfetti, I. Rieben & M. Fayol (Eds.), *Learning to spell. Research, theory and practice across languages* (pp. 21–38). Mahwah, NJ: Lawrence Erlbaum.

Read, C. (1986). *Children's creative spelling*, London: Routledge & Kegan Paul.

Rice, J. M. (1897). The futility of the spelling grind, *Forum, 23*, 163–172, 409–419.

Schonell, F.J. (1932). *The essential spelling list*. London: Macmillan.

Thompson, G. B., & Fletcher-Flinn (1993). A theory of knowledge sources and procedures for reading acquisition. In G. B. Thompson, W. E. Tunmer & T. Nicholson (Eds.), *Reading acquisition processes,* (pp. 20–73), Cleveland, England: Multilingual Matters.

Treiman, R. (1993). *Beginning to spell: A study of first-grade children*, New York: Oxford.

Treiman, R. (1994). Sources of information used by beginning spellers. In G. D. Brown & N. C. Ellis (Eds.), *Handbook of spelling: Theory, process and intervention* (pp. 75–91). New York: John Wiley.

# READING COMPREHENSION

### What is Reading Comprehension?

There are two different views about the process of reading comprehension (Nicholson, 1999). One view is that comprehension is very much text-based. The reader does a complete processing of text information, bringing in background knowledge only when necessary. Another view is that comprehension is very much driven by background knowledge, so that it involves not much more than filling in the blank spaces in the knowledge we bring to the text. The first view is a text-driven view of comprehension and the second is a reader-driven view.

### An example

It is tempting to think that comprehension is reader driven, that we bring our own ideas to the text and that the meaning of the text is a construction, based on our prior knowledge, and on the text. For example, in a study by Nicholson and Imlach (1981), eight-year-old pupils were asked to read a short passage. The passage (see following page) described how a pet lamb became frightened and ran amok in a store. Pupils had to answer various questions, but the one that interested us was the question 'Why did the lamb run wildly around the store?'.

*Midnight Passage*

Jeremiah went into the store to buy some candy. He took his little black lamb, Midnight, with him. 'I want to buy some candy,' Jeremiah said. 'I'll keep Midnight right beside me.'

'Well, buy your candy quickly and get the trouble-maker out of here,' said Mr. Grundy. He smiled as he said it, so Jeremiah knew he wasn't angry. Midnight was so quiet that Jeremiah kept looking. It was hard to make a choice. Jeremiah kept looking.

Then it happened. A train whistled as it went past. Midnight began to run wildly around the store. He butted into pans and pails that were hanging on one side of the store. Down they came. He knocked jars and boxes off the candy counter. The floor was covered with candy and broken glass. He leapt wildly over the counter and knocked groceries all over the floor.

Mr Grundy decided that something had to be done. He picked up a broom and tried to chase Midnight out of the store.

Just then, Uncle Hiram walked into the store. He saw at once what was happening. As the frightened lamb tried to leap over the candy counter, Uncle Hiram caught him. The wild chase was over.

Question: *'Why did Midnight begin to run wildly around the store?'*

In the text, the little lamb was described as a 'black lamb', and the shopkeeper referred to the lamb as a 'trouble-maker'. The text also implied that a 'whistle' from a passing train might have frightened the lamb. Pupils' responses to the question were so varied that we suspected they were comprehending in a reader-driven way. The question asked was why had the lamb ran wildly around the store. Pupils replied with answers like:

- 'He was frightened.'
- 'He did not like it.'
- 'He was naughty.'
- 'He wanted to get Mr Grundy.' [the shopkeeper]
- 'He was bored.'
- 'He smallet [smelled] the candy.'

Yet we concluded that a text-driven view of comprehension was a more plausible view. Although pupils' answers can give the impression that they are relying on prior knowledge, there may be other reasons for their answers. First, the writer of the text may not have clearly explained why certain things happened. Second, the children may not have completely understood the content material (e.g. city pupils may not know very much about lambs). Third, some of the words in the text may have been hard to pronounce, so that some students may have gleaned only a partial understanding of the text. There are several possible reasons for the differing responses. Thus, although sometimes it seems that reading is reader-driven, it may well be that most of the time this is not the case. Readers may construct different meanings for texts, and as shown above, there may be several explanations for why they do this.

### The Language Comprehension Process

There are at least two reasons to favour a text-driven view of reading comprehension. One reason is that the text-driven view fits in better with what we know about how spoken language is processed (Pinker, 1994). The reader first decodes (i.e. phonologically recodes) the printed forms of words. At almost the same time, the reader looks up the meanings of those phonologically recoded words in his or her mental dictionary. Once the reader mentally accumulates meanings of several words, these phrases or clauses are then interpreted for their wider meaning. In this way, sentence by sentence, paragraph by paragraph, the overall meaning of the written material is worked out.

Comprehension processes occur very quickly (Matthei & Roeper, 1983; Rayner & Pollatsek, 1989). We make decisions about the meanings of words and sentences virtually on-line, as we read. These processes are very complex and not well understood, but every person has a language capability that makes it possible for them to understand most of what they read almost as soon as they read it. Our language ability is an 'instinct', like the ability to see and hear, that is passed down to humans by evolution. As Pinker puts it, 'Language is not a cultural artefact that we learn the way we learn to tell the time or how the federal government works. Instead, it is a distinct piece of the biological makeup of our brains' (1994: 18).

This is why I favour the text-driven view. Even though it seems to be a lot of work to read through a text in detail, it is in fact very easy for our language system to do this. We have a hugely successful mechanism for taking in words, sentences and paragraphs, figuring out what they mean, and storing those meanings in memory.

Another reason for favouring the text-driven view is that it seems a more efficient way of constructing the meaning of the text. Accessing prior knowledge in order to out-guess the writer, as is suggested in the reader-driven view, may require more mental energy than is needed to comprehend the text in a text-driven way. Instead, research suggests that guessing what parts of the text do not need reading may be risky. What if the guess is wrong? Prediction is not always successful. Skimming the text looking for information that is new and not part of the reader's prior knowledge may help the reader to gain the gist of the text. But good readers read almost every word of the text: skimming, or reader-driven processing, is not the normal way we read (Just & Carpenter, 1987; Rayner & Pollatsek, 1989).

## Can Reading Comprehension Be Taught?

This is a difficult question to answer. Carver (1987) has argued that although many studies have claimed to teach reading comprehension, the effects of such instruction have been very limited. Carver's argument is that comprehension instruction usually has local effects. These effects extend to comprehension of passages that teachers have explicitly used for instruction, but the effects do not usually extend to comprehension of new text or to reading comprehension in general. Comprehension instruction is very good at producing better comprehension, but only of the material that is studied. These results do not extend to standardised tests of reading comprehension.

Carver argued that much of what passes for comprehension instruction is nothing but extra practice and time spent revising text material. For example, teaching pupils strategies for answering questions might produce better comprehension scores on a test, but the better scores may have nothing to do with the strategies. Instead, it may be that the process of applying these question-answering strategies means that pupils have to spend more time on the task. Thus, it may well be the 'time on task' factor that accounts for the improvements. Of course we will understand things better if we spend more time on them.

Does this mean that comprehension instruction is a waste of time? Not necessarily. Many comprehension studies have been short term. Not many studies extend over a long period of time, which is what is probably needed for general comprehension to increase. We are talking about making significant gains in students' general vocabulary and content knowledge. This does not happen overnight.

Teaching pupils about text structure and about question-answering, and asking them to do extensive reading can still be useful, even though the effects of such instruction may be limited to the specific material studied. The reality of gaining school qualifications is that a lot of what students study is specific content that has to be learned, and which is likely to be assessed in class tests or examinations. Students often have to answer comprehension quizzes in school examinations. The pupil who is 'test-wise' and understands how questions are designed will be in a better position to work out the answers that examiners are looking for.

**Strategy Instruction**

This is sometimes called 'reciprocal teaching'. It involves teaching pupils four key strategies of clarifying, questioning, summarising and predicting. The first strategy is to ask questions. For example, pupils will read the first paragraph of a text and then question themselves to check that they understood the material. The second strategy is to clarify understanding. For example, pupils may check the meanings of some new words in the paragraph by looking them up in a dictionary. The third strategy is to summarise what the text is about. For example, pupils may look for the topic sentence in the paragraph. The fourth strategy is to predict. For example, pupils might anticipate (to themselves) what the next paragraph will be about. The pupil then reads the next paragraph and applies the four strategies all over again, and so on until the text is fully read.

Research on strategy training is inconclusive. Aarnoutse *et al.* (1998) reported a study where they taught the four reading strategies to 95 pupils whose ages ranged from nine to 11 years. There was an experimental group of 48 pupils and a control group of 47 pupils. They were all poor decoders. Half the pupils were poor listeners; half were normal listeners. To avoid decoding problems, the texts were read aloud to the pupils. The training programme involved 20 lessons, each taking half an hour. The results showed that pupils did learn how to use the strategies for reading, but that the training did *not* improve their reading comprehension as measured by a standardised test.

Paris, Cross and Lipson (1984) taught pupils how to read strategically. Their programme was called 'informed strategies for learning' (ISL). There were 87 third graders (eight-year-olds) and 83 fifth graders (ten-year-olds) in the study. The experimental group was taught ISL strategy training for four months, with 30-minute lessons given twice each week. The control group received regular classroom instruction. The findings were that the training did not result in any significant improvements in reading comprehension.

Are these non-significant findings typical? Rosenshine and Meister (1994) compared the results of 16 studies of strategy training and found a similar pattern. Strategy training was useful for improving comprehension of specific text material, but had weak effects on general reading comprehension as measured by standardised tests.

**Text Structure Instruction**

Is it useful to teach students about the ways in which texts are built? Narrative texts (novels, short stories, plays) are stories. They have a basic structure of a setting, a plot, and some characters. Expository texts are not stories. They tell you things. They have a variety of structures. For example, information may follow a sequence; information may be about a specific topic; information about one thing may be contrasted with another thing, and so on.

One reason for teaching pupils about text structures is that it will show them how to 'see' the structures of narrative, expository, and dramatic texts (Calfee & Patrick, 1995; Dymock & Nicholson, 1999). Pupils can learn how texts are designed by writers. They learn to 'see' the design of a text the way an architect sees the design of a house. This helps them to gain a better understanding of text content. As a bonus, they can also use their text structure knowledge to organise their ideas when writing.

Structural analysis applies to expository and narrative texts. Calfee and Patrick (1995) separate narrative text from expository and teach students to visualise them differently. Diagrams are used to show different structural patterns. There are a wide range of structures taught in the structural analysis approach to comprehension. We will look at some of them (for more detailed discussion, see Dymock & Nicholson, 1999).

## Narrative

A definition of narrative is that it is a story. Narratives have a plot and characters. Characters can be analysed by using web (one character) or matrix structures (comparison of several characters). One way to show the plot is to use a 'time-line'. This can be drawn on a large sheet of paper to show high and low points of the story over time. Events in many narratives build slowly toward a high point, or climax. Students chart the key events, in order, and think about their relative importance in the flow of the story. During discussion, pupils can be asked to justify their decisions about high and low points in the action. They can also refer back to the text for support when making decisions about the order of key events.

## Expository

Expository texts are 'not' stories. This makes them different to narrative texts. There are various kinds of expository structural designs. A sequence text (like a continuum) shows something happening over time, like the life cycle of the monarch butterfly. There is a cause–effect structure in this life cycle pattern. The events follow a set order. They can't be scrambled. Again, in discussion, students should talk about why the sequence is the way it is, and they can check the text to verify their ideas. A description text, on the other hand, can have a list structure where there is no set order. It may be a list of things to take when you go fishing, or a list of animals found in Australia, or a list of products made in Japan. It doesn't matter what goes first in the list. Pupils discuss whether or not the text fits a list structure. Could it be sequence? Why not? And so on. Other kinds of description text include the web structure (like a spiderweb), and the matrix structure (like a criss-cross weave). The use of structural strategies will work better if students are already fluent decoders of words, since they will not get stuck on pronunciation of difficult words. If pupils are not good decoders, then the texts can be read aloud to them. The aim of structural analysis is to show students how to 'see' specific design patterns in text.

*Practical applications*

We can illustrate structural analysis by looking at some specific examples. We will start with narrative text, a story called 'The Million Dollar Smile' (Dunlop, 1983). In this story, Dad is always boasting to Mum that his teeth are stronger than hers. Mum has false teeth. But Dad comes to grief when he gets a toothache and has to have his tooth removed. Dad's pride is broken and he loses his old sense of humour. The story ends happily with Dad getting a new gold crown. The gold tooth makes him feel important again. How do you structure a story like this? One possibility is to use a story graph (Calfee & Patrick, 1995; Nicholson, 1997) with time on the horizontal axis and levels of action on the vertical axis (see illustration on next page). After reading the story, children are asked to describe the plot. Their ideas are listed on pieces of paper and placed on the graph, following the time-line from the start of the line until the end. The time-line is a concrete representation of the fact that the plot of a story is a sequence of events that take place over time. The teacher then takes each scrap of paper and asks the children to place it vertically according to whether it was a high or low point in the action of the story, which signals to children that events in the story differ in dramatic impact. The final product is a visual representation which shows how the plot develops over time, and also shows the exciting high points. The aim is to show children that stories have a design, just like a house is built around an architect's designs, and that it is possible to 'see' the design.

It is also possible to use structural analysis to study the characters in a story. Calfee and Patrick (1995) recommend 'character matrixes'. For example, in 'The Million Dollar Smile', the teacher can draw an empty grid pattern which looks like the start of a game of noughts and crosses. Down the vertical side of the grid, list the characters: Mum, Dad, Mr Holman and Mrs Holman. Along the horizontal side of the grid, list some character attributes (e.g. gender, teeth, country of birth, personality). Children then fill in the blank squares. For example, in the story, Dad was born in Russia, Mrs Holman was born in Holland, Mum and Mr Holman were born in New Zealand. Children write this information into the matrix. In regard to personality, they might want to write that Dad was boastful, Mum was embarrassed, and so on. The aim of the matrix is to 'see' in a simple but clear way the similarities and differences of characters in the story.

# Million Dollar Smile

## Character

| Major | Minor |
|---|---|
| Dad, Mum | Mr Holman, Mrs Holman<br>Dentist<br>Children |

## Plot

1. Dad boasts about his teeth.
2. Dad gets toothache.
3. Dentist removes tooth.
4. Dad gets new false tooth.
5. Dad brings home presents.
6. Everyone is happy.

## Story graph

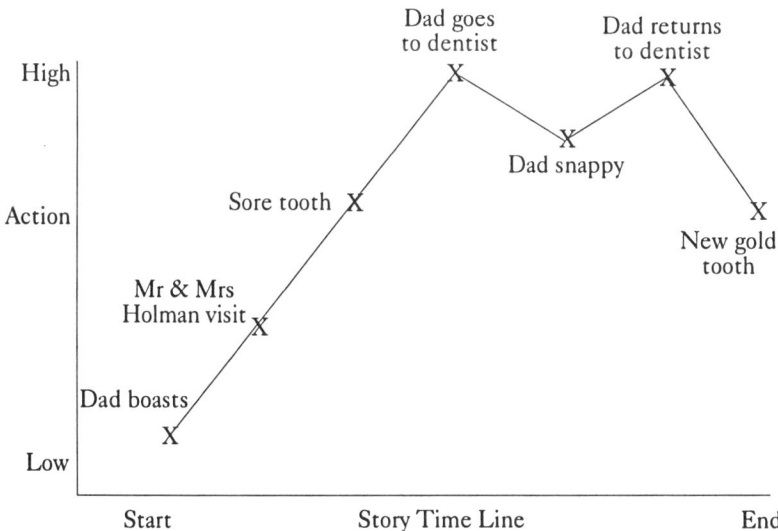

Now let's look at some expository text structural patterns. While there are various kinds of expository texts, we will look at just those that involve description and sequence. Why? The reason is that these texts are very common. They also have distinctively different design features. Description texts usually follow one or other of two different design plans. One type of design is where the article focuses on one topic, event, or person. For example, imagine reading an article about 'White-eyes'. This bird is a native of Australia but flew all the way to New Zealand many years ago. The article describes what this pretty little bird looks like, its habitat, its offspring, and its enemies. The information in the article can be diagrammed in a 'spider-web' structure. At the centre of the web is the topic focus, which is the white-eye bird. Around the web centre, and connected to the centre, are categories relating to this bird (e.g. origins, features, etc.).

A second design is where two or more things, events or persons are compared. In the article 'Sparrows' (Brockie, 1970), for example, two kinds of sparrow are compared – the bush sparrow and the house sparrow. The bush sparrow eats seeds but the house sparrow eats aphids; they are different in colour, nesting patterns, and in other things. This text can be represented as a matrix structure, just like a character matrix, comparing the two kinds of sparrows on different dimensions: appearance, habitat, food and 'other things' (a catch-all category).

Another kind of expository text structure is where a process or series of events is described. This is a sequence structure. It is different to the sequence of a plot in a narrative text in that the sequence is not a story. An example of a sequence structure is an article called 'The Monarch Butterfly' (Richards & Richards, 1978). This describes the life cycle of the butterfly. It follows a specific sequence of events. Sequence texts can be diagrammed by writing each step in the sequence on cards, and then placing these cards one after the other, joined by arrows, so that children can see that it is a linear sequence. Children can be challenged to question whether the order in the sequence can be changed, but in this kind of structure, that is unlikely.

The rationale for teaching text structure makes sense, but does such teaching increase reading comprehension? Calfee and Patrick (1995) charted the reading progress of pupils in One Hundred and Second Street School in Los Angeles over a ten-year period. The children in this school were taught text structure analysis. The chart showed steady improvements each year. The reading growth curve of the One Hundred and Second Street School was much steeper than that of the average for the whole of the Los Angeles area school district. While the result is positive, it was not a controlled study, so it is hard to rule out other factors (e.g. more resources, a new principal) that might have caused the improvements.

Dymock (1998) found that teaching text structure strategies was as effective as more general strategies such as guided reading (which is a kind of 'reciprocal teaching' approach) and sustained silent reading. There were 90 pupils in her study. The pupils were between eight and ten years old, and were all below average in reading comprehension. Their decoding skills were average or better. The 90 pupils were allocated randomly into programmes that involved learning about text structures or guided reading or sustained silent reading. The programme ran for 17 weeks, in 30 minute sessions, twice each week. The findings were that pupils in all three groups made significant gains in reading comprehension as measured by standardised tests, although there was no distinctive advantage for the text structure training. It was hard to be sure whether the overall significant gains in reading comprehension for all three groups were due to extra teaching provided in the study or to a regression effect. This is an effect where children who are initially assessed as below or above average, 'regress' toward the average when re-assessed. These pupils were below average in reading comprehension to begin with. Thus, their gains in reading comprehension could be put down to a regression effect.

It seems that text structure teaching has positive effects on comprehension of specific texts, even though the teaching may not transfer to general reading comprehension abilities. One reason why the training transfers to specific texts is that pupils are able to spend more time reading and thinking about specific texts. Extra study time helps comprehension of a specific piece of reading material. Also, the approach is very structured and produces a tangible structure, or product. This may not be the only reason for improved understanding. Further study would be needed to find out which explanation is correct.

Lipson (1995) taught 'semantic mapping' to a group of 40 below-average university freshmen. Semantic mapping is basically a 'spider web' text structure. The students were in their 20s, on average, and enrolled in compulsory remedial reading classes. They were placed into three groups and were given either mapping training, a study guide, or were asked to read text material and then discuss it. The students were pre-tested on a passage about 'memory'. Each group got similar pre-test results, indicating they were matched in comprehension levels at the outset of the study.

The training was carried out over eight weeks, four hours each week. Students in the mapping group were shown how to break textbook passages into categories and list supporting details under each category heading. Students had to produce a map each session. The study guide training involved giving students a study guide that related to the passage. Their job was to check statements in the guide in terms of whether the statements were right or wrong. Students also wrote some study guide questions of their own each session.

The students were post-tested on a new passage about 'emotions'. The results showed that students who received the mapping training were significantly better than the other groups in answering explicit and implicit questions about the passage, which focused on factual information in the text. However, questions that focused mainly on prior knowledge, rather than on information mentioned in the text, were not answered any better by the mapping group.

Why did the mapping have an effect? Lipson gave two possible explanations. First, the mapping strategy helped students understand the text more efficiently. Second, it may not have been the mapping instruction that made the difference, but rather the work involved in creating a semantic map. This extra work and extra time on task may have caused students to read the text more carefully. In other words, the result was due to extra 'time on task'. Lipson's study is a good example of how a structural training programme can have specific effects on the comprehension of certain kinds of text and can generalise to new text. Such training can be important, since pupils are often required to have good comprehension of specific textbook material that has a 'spider web' type of design.

### Question-answering

Students are often required to answer quizzes about text material, not just for class revision, but also for formal examinations. They must become test-wise. Learning about the process of answering questions can assist students to produce more effective answers to questions.

Ezell *et al.* (1996) reported a longitudinal study looking at the effects of teaching question-answering strategies to 34 children in two grade-four classrooms. The pupils were of average reading ability. The classes were given 36 weeks of question-answering lessons. They were taught four kinds of questions, based on a taxonomy developed by Raphael (1986). The first type of question was 'Right There', where the answer was stated in a single sentence in the text. The second question type was called 'Putting It Together', where the answer was stated in the text, but in two or more different places. The third question was called 'Author and You', where the answer is implied in the text but not stated explicitly. The fourth question was 'On Your Own', where the answer was not stated in the text at all. The pupil had to find the answer from his or her own general knowledge.

The children were assessed at baseline in fourth grade. They were given 36 weeks of instruction in question-answering strategies in their fourth-grade year. They were tested again midway through fifth grade to see if the training from the previous year had been maintained. Results showed that pupils were still better at answering 'Right There' and 'Putting It Together' questions than they had been at baseline back in fourth grade. Their ability to answer 'Author and You' questions was slightly better than baseline. Pupil performance for 'On Your Own' questions was still at baseline level, which is where it had been even during the special training period.

The conclusion was that the question-answering instruction was effective for text-based questions, but not for questions which required prior knowledge. To answer prior knowledge questions pupils need access to a dictionary or an encyclopaedia, because answers to these kinds of questions are not stated in the text.

These findings support the idea of teaching pupils about types of questions. The children in the study were average readers so the findings might not hold for poor readers. The findings also only applied to the material given to the children. It did not necessarily improve their overall reading comprehension since no standardised reading tests were given, but it did show that teaching how to answer questions helped to answer questions about specific passages.

Do school reading assignments ask text-based, 'Right There' questions? I did my own informal survey by looking at comprehension questions asked in some School Certificate English examination papers. My impression was that nearly all the questions were 'Author and You', but when I looked at some School Certificate Science examination papers I found some 'Right There' questions.

A more rigorous analysis was done by Hanus and Moore (1985). They analysed all the comprehension questions asked in two secondary school literature textbooks. One of the books was designed for good readers, and the other was for poor readers. The textbook for good readers had only one per cent 'Right There' questions, but had 44 per cent 'Author and You' questions, and 55 per cent 'On Your Own' questions. The textbook for poor readers was more heavily weighted toward low-level factual questions, with 14 per cent 'Right There', 70 per cent 'Author and You', and 16 per cent 'On Your Own'. If this is the case, then teaching about question–answer relationships may not be so productive, since it seems to be most effective for text-based 'Right There' questions. On a positive note, teaching about question types is still appropriate for factual material where the text content is very important. There are many instances where text-based answers are necessary. For example, questions about the Road Code for intending drivers are unlikely to target creative thinking about what the road rules might be or should be.

### Teaching vocabulary

There is evidence that many readers, especially below-average readers, do not learn the meanings of words easily from context while reading. As a result, their comprehension of what they read may be disadvantaged. Nicholson and Whyte (1992) found problems in vocabulary learning among a group of 57 children aged eight to ten years, especially among those children who were average or below average in reading skills. There were 18 below-average, 19 average, and 20 above-average readers. The story was *Farmer Palmer's Wagon Ride* by William Steig. We selected ten words from the story. Children were pre-tested, before they heard the story, on their understandings of those ten words. The meanings of the words (e.g. 'tripod') were unfamiliar to most of the children.

After the story reading we assessed each child's understanding of the words to see if they had learned their meanings by hearing them read in the context of a story. We first asked what each word meant. We said the word and the child had to explain it. We found that the gains from pre-test to post-test were very small. The below-average readers made a one per cent gain (learned virtually no words), the average readers made a four per cent gain (learned about half a word), and the above-average readers made a ten per cent gain (learned one new word).

In order to help, we also showed each pupil the page on which the word appeared, and we re-read the sentence in which the word appeared in the story. This gave the child time to reflect on the meaning. It also gave direct context clues. This careful focus on the word in context led to better results. This time, the below-average readers made a nine per cent gain (learned one new word), the average readers made a 16 per cent gain (learned 1.5 new words), and the above-average readers made a 23 per cent gain (learned just over two new words).

These findings showed that poor readers may be very disadvantaged in learning new words when listening to stories. It was much more effective to give them a chance to focus on the words specifically in context. Nevertheless, the amount of new word learning in context was still small. This raises the question, should vocabulary meanings be taught more formally?

Roser and Juel (1982) conducted a study where they pre-taught the meanings of words that children would encounter when they read them in stories from their classroom basal readers. There were 66 children in the study, from first grade through to fifth grade, in 12 different classrooms. They were pre-tested on words from the two basal stories they would be reading next in their classroom reader. For one of the stories, teachers provided the children with a list of sentences, each with one word missing. There was another list of words alongside the sentences. Children had to figure out which of the words went into each sentence. When meanings were unclear, teachers helped out with explanations of the words. For the other story in their reader, the children received no vocabulary instruction. The impact of the vocabulary teaching was assessed by asking children 'Right There' questions about what happened in the story. All the questions focused on sentences in the story that contained the taught words.

What they found was that the instruction was most beneficial to below-average readers at each grade level. The below-average readers in third, fourth and fifth grades were significantly better at answering questions about the story if they had been pre-taught the vocabulary. Roser and Juel concluded that below-average readers were the ones who benefited most from direct instruction in the meanings of words. Although these results only applied to the specific stories that the children were reading in class, the instruction still seemed worthwhile. The below-average readers gained more meaning from their reading than if they had not received the vocabulary help.

Vocabulary instruction can take many forms. Roser and Juel (1982) involved children in discussion of 'fill in the blank space' quizzes. Nicholson and Whyte (1992) focused children on the exact part of the story in which new vocabulary occurred. Calfee and Patrick (1995) taught children to use structural strategies such as webs and matrixes to organise and clarify new vocabulary. Other traditional techniques such as looking up the meanings of words in a dictionary are also helpful (Stahl, 1983). Why else do we have dictionaries? I remember using this simple strategy at school. I read classic novelists like Charles Dickens, whose stories are brimful of unusual vocabulary. I would look up the new words in my dictionary as I was reading. At one point, I even kept a notebook in which I wrote down the meanings of these words. I then used to study the words so as to remember them. Boring, but it seemed to work. I often found ways of using these words in conversations. My friends used to hate me saying words like 'iconoclastic', but it helped me to remember them.

However it is done, teaching children the meanings of words they read in their textbooks or in stories they are reading can help with comprehension of specific texts. This is not only good in itself, but it might have other positive spin-off effects. For example, children might be more willing to write about what they have read. They may even want to read another story.

### Sustained silent reading

This is a popular technique for improving reading comprehension. It is sometimes called USSR (Uninterrupted Sustained Silent Reading) or DEAR (Drop Everything and Read). But how effective is the technique in terms of improving children's overall reading abilities? One problem for USSR and DEAR is that many pupils appear to read silently but are not concentrating and so do not gain from this open-ended reading activity (Widdowson, Moore & Dixon, 1998). How are they to be motivated to read? One possibility is to combine free reading with quizzes. The Electronic Bookshelf (EB) does this. EB has hundreds of quizzes on computer disks to assess comprehension of hundreds of well known children's books. Pupils read a book, then complete a quiz to verify comprehension. They can re-take quizzes if necessary. There are some reservations about EB, especially in regard to possible negative effects on motivation to read, although this seems unlikely (for more detailed discussion see Dymock & Nicholson, 1999).

Dymock (1998) reviewed 14 studies of sustained silent reading. She found that in nine of the studies there were no improvements in reading comprehension as measured by standardised tests. In some of the studies pupils made gains, but they would possibly have made similar gains anyway, since pupils usually improve in reading during each year of school. Perhaps it is expecting too much to look for improvements in reading comprehension as a result of reading practice. Carver and Liebert (1995) have questioned whether sustained silent reading is powerful enough to produce improvements in reading comprehension.

A study that has gone against this trend is one that involved a sample of third-grade and fourth-grade poor readers (Shany & Biemiller, 1995). It was not a typical sustained silent reading study. In a typical sustained silent reading period, pupils read books on their own; in this study, pupils were given assistance with their reading. A group of 19 poor readers engaged in assisted reading. The assisted reading pupils either read to the teacher and the teacher helped with mistakes, or they listened to audiotaped versions of the text material. A control group of ten children received no extra help. The assisted reading practice was provided over a four-month time period. It involved 30 hours of reading practice.

The results showed that the pupils who received assisted reading improved in reading comprehension more than the control group who had no extra help. This is a positive result, but it is different from the usual brand of sustained silent reading where no assistance is given. In fact, in sustained silent reading the teacher is expected to read as well, rather than provide help to pupils. Another unusual aspect of the study was that the poor readers improved in decoding as well as reading comprehension. Could it be that the assisted reading helped their decoding, which in turn helped their reading comprehension? Let's consider this possibility.

### Decoding and reading comprehension

Research suggests that teaching children to read words quickly and accurately can increase their reading comprehension (Tan & Nicholson, 1997). The theory behind fast and accurate word reading is that good readers are very good at reading words. They have acquired this level of skill through much reading practice. As a result, like skilled musicians and athletes, they have developed "automaticity" as a result of many hours of word-reading practice. What this means is that they have learned word-reading skills to the point where they require little or no mental effort. Thus, they are able to put all their mental energies into reading for meaning.

There is a myth that concentrating too much on word reading can interfere with comprehension. The belief is that children can become too concerned about getting every word correct and as a result they do not attend to meaning. But the pay-off from learning to read words quickly is that children do not have to worry about whether or not they are reading correctly. This is because the ability to read words quickly guarantees that the reader is reading accurately and effortlessly.

Tan and Nicholson (1997) were able to show the importance of reading words quickly in terms of effects on reading comprehension. They divided a sample of 42 poor readers, aged between seven and ten years, into three groups. The first group received training in reading single-word flashcards; the second group were trained with sentence flashcards (to give context clues); the third group discussed the meanings of words but received no help in reading them. In the flashcard training groups, each child was shown sets of 15 to 25 words and were to read them as quickly as they could. This took about 15 to 20 minutes. The child then read aloud a passage that contained the flashcard words. The passage was no more than a year above the child's reading level. The flashcard words were in the passage, but pupils didn't know that. The trained pupils read the passage aloud, answered comprehension questions, and then recalled what they remembered of the passage. This procedure was repeated for five different passages for each pupil in the study.

The results showed that the poor readers who had received the flashcard training were significantly better than the control group pupils in their comprehension of the passages they had read. The results support the theory that if pupils can develop their word-reading skills to the point where they can read words easily, then their reading comprehension will improve as well. Similar improvements in reading comprehension as a result of word training have been obtained by Taka (1997) and Levy *et al.* (1997).

Calfee and Patrick (1995) argue that it is very important to teach children the origins of the English spelling system. Many children do not know the historical background of English spelling – that English consists of layers of spelling influences. The basic layer is Anglo-Saxon spelling. The second layer of spellings comes from borrowed Latin and French words (recall the Roman and French invasions of England). The third layer is the scientific layer of spellings borrowed from Greek. Each layer has its own spelling rules. The Anglo-Saxon layer, though, has all the 'common' words we use. Children need to start by learning to decode Anglo-Saxon words. The 'classy' Latin and French words and the scientific Greek words can come later. Ideas for teaching the basic decoding patterns of Anglo-Saxon English are in Calfee and Patrick (1995) and in Nicholson (1997). The appendix to Chapter 3 focuses on basic Anglo-Saxon spelling patterns.

To summarise, it can be argued that one direct way of making gains in reading comprehension is to ensure that pupils are fluent and accurate word readers. The ability to read words quickly is a skill that will apply to all text material. These are direct benefits. In contrast, attempts to improve reading comprehension by improving general knowledge and vocabulary will have less direct effects since each text a child reads will require different kinds of vocabulary and knowledge. Yet every text will require decoding skill. Decoding contributes to reading comprehension across all texts, while language knowledge will make different contributions, depending on what the text is about (Gough, Hoover & Peterson, 1996).

## Conclusion

Let us personalise the topic of reading comprehension. What would a phonics teacher predict to be causes of problems with reading comprehension? If one of their pupils, Janet or John, had problems with comprehension, phonics teachers would suspect problems with decoding. They would be thinking, 'Janet lacks fluency. She reads fairly accurately, but it's a real effort. I've got to improve her decoding skills'. In contrast, whole-language teachers would suspect that problems with meaning were causing comprehension difficulties. They will think, 'Janet's not understanding. The book is probably not interesting to her. Maybe I can find a more exciting book. I will have a conference with her to discuss the meanings of some of the words in the book'. Strangely enough, if the phonics and whole-language teachers combined forces, then Janet might get exactly the help she needs: extra skills in decoding and extra understanding of the meaning of what she reads.

Reading comprehension requires the pupil to read accurately and quickly, but it also requires the ability to gain a complete understanding of the meaning of what has been decoded. Research on comprehension is still not entirely clear about how best to teach comprehension. Most researchers agree that decoding skills are very important. How best to improve reading comprehension by using other strategies is still being debated. One thing seems clear. Teaching students how to learn new words, look for structure, show understanding of question-types, be able to read strategically, and be able to read fluently requires a long-term commitment.

## References

Aarnoutse, C. A., Van den Bos, K. P., & Brand-Gruwel, S. (1998). Effects of listening comprehension training on listening and reading. *The Journal of Special Education, 32*, 115–126.

Brockie, R.E. (1970). Sparrows (Part One). *School Journal*, Part 2, Number 1, pp. 36–40.

Calfee, R. C., & Patrick, C. L. (1995). *Teach our children well*. Stanford, CA: Stanford Alumni Association.

Carver, R. P. (1987). Should reading comprehension skills be taught? In J. E. Readance & R. S. Baldwin (Eds.), *Research in literacy: Merging perspectives* (pp. 115–126). Rochester, NY: National reading Conference.

Carver, R. P., & Liebert, R. E. (1995). The effect of reading library books at different levels of difficulty upon gain in reading ability. *Reading Research Quarterly, 30*, 26–48.

Dunlop, B. (1983). The million dollar smile. *School Journal*, Part 2, Number 3, pp. 32–39.

Dymock, S. J. (1998). A comparison study of the effects of text structure training, reading practice, and guided reading on reading comprehension. Unpublished Ph.D. thesis, The University of Auckland.

Dymock, S. J., & Nicholson, T. (1999). *Reading comprehension. What is it? How do you teach it?* Wellington: New Zealand Council for Educational research.

Ezell, H. K., Hunsicker, S. A., Quinque, M. M., & Randolph, E. (1996). Maintenance and generalisation of QAR reading comprehension strategies. *Reading Research and Instruction, 36*, 64–81.

Gough, P. B., Hoover, W. A., & Peterson, C. L. (1996). Some observations on a simple view of reading. In C. Cornoldi & J. Oakhill (Eds.), *Reading comprehension difficulties: Processes and intervention* (pp. 1–13). Hillsdale, NJ: Lawrence Erlbaum.

Hanus, K. S., & Moore, D. W. (1985). Reading comprehension questions in secondary literature textbooks for good and poor readers. *English Quarterly, 18*, 93–103.

Just, M. A., & Carpenter, P. A. (1987). *The psychology of reading and language comprehension*. Boston: Allyn & Bacon.

Levy, B. A., Abello, B., & Lysynchuk, L. (1997). Transfer from word training to reading in context: Gains in reading fluency and reading comprehension. *Learning Disabilities Quarterly, 20*, 173–188.

Lipson, M. (1995). The effect of semantic mapping instruction on prose comprehension of below-level college readers. *Reading Research and Instruction, 34*, 367–378.

Matthei, E., & Roeper, T. (1983). *Understanding and producing speech*. Bungay, Suffolk, England: Fontana.

Nicholson, T. (1997). *Solving reading problems across the curriculum*. Wellington: New Zealand Council for Educational Research.

Nicholson, T. (1998). The flashcard strikes back. *The Reading Teacher, 52*, 188–192.

Nicholson, T. (1999). Reading comprehension processes. In G.B. Thompson & T. Nicholson (Eds.), *Learning to read: Beyond phonics and whole language* (pp. 127–149). New York: Teachers College Press.

Nicholson, T., & Imlach, R. (1981). Where do their answers come from? A study of the inferences which children make when answering questions about narrative stories. *Journal of Reading Behavior, 13*, 111–130.

Nicholson, T., & Whyte, B. (1992). Matthew effects in learning new words while listening to stories. In C. K. Kinzer & D. Leu (Eds.), *Literacy research, theory, and practice: Views from many perspectives* (pp. 499–503. Chicago: National Reading Conference.

Paris, S. G., Cross, D. R., & Lipson, M. Y. (1984). Informed strategies for learning: A programme to improve children's reading awareness and comprehension. *Journal of Educational Psychology, 76*, 1239–1252.

Pinker, S. (1994). *The language instinct*. New York: Morrow.

Raphael, T.E. (1986). Teaching question–answer relationships revisited. *The Reading Teacher, 39*, 516–522.

Rayner, K., & Pollatsek, A. (1989). *The psychology of reading*. Englewood Cliffs, NJ: Prentice Hall.

Richards, G., & Richards, L. (1978). Monarch butterfly. *School Journal*, Part 1, Number 5, pp. 28–32.

Rosenshine, B., & Meister, C. (1994). Reciprocal teaching: A review of the research. *Review of Educational Research, 64*, 479–530.

Roser, N., & Juel, C. (1982). Effects of vocabulary instruction on reading comprehension. In *New inquiries in reading research and instruction* (pp. 110–118). Chicago: National Reading Conference.

Shany, M. T., & Biemiller, A. (1995). Assisted reading practice: Effects on performance for poor readers in grades 3 and 4. *Reading Research Quarterly, 30*, 382–395.

Stahl, S. (1983). Differential word knowledge and reading comprehension. *Journal of Reading Behavior, 15*, 33–50.

Taka, M. L. (1997). Word game bingo and adult literacy students: Sight word acquisition and reading comprehension. Unpublished master's thesis, The University of Auckland.

Tan, A., & Nicholson, T. (1997). Flashcards revisited: Training poor readers to read words faster improves their comprehension of text. *Journal of Educational Psychology, 89*, 276–288.

Widdowson, D. A., Moore, D. W., & Dixon, R. (1999). Engaging in recreational reading. In G. B. Thompson & T. Nicholson (Eds.), *Learning to read: Beyond phonics and whole language*. New York: Teachers College Press.

# REDING DIFFICULTIES

To understand reading difficulties, it is helpful to have a model in our heads about the basic anatomy of reading. Then, when someone asks us why a child can't read, we can consult the model and we will know what to look for. If the child can't read, then the problem must be in one of these locations. That's the ideal. We can go straight to the heart of the matter. When it comes to diagnosing reading problems there are often all kinds of explanations about why difficulties happen. Everyone has an opinion. Explanations can vary from problems with diet to the wrong colour of the paper in books to dull and unimaginative teaching. There are all sorts of things that can be focused on. But we have to distinguish between what might be the direct cause of a reading problem and what might be a consequence of not being able to read. My preference is to work from a simple model of reading and reading disabilities. It means that I can go to the core of the problem and focus my energies on that area.

## What is Reading?

When we think of the reading process, we can either focus on its complexity or its simplicity. Let's look first at its complexity. Reading is a multi-component process. It involves decoding printed words into their linguistic forms, accessing the meanings of those words, parsing of groups of words, in phrases and sentences, semantically analysing those sentences, and finally putting together the overall meaning of all those sentences and paragraphs that make up a text. These reading components have been illustrated in a simple way by Calfee (1981) as follows:

Reading = Decoding Print → Accessing Word Meanings→Syntactic Analysis→Semantic Analysis→Meaning

The advantage of dividing the reading process into separate components like this is that the reading process seems more transparent. No one would deny that each component itself is extremely complicated. Implicit in the above description are all the complexities of visual processing, language processing, thinking, remembering, recalling, and problem-solving. It represents huge challenges for researchers. When we talk about the reading process, we are talking not just about the psychology of reading, but the psychology of language and cognition.

### A simple view of reading

Is it possible that there is *less* to reading than this? Such a question seems terribly reductionist, but there is value in seeing a topic in the simplest possible way. A simple view of reading can inspire research. Some researchers think so anyway. They have argued that the 'decoding' part of reading can be separated out on its own and that all the other components can be clustered together under the heading 'language'.

The reason for separating out decoding is that it is the only component of the reading process that it is *not* part of our evolutionary ability to produce and understand language. All the other components, such as vocabulary knowledge, sentence comprehension, and so on, are there for nearly everyone, for both readers and non-readers alike. For example, consider 'talking books'. You can listen to a popular novel while you are driving to work. The novel is decoded for you. All you have to do is operate your language knowledge system in order to comprehend the 'text'. Thus, a very simple anatomy of the reading process would represent that reading consists of just two parts: the ability to decode written language and the ability to comprehend spoken language. This very simple view can be expressed as:

Reading = Decoding Print + Language Comprehension
(or, R = D + C)

Perfetti (1977) put forward this formula in a bid to describe the anatomy of reading in the simplest possible way. He included a third factor, which he called X, but X was meant to be a very small part of the equation. Perfetti reasoned that the skilled reader was adept in both decoding and language comprehension. In contrast, the unskilled reader, according to the formula, must be deficient in either decoding or language comprehension or both. Perfetti has argued that at the heart of reading skill was the ability to read words automatically. He called this 'verbal efficiency' (Perfetti, 1985). The poor reader is typically hamstrung with decoding difficulties which results in slow, inaccurate processing of the print, thus leading to verbal inefficiency. Language comprehension, however, could also play a part in reading difficulty, in that the poor reader may have problems in understanding vocabulary or in processing the meanings of sentences and so on.

The Perfetti formula had the virtue of simplicity in that researchers could challenge it. A very complex formula is an obstacle to research because it is very hard to prove wrong. But something as simple as this invites researchers to have a look at its viability. This is what Gough and Tunmer (1986) did. They checked whether the formula could account for reading difficulties of various kinds, such as dyslexia. They concluded it was not completely accurate in its additive form. An additive formula left open the highly unlikely possibility that a reader who had no decoding skill (e.g. 0 per cent) yet had excellent language comprehension (e.g. 100 per cent) could have perfect reading comprehension (100 per cent plus 0 per cent = 100 per cent).

As an alternative, Gough and Tunmer proposed a multiplicative formula: R = D x C, where R = reading comprehension, D = decoding and C = language comprehension. Using this formula, if D = 0 per cent and C = 100 per cent, R would still be 0 per cent. At the other extreme, if D = 100 per cent and C = 0 per cent, then R = 0 per cent. This seemed a more realistic way to express the formula in that if decoding or language comprehension was zero, reading comprehension would also be zero. It didn't make sense that a person could have zero decoding or language skills, yet still be able to read with comprehension.

Foss (1988) has described the Gough and Tunmer (1986) 'simple view' of the anatomy of reading as 'one of the boldest approaches to the theory of reading' (p. 334). Why? As Foss puts it, the simple view 'conjectures that what is unique to reading is *simply* the decoding of words. Thus, one cannot be a good decoder, a good listener, and a poor reader' (p. 334–335). If the simple view is correct, then the challenge in understanding reading is to understand decoding.

### Reading and Reading Disabilities

This is not to say that reading is *merely* decoding. Gough and Tunmer's 'simple view' argued that decoding was unique to reading, but they acknowledged that poor language comprehension could also contribute to reading problems. They described the phenomenon of hyperlexia as an example of poor reading ability that was not due to poor decoding. The hyperlexic is a person who is a native speaker, has good decoding skills, yet has poor reading comprehension. Yet survey data show that very few poor readers fit this category. Hyperlexics appear to have a language impairment (Healy, 1982; Cohen *et al.*, 1997).

Many teachers, however, would argue that there are children who can decode, but don't understand what they read. They 'bark' at print. This is not the same as the clinical case of hyperlexia. What teachers mean is that some children focus so much on reading words correctly that they lose meaning. The question is, how common is this phenomenon of good decoding but poor comprehension among poor readers? Stanovich (1986) has been sceptical about the numbers of such children. He argues that very often they are not good decoders at all. When this issue was discussed on the National Reading Conference (NRC) Internet Listserv, Gough wrote:

> I'm skeptical that there are children who can decode well but not understand (sounding out and blending is not good decoding.) Joe Danks once (1986) gave a paper at NRC, telling us how he scoured Cleveland to find one, and couldn't. There evidently are hyperlexics (cf. Jane Healy, RRQ [Reading Research Quarterly], 1982), but they are very rare.
>
> (NRC Email Listserv, 14 April, 1998)

Dymock (1998) located children who appeared to be good decoders yet were poor readers. She suggested that perhaps one child in ten is in this category. Whether or not this is an accurate figure may depend on how 'good decoding' is defined. A child may be good at decoding, but may still find decoding much more of an effort than should be the case if someone is really good at decoding. As a result, they have less mental energy for comprehension than they should have. Good decoding should be effortless. In order to be absolutely sure that a child is a good decoder, assessment would have to focus on the extent to which they have achieved automaticity in decoding.

What should we conclude? The simple view (Gough & Tunmer, 1986) accepts that reading disabilities will be due to problems with either decoding or language comprehension and this view enables us to categorise different kinds of reading disabilities (see Table 11.1).

**Table 11.1: Different kinds of reading disabilities**

|  | Poor Decoder | Good Decoder |
|---|---|---|
| **Good Language Comprehension** | Dyslexia | Skilled Reader |
| **Poor Language Comprehension** | 'Garden Variety' | Hyperlexia |

In the case of dyslexia, we have a poor reader who has good language comprehension. Hence the problem is located in poor decoding. In the case of hyperlexia, we have a poor reader who has good decoding skills. Hence, poor language comprehension is the problem. Finally, there is the 'garden variety' poor reader. The term 'garden variety' is meant to characterise the typical disabled reader, because in most instances of poor reading, children have both poor decoding skills and also poor language comprehension skills. These are the most prevalent poor readers.

Yet even for 'garden variety' poor readers, it seems to be the case that poor language comprehension was probably not the original cause of their problems with reading. Stanovich (1988) has argued that poor language comprehension amongst many poor readers is probably a result of poor decoding. Children who are unable to read words fluently find vocabulary and new ideas though reading. This in turn has a negative effect on their language knowledge in general. Thus their reading problems did not necessarily begin with language. Instead their language skills have suffered over time as a result of their difficulties with reading.

So, when we search for the causes of reading problems, the simple view tells us that there are two causes – poor decoding or poor language comprehension. Which is more important in accounting for reading problems? In the end the path keeps coming back to decoding as the key factor that holds back many poor readers. For this reason, we will spend some time looking at what decoding is.

## The Heart of Reading Problems: Difficulties with Decoding

What do our eyes do when we decode? Do our eyes decode a sentence at a time? A word at a time? Many skilled readers are oblivious as to what they do when they read words on the page. As Foss and Hakes (1978) pointed out, our knowledge of exactly what our eyes do when we read is only about 100 years old, even though humans have been reading for thousands of years. The problem is that our intuitions about what our eyes do are not correct.

Many adults think that we don't really look at words very much at all. Most of the time we feel as if our eyes are on the move, skimming across each line of print. If you ask adult readers to tell you what proportion of the time their eyes are moving, many will say that they are moving just about all the time. If you ask adult readers to draw in the air with their finger what their eyes do when they read, they will probably make their finger move smoothly from left to right across an imaginary line of print in the air, then sweep back to beginning of the next imaginary line, and so on.

But our eyes don't move smoothly across each line of print (see Rayner & Pollatsek, 1989; Underwood & Batt, 1996). Instead of moving smoothly, they jump from word to word in a very fast ballistic movement. Instead of being on the move most of the time, our eyes are actually perfectly still. While we read, our eyes are fixated on the print for 95 per cent of the time. Obviously our eyes do move – they cover about 200 words per minute. But time spent moving from word to word is extremely short, about five per cent of the time. The typical pattern of eye movements has the eye fixating for about 250 milliseconds (one fourth of a second) on a word, then jerking to the next word in a saccadic motion that takes 20 milliseconds (two one hundredth of a second). We rarely skip words. Instead we are jumping from one word to the next, processing almost all of what is on the page. Poor readers, however, do not do this. Their fixation times are often much longer than 250 milliseconds, because it is difficult for them to decode words.

### The direct access hypothesis

How do we identify words? Do we identify all the letters as a complete pattern or do we process the letters in small chunks of two or three at a time? Do we identify the first letter, then the next letter and so on? However it is done, most researchers agree that *all* the letters in each word do get processed (Adams, 1990; Gough, 1984; Stanovich, 1991).

Is the processing done by going straight from letters to meaning? The visual route hypothesis argues that this is what we do. We don't recode letters into sound and then go to meaning. Instead, we go directly from letters to meaning. It is possible to read words this way because the skilled reader has identified millions of words through reading. The visual alphabetic forms of many of these words have been remembered. All the reader has to do is match the printed forms with the same visual forms in memory.

This is called the 'direct access' hypothesis (Tunmer & Hoover, 1993). It seems hard to deny that the visual forms of very frequent words like 'the' must be stored in visual memory. Many words that are awkward to decode must also be stored in visual memory (e.g. 'laugh'). This orthographic information in memory is accessed during word recognition.

### The indirect access hypothesis

The 'indirect access' hypothesis says that when we recognise a word we initially recode the letters in words into systematic phonemes. We then search for the word in our mental dictionary, looking for its phonemic representation. For example, the word 'health' is converted into systematic phonemes (e.g. /h-ea-l/ + /th/). We then access the meaning of the word just as if it had been spoken to us (Foss & Hakes, 1978). There is evidence both for and against this hypothesis (see Gough, 1984).

*Are both access routes used?*

Another possibility is that skilled readers use both a visual route to the mental lexicon *and* a phonological route. But how? One idea is that both routes are used in a race to the lexicon. This is the 'dual route' (Coltheart, Patterson & Marshall, 1987). The debate about how we recognise words is still unfinished (e.g. for a review see Underwood & Batt, 1996).

## Implications for Teaching Children with Reading Problems

Adams (1990) argues that decoding is probably a shared task in which we identify words by simultaneously using indirect and direct routes in such a way that they help each other. In addition, context acts very quickly to resolve any ambiguities or mistakes made by these other two systems.

This view of decoding is helpful in terms of teaching. Good readers have excellent knowledge in memory of how words are spelled. They are also very good at converting spelling patterns into phonemes. Less skilled readers, in contrast, have deficient knowledge of the letter patterns within words. Good readers are familiar with letter sequences that are common and uncommon. For example, they are very familiar with the fact that 'th' represents the phonemes that occur in words like /then/. When they see th together they immediately relate those letters to words like /father/, not words like /fat-head/. Poor readers need this kind of orthographic knowledge of spelling regularities as well.

Good readers are able to break words into useful chunks such as syllables. To break words into syllables, the reader must know that a syllable has a vowel sound at its core. Adams (1990) suggests that the great value of vowels is that they signal the presence of syllables in words. This enables the skilled reader to break long words into syllables very quickly. In contrast, poor readers are less aware of syllable structure in long words and thus have trouble reading them. Instructionally, this supports the practice of teaching spelling patterns. The poor reader must be able to break words into syllables, and then analyse syllables in terms of letter blends (e.g. cr-, bl-) and digraphs (e.g. ch-, sh-), and phonogram patterns (e.g. -ill, -at, -up).

But poor readers are often unable to recode words phonologically. The stumbling block is a lack of phonemic awareness. Many kindergarteners have difficulty in breaking spoken words into sounds. If you ask a five-year-old to tell you the first sound (not first letter, but first sound) in his or her name, the child may not be able to tell you. A poor reader still has such difficulties. He or she may know that the two-letter combination 'an' says /an/, but not be aware that /-an/ is part of the spoken word /stand/. For example, a poor reader may be able to write her name (e.g. 'Amanda'), but if you then asked her to draw a circle around the letters in 'Amanda' which make the /an/ sound in her name, she might not be able to do it. Why not? Poor readers have difficulty in breaking spoken words into sounds. They are often not clearly aware that words are made up of sounds. This is a real problem for them if they want to recognise words through the indirect route of print to sound to meaning. Hence, the huge amount of recent research designed to find better ways of teaching poor readers to be phonemically aware (for a review, see Nicholson, 1997, 1998a).

Reading words quickly is also a characteristic of skilled reading. Poor readers are often slow and inaccurate. One way to break this pattern is to automate their reading and spelling of the most frequent words in their text materials. This should make their reading more fluent and their spelling more accurate. One way to do this is by practising the reading of high frequency words using flashcards (Nicholson, 1998b). This has been shown to be a simple and effective way of teaching poor readers to read words more quickly and accurately. Reading words more quickly can improve poor readers' comprehension of what they read (Tan & Nicholson, 1997; Nicholson & Tan, 1999).

Adams (1990) makes the point that context is very important *after* a word is recognised. This is especially the case for ambiguous words (e.g. 'bug' can be an insect or a listening device). The meanings of such words are both accessed initially. Context resolves these ambiguities very quickly.

While context is important in resolving the meanings of words, it is less useful for recognising words except as a temporary support system until decoding skills are well developed. As already discussed, the research on context effects shows context is not usually used by the skilled reader for recognising words. It does get used by the beginning reader and the poor reader, but as Adams (1990) puts it, 'overreliance on contextual clues should be a source of concern for the educator rather than a source of pride, for it is a strong sign that the reader's orthographic knowledge and skills have not been properly developed' (p. 140). The context processor is responsible for the language comprehension side of what is read. In skilled reading, word recognition is not done by the context processor; what it does is work out the meaning of the text as words are identified.

### Reading Interventions

In New Zealand the biggest single intervention strategy is Reading Recovery. It is a programme that was designed by Dame Marie Clay in the late 1970s when she was a professor of education at the University of Auckland. It involves daily, one-on-one tuition, and is for six-year-old children who are falling behind in reading and writing relative to their classmates. The proportion of children who enter Reading Recovery can range from five per cent to 30 per cent, depending on the school. The programme in 1997 was available in 71 per cent of state schools, accounting for 87 per cent of all six-year-olds. In 1997, 13,416 children (22 per cent of all six-year-olds) were involved in the programme (Kerslake, 1998); 66 per cent of children in Reading Recovery were boys.

What does Reading Recovery involve? A typical Reading Recovery programme for a child runs every day for 30–40 minutes for ten to 12 weeks. The programme is discontinued when the child 'can read a text which the average child in the second year at school can read', and the child 'can write a couple of sentences for a story, requiring only one or two words from the teacher' (Clay, 1993: 59). The Reading Recovery teacher is expected to monitor progress after the child has returned to the regular classroom to ensure that progress continues. Children are taught to make sense of what they read, to use a range of cues to cross-check, to re-read if the meaning is unclear and to self-correct. In the first two weeks of teaching, teachers 'roam around the known' (p. 12) to get to know the child and to find out what the child can do. After that, the teaching settles to a daily routine which involves seven steps (p. 14):

1.  Re-reading two readable texts that the child can read at 90 per cent

accuracy or better. These are books that have been read in previous lessons.

2. Re-read the previous lesson's text while the teacher records the child's oral reading accuracy ('running record').
3. Identifying letters; making words ('making and breaking', using onsets, rimes and analogy).
4. Writing a story (making words; hearing sounds in words).
5. Cut-up story rearranged.
6. New book introduced.
7. New book attempted.

*Two case studies of reading recovery children*

These case studies are from a longitudinal research study in Auckland schools (Nicholson, Ell & McIntosh, 1999). The first case study is Sam, who was attending school in an upper-middle-class neighbourhood. He was of European background. We assessed him in his first few months at school when he was just five years of age. He was of average intelligence and could write his name, but could only identify six or seven letters of the alphabet. He also had low phonemic awareness skills, scoring two out of 42 on our test. Toward the end of his first year of school his knowledge of the alphabet was nearly perfect, and his phonemic awareness was improving (17 out of 42). He could read some sight words as well. When we asked 'would you rather watch TV or read?', he said, that he would rather watch TV because 'you don't have to read words'.

When we next assessed him after he had completed Reading Recovery, he was six years and nine months, and his reading age was six years and three months. Phonemic awareness was much improved, with 30 out of 42. His invented spelling showed good phonemic awareness: 'The crorocadiel is drivn the car. The crorocadiel has a apole in heis mathe'. He said he liked reading and read every day to his mum and dad.

The next case study is Sally, who is also a child from an upper-middle-class neighbourhood. She was European, well above average in intelligence, and just five years of age when we first assessed her reading and writing. She could write her name, and knew 26 of the uppercase letters, but only seven lowercase letters. Her phonemic awareness score was three out of 42. We assessed her again toward the end of the year. Her phonemic awareness had much improved (27 out of 42) and she knew most letters of the alphabet (26 uppercase, 19 lowercase). She recognised five sight words. When we asked if she liked to read she said, 'Yes, because it's fun because you learn to read.'

We assessed her again after she had completed Reading Recovery. She was just over six and a half years old. Her phonemic awareness score was now almost at the top of the scale (37 out of 42). She had a reading age of seven years, three months. Her writing showed good phonemic awareness: 'a crochadiel is driving the car There has been an axsdt'.

These two case studies suggest that Reading Recovery works reasonably well. After going through Reading Recovery, the first case study, Sam, was a little below average in reading for his age, but not too far behind. The second case study, Sally, was quite a way ahead for her chronological age. But what evidence is there to say that Reading Recovery is successful or unsuccessful for children in general?

### How effective is reading recovery?

Clay (1993) summarised her research findings in relation to Reading Recovery. In her first study in 1978, 80 children completed the programme successfully and were able to progress to a reading level similar to that of a comparison group of 160 children. The comparison group initially had higher reading scores than the Reading Recovery children. After receiving tuition, however, the Reading Recovery children caught up to the comparison group in terms of reading scores. Clay (1993) reported a one-year follow-up of the children in 1979 and found that the Reading Recovery children (76 of them) were still at a similar reading level to the comparison group (153 children). She followed up the same children two years further on, in 1981, when they were nine years old. She found that the 68 follow-up Reading Recovery children were still reading within the average range for nine-year-olds. Results were similar for European, Maori and Pacific Islands children from the original Reading Recovery study. Clay replicated the original Reading Recovery study in 1979 and gained similar results to those of the group involved in the programme in 1978. These results suggested that Reading Recovery gains were not just a one-off result, but could be replicated by different teachers with different students.

Clay's research in New Zealand has been queried by some researchers in terms of the technical design of the studies, especially the lack of a proper control group for comparison purposes (Shanahan, 1987; Nicholson, 1989). The Reading Recovery programme has been implemented in countries such as Canada, the United States, Australia and England. A recent review of Reading Recovery research by Shanahan and Barr (1995) concluded that it was effective, but not as dramatically as had been claimed by its supporters. Also, it is an expensive intervention that might be made more cost-effective. For example, Iversen and Tunmer (1993) reported a study in which the addition of phonological recoding instruction enabled children to complete the programme in a third less time than normal. In New Zealand there have been two independent evaluations of Reading Recovery that are summarised here.

### The Glynn et al. study

An independent evaluation of Reading Recovery was carried out in the Otago-Southland region in 1986 where ten Reading Recovery teachers worked with the children. In the Reading Recovery sample, there were 26 boys and 16 girls; in the comparison sample, there were 22 boys and 19 girls. Reading Recovery children were selected by their schools as those in most need of extra instruction. The researchers thought it would be unethical to randomly assign children in need of instruction to a control group because they would miss out on extra instruction. As a result, the comparison group of children were those children not eligible for Reading Recovery. They were, however, children who were relatively low in reading level.

The total sample from 12 schools was 83 children, with 42 children in Reading Recovery and 41 in the comparison group. Each child was assessed on entry to the Reading Recovery programme. At the same time a comparison child was also assessed. Each pair of children was then assessed several times over a two-year period. Unfortunately children began and finished Reading Recovery at different times during the first year, so at each assessment period there were different numbers of children in each group. The first assessment, for a group of 21 children who had reached 'discontinuation', showed that Reading Recovery children were reading at the same book level as the comparison group even though they started behind them. The Reading Recovery group had gained almost 11 book levels (4.1 to 14.7) from pre-test to post-test, while comparison children gained only six book levels (8.5 to 14.5).

At the next assessment at the end of the year, the Reading Recovery children were nearly two book levels ahead of the comparison children (16.7 versus 15.1). When assessed in the first term of the next year, Reading Recovery children had slipped behind the comparison group. They were now two book levels behind (16.6. versus 18.8). When assessed in the second term, they were one and a half book levels behind (18.9 versus 20.5). When assessed in the third term of that year, they were two book levels behind (20.5 versus 22.7). In summary, these data suggested that the initial gains in Reading Recovery had 'washed out' once children were discontinued from the programme.

There were interesting qualitative data in this study, showing some differences in the kind of instruction provided by different Reading Recovery teachers. One of the Reading Recovery procedures is to 'cut up' a child's story into its component words and then re-assemble it. In one school the Reading Recovery teacher put the child's cut-up story in the rubbish bin. When the child asked why she did this, the teacher said it was because she didn't have time to put his story into an envelope. Another observation was that 'sound boxes' for phonemic awareness instruction were used by all teachers at least some of the time, but that one teacher did not use the boxes at all.

When children were asked about Reading Recovery they were mostly positive, for example, saying that they did 'lots of reading'. One child said that the lessons were helpful because 'it helps me learn more words that I can be teached' (p. 48). Although the vast majority of Reading Recovery children said they enjoyed their lessons, one or two did not. One child said he did not like it 'when the teacher smacks you' (p. 48). Another child complained that he did not like 'the smoke in my face' (from the teacher's cigarette).

### Tunmer et al. (1998); Chapman et al. (1999)

This was a longitudinal study of children from the Manawatu region. In this study 152 children were followed through their first three years of school. In the second year of school, 26 of the children completed the Reading Recovery programme. Their progress was compared with a group of 98 children who had not received Reading Recovery. The results showed that the Reading Recovery children never caught up with the comparison group. One of the findings of the study was that reading and spelling skills were insufficiently developed through Reading Recovery. The children were tested at the end of Year 1 and midway through Year 2 of school. By this time, all the Reading Recovery children had completed the programme. On a test of invented spelling, the Reading Recovery children made considerable progress, moving from a score of 16.8 to 38.2, but they were still behind the comparison group who had moved from 43.9 to 53.4. The word-reading scores of the Reading Recovery children had moved from 4.2 to 11.7 on a standardised Word Reading Test, but the comparison group had moved from 21.8 to 32.3. When assessed midway through Year 3, the total group of children in the study had an average chronological age of seven years, six months. But Reading Recovery children had a reading age of six years, six months. They were still behind the comparison group of poor readers, who had a reading age of six years, 11 months. These data suggested that the Reading Recovery children had been discontinued too soon and had acquired an insufficient level of phonological reading skill to continue to grow as readers. The results also showed that Reading Recovery children had consistently lower reading-self-concept scores than the normally progressing children, and exhibited more classroom behaviour problems. They had graduated from the programme before they had caught up to their classmates in reading and spelling.

So why is it that children are helped when they stay in an intervention programme, but fall back when the interventions are completed and they have to survive on their own? As Pressley (1998) points out, most interventions have the same long-term problems faced by Reading Recovery. What can be done? Two things. Chapman *et al.* (1999) suggest much stronger teaching of spelling patterns, and much less reliance on context clues for reading of words. Second, children experiencing reading difficulties may need long-term interventions, just as do some children with chronic illnesses. This same point was made by Balow (1965), who argued that short-term interventions are not 'magic bullets'. Yet to what extent are long-term interventions possible?

*Resource teachers of reading*

In New Zealand, children who do not respond to Reading Recovery have an opportunity for further intervention by working with Resource Teachers of Reading (RTRs). In 1997, 1,638 students were taught by RTRs. Sixty-six per cent were boys, 60 per cent were Pakeha, 30 per cent Māori and eight per cent were Pacific Island (Dewar, 1998). Tutoring is usually three to five times each week. Of the 1,034 children admitted to RTR teaching in 1997, 48 per cent had not been in Reading Recovery, while 41 per cent had been either discontinued from Reading Recovery or referred on because they were not responding to the instruction. Children eligible for RTR help have to be seven years or older (usually up to 12 years), below average in reading for their age, having difficulty with spelling or language, and unresponsive to school interventions. In 1997, 1,527 children were on waiting lists for RTRs. As in the health system, the problem of providing long-term help to children in need of reading assistance is one of insufficient resources. Another problem is that we need independent research studies of the effects of long-term interventions such as those provided by RTRs. It is one thing to *say* that children need long-term help, but we need to verify this idea. We also need to find out which long-term approaches are most effective. For many children, continuous reading assistance throughout their schooling may be the only realistic solution.

## Conclusions

If we personalise this topic, relating it to a fictional Janet and a fictional John, how would their reading problems be diagnosed by phonics and whole-language teachers? A phonics teacher would hone in on decoding as the most probable cause of reading problems. If Janet or John were struggling with reading, a phonics teacher would find ways of building their decoding skills. They may have not learned some letter–sound patterns (e.g. 'ph' represents /f/, as in 'photo'), or they may have trouble breaking words into syllables. A phonics teacher would work on this area, teaching them that words are made of syllables. A syllable has a vowel. Long words can be broken into syllables by mentally drawing a line after the first consonant following each vowel, and then pronouncing the word syllable by syllable (e.g. Con/stan/tin/ople, No/vem/ber, kan/gar/oo).

In contrast, the whole-language teacher may think that Janet and John are struggling because they are relying too much on sounding out each letter of each word. The whole-language teacher will work on prediction and guessing skills. Some strategies will be taught, like

- read to the end of the sentence and think of what the word might be
- go back to the start of the sentence and read it again
- look at the first letter of the word and guess what it means
- if it's too hard, skip it.

The whole-language teacher may think that teaching letter–sound skills will be the wrong thing to do. These children have probably been drilled out of their minds with phonics. What they need is to make better use of their language skills.

Who is right? It may be that Janet and John would be better off if both teachers worked with them. The phonics teacher builds up the poor decoding skills of Janet and John. The whole-language teacher encourages these children to put their skills into real reading. I remember once teaching a child how to decode lists of words quite well, but when I gave her a book to read, she froze. She had become used to the structure of the phonics lessons and was reluctant to tackle new words and letter–sound patterns in the context of a book. By combining phonics and whole language strategies, I may have been able to help her more effectively.

The simple view of reading predicts that improvements in decoding and/or language comprehension will improve reading comprehension. Both are necessary for reading. Deficiencies in one or both areas will cause reading problems. The simple view also suggests that for the vast majority of struggling readers the heart of their problem is to do with decoding. The simple view does not take a position on which is the best way to teach poor readers. The fact that many children learn to read, no matter what the method, suggests that every reading method has the basic ingredients for learning to read. Some researchers feel that if every kindergarten child was helped to become phonemically aware before starting school, then learning to read would be a breeze no matter what the reading method. This is why the recent discovery that most poor readers have problems with phonemic awareness has been hailed as reading's most significant breakthrough. We should also be wary of waiting too long to intervene when children are having difficulty learning to read and write. Reading Recovery has been put in place in New Zealand schools as an intervention to help struggling six-year-olds, yet research indicates that this is not enough to bring about long-term benefits and that we should be looking at interventions that start early and last for many months, perhaps even years, to ensure that these children find success.

Many children have difficulty in learning to decode. We have discussed various reasons why this is so. We have had to consider why decoding difficulties happen, and how we can make decoding skills easier to acquire. How this is best done has been the topic of long and deep debate over the decades. There has been and still is much discussion about how to teach reading effectively so that children can read with ease and enjoy reading. In the last decade (at least) the focus of much debate has been on the relative merits of phonics or whole language. The debate is still in progress. If the simple view is correct, then no matter which way we teach, the important goal is that children learn as quickly as possible how to be expert code-breakers.

## References

Adams, M.J. (1990). *Beginning to read*. Cambridge, MA: MIT Press.

Balow, B. (1965). The long-term effect of remedial reading instruction. *The Reading Teacher, 18*, 581–586.

Calfee, R. C. (1981). Cognitive psychology and educational practice. *Review of Research in Education, 9*, 3–72.

Chapman, J.W., Tunmer, W.E., & Prochnow, J.E. (1999). *Success in Reading Recovery depends on the development of phonological processing skills*. Report to Ministry of Education (New Zealand), Massey University.

Clay, M.M. (1993). *Reading Recovery*. Auckland: Heinemann.

Cohen, M.J., Hall, J., Riccio, C.A. (1997). Neuropsychological profiles of children diagnosed as specific language impaired with and without hyperlexia. *Archives of Clinical Neuropsychology, 12*, 223–229.

Coltheart, M., Patterson, K.E., & Marshall, J.C. (1987). *Deep dyslexia* (2nd ed.). London: Routledge and Kegan Paul.

Dewar, S. (1998). A summary of the 1887 data on students taught by resource teachers of reading. *The Research Bulletin* (pp. 59–66). Wellington: Ministry of Education.

Dymock, S. J. (1998). A comparison study of the effects of text structure training, reading practice, and guided reading on reading comprehension. In T. Shanahan (Ed.), *National Reading Conference Yearbook* (Vol. 47, pp. 90–102). Chicago, IL: National Reading Conference.

Foss, D. J. (1988). Experimental psycholinguistics. *Annual Review of Psychology, 39*, 301–348.

Foss, D. J., & Hakes, D. T. (1978). *Psycholinguistics: An introduction to the psychology of language.* Englewood Cliffs, NJ: Prentice Hall.

Glynn, T., Crooks, T., Bethune, N., Ballard, K., & Smith, J. (1989). *Reading Recovery in context.* Wellington: Ministry of Education.

Goodman, K. S. (1970). Reading: A psycholinguistic guessing game. In H. Singer & R. Ruddell (Eds.), *Theoretical models and processes of reading* (pp. 259–271). Newark, DE: International Reading Association.

Gough, P. B. (1984). Word recognition. In P. D. Pearson, R. Barr, M. L. Kamil & P. Mosenthal (Eds.), *Handbook of reading research* (Vol. 1, pp. 225–253). White Plains, NY: Longman.

Gough, P. B., & Tunmer, W. E. (1986). Decoding, reading, and reading disability. *Remedial and Special Education, 7*, 6–10.

Healy, J. (1992). The enigma of hyperlexia. *Reading Research Quarterly, 17*, 319–338.

Iversen, S.A., & Tunmer, W.E. (1993). Phonological processing skill and the Reading Recovery program. *Journal of Educational Psychology, 85*, 112–125.

Kerslake, J. (1998). Annual monitoring of Reading Recovery. The data for 1997. *The Research Bulletin* (pp. 43–48). Wellington: Ministry of Education.

Nicholson, T. (1989). A comment on Reading Recovery. *New Zealand Journal of Educational Studies, 24*, 95–97.

Nicholson, T. (1993). The case against context. In G. B. Thompson, W. E. Tunmer, & T. Nicholson (Eds.), *Reading acquisition processes* (pp. 91–104). Clevedon, England: Multilingual Matters.

Nicholson, T. (1997). Closing the gap on reading failure: Social background, phonemic awareness, and learning to read. In B. A. Blachman (Ed.), *Foundations of reading acquisition and dyslexia: Implications for early intervention* (pp. 381–407). Mahwah, NJ:

Lawrence Erlbaum.

Nicholson, T. (1998a). Phonological awareness and learning to read. In L. van Lier & D. Corson (Eds.), *Knowledge about language* (Encyclopedia of language and education, Vol. 6, pp. 53–61). Dordrecht, The Netherlands: Kluwer.

Nicholson, T. (1998b). The flashcard strikes back. *The Reading Teacher, 52,* 188–192.

Nicholson, T., Ell, F., & McIntosh, S. (1999). The rich get richer and the poor get poorer. A longitudinal study of children's literacy development through Years 1 to 4. Paper presented to the Australian Association of Special Education. Sydney, September.

Nicholson, T., & Tan, A. (1999). Proficient word identification for comprehension. In G. B. Thompson & T. Nicholson (Eds.), *Learning to read: Beyond phonics and whole language* (pp. 150–174). New York: Teachers College Press.

Perfetti, C. A. (1977). Language comprehension and fast decoding: Some psycholinguistic prerequisites for skilled reading comprehension. In J. T. Guthrie (Ed.), *Cognition, curriculum and comprehension* (pp. 20–41). Newark, DE: International Reading Association.

Perfetti, C. A. (1985). *Reading ability.* New York: Oxford University Press.

Pressley, M. (1998). *Reading instruction that works. The case for balanced instruction.* New York: Guildford Press.

Rayner, K., & Pollatsek, A. (1989). *The psychology of reading.* Englewood Cliffs, NJ: Prentice Hall.

Shanahan, T. (1987). [Review of the book. *Early detection of reading difficulties.*] *Journal of Reading Behaviour, 19,* 117–119.

Shanahan, T., & Barr, R. (1995). Reading Recovery: An independent evaluation of the effects of an early instructional intervention for at-risk learners. *Reading Research Quarterly, 30,* 958–996.

Smith, J. W., & Elley, W. B. (1994). Learning to read in New Zealand. Auckland: Longman Paul.

Stanovich, K. E. (1980). Toward an interactive-compensatory model of individual differences in the development of reading fluency. *Reading Research Quarterly, 16,* 32–71.

Stanovich, K. E. (1986). Matthew effects in reading: Some consequences of individual differences in the acquisition of literacy.

*Reading Research Quarterly, 20*, 360–406.

Stanovich, K. E. (1988). The right and wrong place to look for the cognitive locus of reading disability. *Annals of Dyslexia, 38*, 154–177.

Stanovich, K. E. (1991). Word recognition: changing perspectives. In R. Barr, P. D. Pearson, M. L. Kamil & P. Mosenthal (Eds.), *Handbook of reading research* (Vol. 2, 418–452). White Plains, NY: Longman.

Tan, A., & Nicholson, T. (1997). Flashcards revisited: Training poor readers to read words faster improves their comprehension of text. *Journal of Educational Psychology, 89*, 276–288.

Tunmer, W.E., Chapman, J.W., Ryan, H.A., & Prochnow, J.E. (1998). The importance of providing beginning readers with explicit training in phonological processing skills. *Australian Journal of Learning Disabilities, 3*, 4–14.

Tunmer, W.E., & Hoover, W.A. (1993). The components of reading. In G.B. Thompson, W.E. Tunmer, & T. Nicholson (Eds.), *Reading acquisition processes* (pp. 1–19). Cleveland, England: Multilingual Matters.

Underwood, G., & Batt, V. (1996). *Reading and understanding*. Oxford: Blackwell.

# 12

# READING AND MOTIVATION

By the time it is realised that a child is having difficulty with reading, he or she may have come to dislike reading and be on the defensive. When asked about reading, the child may not be able to explain why reading is difficult. The child lacks the skills to read easily and confidently, and thus a dislike of reading is a result of embarrassing experiences in reading. For example, a poor reader once said to me, 'I can't explain why, but I hate reading. I just hate it.' I told him that he hated it because it was difficult for him. No one likes something that is too difficult. He then said, 'How come none of my teachers are able to explain that to me?' This was a boy who had told a counsellor that he sometimes felt like ending his life. His mother was very concerned. His difficulties with reading had affected his overall feelings about himself. Let's look at this issue in more detail.

Reading self-efficacy refers to a person's perception of themselves as a reader. This can be different from a person's attitudes towards reading in general. A pupil can like reading, but not like themselves as a reader. For example, a question like 'How do you feel about getting a book for a present?' may not discriminate between a good and a poor reader. A poor reader might actually like getting books as presents simply because it's nice to get presents. Another question that might miss the mark is 'What does your teacher think about your reading?' A poor reader, with a very supportive teacher, may say that the teacher really likes his or her reading. And this may be true, in that the teacher gives lots of positive feedback to all pupils, no matter how good or poor they are. In contrast, a question like 'Do you think you are a good reader?' cuts to the quick. Such a question targets the reader's own assessment of themselves as readers. When using reading assessment measures, it is worth looking at the items. Some may be more diagnostic than others. Several assessment measures are available in the literature (e.g. Dymock, 1995; McKenna & Kear, 1990; Henk & Melnick, 1995). See also the appendix to this chapter for a checklist of possible questions to ask.

### Reading and Liking Reading: There Can Be a Difference

Good readers usually enjoy reading. But does this mean that if teachers emphasise enjoyment of reading then children will learn to read? The reality seems to be that enjoyment of reading is not a cause of learning to read, but a consequence. Stanovich (1986) and Juel (1988) have both argued that children's enjoyment of reading is related to their experiences while learning to read. The 'Matthew effects' hypothesis is that getting off to an advantageous start in reading will have strong spin-off effects on other reading-related behaviours such as general knowledge, vocabulary, self-esteem as a reader, and the love of reading. Children who experience early success in learning to read are more likely to want to read and to enjoy reading. This is a positive Matthew effect that derives from learning to read (i.e. 'the rich get richer'). In contrast, children who experience early difficulty in learning to read aren't as likely to want to read, or to want to engage in reading tasks. This is a negative Matthew effect (i.e. 'the poor get poorer'), in that these children will not gain access to the world of books, and the benefits they bring (e.g. new ideas, new vocabulary).

### How Long Does it Take to Feel Bad About Yourself?

What are some of the long-term effects of not learning to read on children's enjoyment of reading? Juel (1988) assessed the reading and writing progress of 129 pupils as they moved through grades one to four. The children were learning to read with a mix of programmes, including regular phonics teaching. At the end of her study, many of the original 129 children in the study had left the area; only 54 remained. There were 24 poor readers and 30 average-to-good readers. Juel found that of the remaining children in the study, those who were poor readers at the end of grade one were almost 90 per cent likely to be poor readers at the end of grade four. To put it another way, there was only about a ten per cent chance of a child becoming an average reader in fourth grade if he or she was a poor reader in first grade.

In addition, the motivation of these poor readers to read became more and more negative as they progressed through the grades. They read less than good readers, and disliked reading more. Poor readers started school with virtually no phonemic awareness skills. Good readers acquired phonemic skills rapidly, so that they were virtually scoring 90 per cent correct on tests of phonemic awareness by the end of first grade. In contrast, poor readers didn't approach 90 per cent correct on the phonemic awareness test until the end of third grade. Almost all of the poor readers still had poor decoding skills in fourth grade. Only two did not. These two children lagged behind in language knowledge, and this was causing their poor reading scores. Three children had average language knowledge in fourth grade but lagged behind in decoding. These children fitted the profile of dyslexia. The vast majority, however, lagged behind in ability to read words accurately and in language knowledge. The gap in language knowledge had not been there in grade one. The widening gap had formed after first grade, presumably because good readers were able to use their superior decoding skills to read lots and lots of books. This extra reading opportunity would have helped to acquire new vocabulary and new general knowledge, both important aspects of language knowledge.

By fourth grade, poor readers did much less after-school reading than did good readers. Their ability to read their primers aloud was also far less fluent and accurate than was the case for good readers. Juel (1988) reported, 'The poor readers rarely correctly read even 80 per cent of the words' (p. 442). Reading had become an unpleasant activity for many of the poor readers, as was revealed by interview questions asked of the fourth grade sample. One question was, 'Would you rather clean your room or read?' Only five per cent of the good readers said they would rather clean their room, but 40 per cent of the poor readers opted to clean their room. One poor reader said, 'I'd rather clean the mould around the bathtub than read' (p. 442). Another question was, 'Do you like to read?' Of the 30 good readers, 26 said 'yes'. Of the 24 poor readers, only five said 'yes'. Several of the poor readers said they hated reading; most said it was boring. Similar data have been reported by Dymock (1993). She asked questions of 16 good and 16 poor readers aged 11 and 12 years. Dymock asked, 'Would you rather watch television or read?' Of the good readers, 73 per cent said they would rather read. Of the poor readers, only 27 per cent said they would rather read.

Nicholson (1999) reported a longitudinal study of a group of five-year-old children who were in whole-language reading programmes. Some of the children were already negative about reading even at the end of their first year at school. One child was asked, 'How often do you read at home?' The answer was 'Never. I hate reading now.' Another child was asked, 'Would you rather clean up your room or read?' The child said, 'Clean up my room, because I can clean up my room, but I can't read'. Another child was asked, 'How do you feel when you come to a new word while reading?' The child said, 'I cry.' Follow-up assessments of a remaining group of 78 children toward the end of their second year of schooling revealed that those children who had made little progress in reading also did not feel good about their own progress. One child was asked, 'Do you like to read?' The child said, 'No. Mum likes me to read, but I read ugly 'cause I don't know how to read.'

## Can You Like Reading Yet Not Feel Good About Your Own Skills?

Chapman and Tunmer (1995) in an experiment involving 771 pupils aged five to ten years, found that the five-year-olds in their study were very positive about their reading abilities, but that the nine and ten-year-olds were less positive. This suggests that low self-esteem in relation to reading is a consequence of a long period of failure. Chapman and Tunmer also found that whether or not a pupil felt bad about reading depended on the questions they were asked. It was better to ask a question that focused on their specific reading skills (e.g. 'Is reading to the class hard for you?') than to ask general questions about reading (e.g. 'Is it fun for you to read books?'). The general questions about reading attitudes weren't related to reading achievement. Good and poor readers were equally likely to say reading was fun. This is possible. Poor readers may enjoy some aspects of reading (e.g. listening to the teacher read a story), even though they personally find reading difficult.

It seems that young children are overly optimistic about their reading abilities in general, even though they admit problems with specific aspects of reading. Why should children feel good about reading, even if it's hard for them? The reason may be that teachers of younger children focus on providing positive learning experiences. Many teachers believe that if children enjoy reading, then this will help them learn to read. Teachers protect children from failure at first. It is not until the child has been in school for several years that their overall sense of competence in reading reflects the impact of continuing difficulties with reading. Even then, children may still enjoy reading in general, even though they know they are not very good at reading.

This was the finding of a study by Wilson, Chapman and Tunmer (1995). The longitudinal study involved a group of 52 children (26 low achievers, 26 competent readers) matched for age, gender and teacher. The researchers initially gave reading self-efficacy tests to all the children. Self-efficacy tests measure the picture you have of your own reading ability and the picture you have about what others think of your reading. As part of this research, a group of low-achieving pupils were assessed both before and after they experienced extra reading tuition in the Reading Recovery programme. The aim of Reading Recovery is to bring children who are below classroom average in reading up to average classroom levels (Clay, 1993). At the end of the Reading Recovery intervention, each matching pair of pupils (low achiever and competent) was re-tested with the self-efficacy measure. It was found that the attitudes of the poor readers about themselves in general were similar to those of the competent readers. But when linked specifically to reading, they had a lower sense of competence and greater sense of task difficulty. Even after they had completed Reading Recovery, the low achieving group's sense of self-efficacy had not changed. The conclusion was that younger children may like reading and also like themselves, even though they are not achieving very well, and feel that they are not good at reading.

## What Sorts of Questions Best Identify Reading Self-Esteem?

If we want to get a more exact look at children's self-esteem in relation to reading, Chapman and Tunmer (1995) suggest that we should focus on children's self-efficacy, which means their opinions of their abilities in relation to specific tasks. Children who feel efficacious in regard to reading will work harder and persist longer at reading tasks. Chapman and Tunmer argue that these attributions about specific aspects of reading accumulate over time and eventually affect their overall reading motivation. Working with a sample of 139 children at the five-year-old level, they found that a reading self-efficacy measure that focused on reading skill was a good predictor of reading progress. The self-efficacy scale consisted of just four questions, with forced-choice answers:

1. What do you do when you are reading and come to a word that you don't know? Do you try to *work out* what the word is, or do you *wait* for someone to tell you? (Expected answer for a good reader was: 'Work it out'.)
2. What do you do when you make mistakes in reading? Do you try to *fix them up*, or do you *keep on reading?* (Expected answer for a good reader was: 'Fix them up.')
3. What do you do when you find words hard to read? Do you like *trying* to work out what the words are, or do you get *tired* and do something else? (Expected answer for a good reader was: 'Try'.)
4. When you find words hard to read, is it *too hard* to get words to make sense, or can you *guess* words that could make sense? (Expected answer for a good reader was: 'Guess'.)

**How Long Does it Take to Feel a Failure?**

Chapman, Tunmer and Prochnow (1998) looked at the effects of reading failure on children's self-concept about reading and their classroom behaviors. The sample was made up of 26 children who had completed the Reading Recovery programme, 20 poor readers who had not received Reading Recovery, and 80 average or better readers. The children in the study all had similar reading self-concepts in year one of school (five-year-olds), before the Reading Recovery programme. But by the end of the second year of school, the poor readers in the sample, including those who had completed Reading Recovery, had lower reading self-concepts and worse classroom behaviour than children in the study who were average or better readers. Why these negative results for the children who had received extra reading tuition? The reason was that the tuition had not succeeded in its aims. The Reading Recovery children had not been brought up to average classroom reading levels. Their reading levels were still similar to those of the poor readers who had not received the extra reading recovery tuition.

### What is the Link Between Reading and Classroom Behaviour?

Why should classroom behaviour be negatively affected by poor reading progress? One reason is frustration. Jorgenson (1977) studied the classroom behaviours of 71 second-grade through sixth-grade students. First, he assessed the reading abilities of the students. Second, the teachers of these pupils were asked to make a note of the pages of the books these pupils were reading at that time. Third, the researcher calculated the readability levels of the pages. Finally, teachers were asked to rate the classroom behaviours of the pupils. Teachers rated behaviours such as the extent to which each pupil was disruptive, impatient, disrespectful, defiant, blamed others for failure, failed to understand what he or she was reading, lacked creativity, and relied on being close to and friendly with the teacher.

The study found that pupils were better behaved if the readability levels of reading materials were below their reading ability levels; that is, pupils were better behaved if they read text that was not too difficult for them. Pupils who were placed with difficult-to-read text materials were more likely to be rated by teachers as disruptive, impatient and demanding of teacher time. Teachers also rated them as having less understanding of what they read, and being less creative. The results suggested that pupils will be better behaved and also make better progress in reading if given easier materials to read. Forell (1985) found some support for this idea. She reported that a school policy of placing pupils in 'comfortable' reading material (i.e. could be read at 95 per cent accuracy or better) was particularly helpful for middle-to-low and low-achieving readers as they progressed from third to seventh grade.

### Quick Summary So Far

To summarise so far, it seems that children's concepts about themselves as readers and even their classroom behaviours depend on whether or not they are successful in learning to read and whether or not they are reading relatively easy material. Children who do not read well feel bad about themselves as readers and are likely to resist the academic tasks of the classroom. If we can get them off to a good start in reading and give them materials that they can 'comfortably' read, they are likely to become better readers, feel better about themselves, and be better behaved in class.

## Learned Helplessness

Some children are more curious than others and try harder to gain control over their environment. Why is this? Such differences in motivation may be due to childhood experiences. It may be that some childhood experiences convince children that they are either 'achievers' or else 'no good'. This may be related to feedback they receive from their caregivers about their efforts (e.g. 'Won't you ever get it right?' versus 'You are terrific!').

Learned helplessness research builds on the idea that intrinsic motivation is influenced by the surrounding environment, especially schooling. Research on learned helplessness suggests that some children react to school tasks in ways that produce either 'helpless' or 'mastery-oriented' patterns of behaviour. Dweck (1986) reported research with fifth graders (ten to eleven years of age) who were given difficult tasks in mathematics. The pupils reacted in two different ways. Some exhibited a helpless pattern of response. Their performance dropped as they continued to experience difficulty with the tasks, and they tended to give up easily. When interviewed, these pupils thought that their failures were due to lack of ability and that their successes were due to luck. Dweck argued that they had an 'entity' theory of their ability (i.e. it is fixed, and that some have more of it than others, so there is no use trying to get better). They internalised the reasons for their failures (i.e. lack of ability) and externalised the reasons for their successes (e.g. luck). Their focus was on performance goals, which involved making their work look good, but not attempting tasks that were challenging.

In contrast, other pupils showed a 'mastery-oriented' response to the mathematics tasks. They had an 'incremental' theory of their ability (i.e. it will improve if I work hard; that it is worth trying to get better). They externalised the reasons for their failures (e.g. lack of time to study) and internalised the reasons for their success (e.g. they were good at the task). They focused on learning goals, which involved trying to get better, taking risks and taking on challenging tasks.

### Individual differences in reactions to failure

Some pupils are resistant to negative feedback from the environment and keep their self-esteem intact. But others react badly. In a study by Heyman, Dweck and Cain (1992), a sample of 107 kindergarten children (five-year-olds) were asked to perform tasks such as drawing houses or writing numbers. The children were asked to imagine that their work was criticised by a teacher (e.g. 'I'm disappointed in your work'). The results showed that 60 per cent of the children were not put off by the criticism. They still thought their work was good. But some (40 per cent) said that they were not good, not smart, not nice people. The positive children were more likely to be angry at the teacher. They also gave more positive responses to the imaginary criticisms.

There also appear to be individual differences in what children think will motivate them. In a study by Thorkildsen (1994), children aged between seven and 12 years were interviewed about the fairness of school practices which influence motivation to learn. The results showed that children were agreed unanimously that praising excellent performances of some children over others would reduce motivation to learn among those not praised.

But they differed in what they thought of as motivating practices. The children showed three different viewpoints. The first was the humanist, whole-child view, that the teacher must help all children in order to get the best out of them. They thought that children would not be motivated if some got special treatment and not others. The second view was called fundamentalist – that children must work hard and this will bring its own rewards. Their thinking was that effort is everything, and that it is wrong to shirk work. The third was the capitalist student-as-worker view, that teachers should use rewards to encourage unwilling workers, and give prizes to the best workers. The idea was that if you provide rewards, this will motivate pupils to try harder. These results suggest that children will react differently to classroom practices. Some will like stickers for achievement and being singled out while others will want everyone to be treated the same, and many will just work hard anyway.

### Learned helplessness and reading

In a study by Butkowsky and Willows (1980), a sample of 123 grade five boys (10–11 years old) were screened for intelligence and reading ability. Of that sample, 72 were selected for the study (24 good readers, 25 average readers, and 24 poor readers). The pupils were given tests of 'reading' that were either solvable or unsolvable. One of the tasks was to untangle anagrams (e.g. chria = chair, ospon = spoon, hroes = horse, trnia = train). To make the task unsolvable, the anagrams were changed slightly, adding in a new letter that could not make a word (e.g. chrua). The researchers interviewed the pupils, asking them to predict how they would go on the tasks. They also interviewed them about their reactions to the solvable and unsolvable tasks. The results showed that poor readers didn't expect to do well. They were also likely to blame failure on lack of ability and success on luck. Finally, it was found that poor readers reacted badly to failure. They were less likely to feel that it was possible to succeed on the anagram tasks. In all, poor readers demonstrated 'learned helplessness' patterns of behaviour.

### Attribution training

Is it possible to change the low levels of reading self-efficacy (i.e. feeling that they are not competent at reading) and general self-esteem (i.e. feeling that they are not good persons) that poor readers have? Dweck (1986) has reported work in attribution training where pupils were given challenging tasks that could be completed but required effort and persistence. Pupils were told that they had the ability to do certain tasks, and that if they put in the effort they would succeed. Dweck was trying to break the pattern of learned helplessness, where children can have ability yet think that they are not good enough. She found that telling them to work hard and encouraging them to do better was a more effective strategy than just giving them successful experiences. This suggests that children with low self-efficacy can be helped to change their attributions about themselves if they are given moderately challenging tasks and encouragement to complete those tasks.

But Nicholls (1995) takes issue with Dweck's idea that students who are not learning should be told that they didn't try hard enough. The reasoning behind the 'try harder' suggestion is that if you say this, then students will realise that they can do better if they work harder. There is hope. Otherwise they will think that their lack of success is due to their personal inability to cope. Thus, by saying 'you didn't work hard enough', the teacher is really saying that the pupil has ability and can succeed if sufficient effort is made. But Nicholls questions whether this really a good idea. Saying that a student is not working hard is also saying that the student is lazy. It's a very negative comment. And it doesn't mesh with what most teachers feel is more productive. If a student fails, then most teachers prefer to do something positive, like finding ways to make the text material easier to learn, or more interesting.

Attribution training is the bread and butter of motivation seminars. It's very difficult to come away from such seminars without a long list of positive self-attributions. It may be that some poor readers will benefit from having their own list. It may inspire them to regain confidence in themselves. Here are some attribution statements:

- 'Success is 85 per cent attitude; 15 per cent aptitude.'
- 'You can only jump as high as the barriers in your mind.'
- 'Believe in yourself.'
- 'Never give in, never give in, never give in.'
- 'There is no gain without pain.'
- 'There is always room at the top.'

### Do Whole-Language Reading Programmes Improve Reading Attitudes?

McKenna *et al.* (1995) looked at the effects of whole-language teaching approaches to children's attitudes to reading. The researchers thought that some aspects of whole-language, such as the emphasis on exposure to good literature, probably have a positive effect on reading attitudes. In comparison, traditional reading programmes, where the difficulty level of texts is highly structured, where the reading material is less exciting, and where there is an emphasis on teaching of decoding skills could very easily have a negative effect on reading attitudes.

To find out which reading approach had a more positive effect on attitudes towards reading, four schools were surveyed. Two schools had a whole-language emphasis, and two had a traditional emphasis. There were 918 pupils (whole-language = 485, traditional = 483), ranging across grades one through five. Each pupil was given a reading attitude questionnaire with questions such as, 'How do you feel about reading instead of playing?', and 'How do you feel when your teacher asks you questions about what you read?' The researchers found no difference in reading attitudes between the pupils in each reading programme. Then they surveyed another school which had an even stronger whole-language philosophy, and got similar results. Interviews with two whole-language teachers, whose pupils differed in reading attitudes, suggested that the teacher whose view of whole-language was more eclectic (i.e. included some skills work such as phonics) had students with more positive attitudes towards reading.

The researchers concluded that the whole-language approach had no advantage over the basal approach in terms of students' attitudes to reading. They also concluded that it may be the way in which whole-language is implemented that is important, in that whole-language teachers with a 'broad' and eclectic way of teaching seem more likely to have students with positive attitudes. This may be because their teaching is more effective and their pupils are likely to read well. In terms of cause and effect, this may be the important factor. If pupils read well, they are more likely to enjoy reading, feel good about themselves and want to read.

### Conclusion

How should we relate the findings of this chapter to our imaginary pupils, Janet and John? If they were having difficulty with reading, a phonics teacher would be thinking that reading problems were causing the low self-efficacy feelings of these children. The phonics teacher might think 'Janet and John say they don't like reading and that it is boring, but I also notice that their reading levels are well below those of their classmates. If I could build up their decoding skills, so they could read long words with ease, then I'm sure their self-esteem would increase along with their reading ability.'

A whole-language teacher might not see it that way. The whole-language teacher might think that low self-efficacy was causing reading problems. The whole-language teacher might think, 'The best way to help Janet and John is to make them feel happy about coming to school.

I should get some easy reading for them. I should let them listen to audiotapes of the books. I should give them lots of positive feedback.' Who is right? Again, both teachers make some good points. There is evidence to show that good readers feel good about themselves. Thus, helping Janet and John to become good readers, as the phonics teacher suggests, is a direct way of making gains both in reading and motivation. But evidence also indicates that even when poor readers improve in reading, they often still lack confidence in themselves. So positive feedback – showing Janet and John how they have progressed – is also important.

Janet and John will need concrete evidence that they are getting better. Keeping a chart of progress, telling them that they are getting better, and saying that you are pleased with them are all useful things to do. But the positive feedback should be genuine. The teacher should be working on reading skills and assessing progress so that the positive feedback is true.

Reading attitudes and reading achievement are linked. Pupils who experience success in reading are more likely to feel good about themselves as readers and will want to read. But pupils who have experienced failure may eventually lose confidence and lose their motivation to want to read. Over time, poor readers don't expect to do well and won't persist if reading seems difficult. They may blame their failure on themselves. Good readers, over time, gain in confidence as a result of repeated success and are more positive about themselves as readers. They seek out challenging tasks and persist with them. If they fail, they externalise the reasons for their failure (e.g. saying that they did not have enough time).

A discouraging finding of the research is that the self-concepts of poor readers don't get better even after they have had remedial reading help. This is probably due to the fact that the extra tuition doesn't necessarily overcome reading failure. What is needed is remedial instruction that is effective, that raises reading performance. In addition, attribution training can give poor readers strategies for feeling good about their efforts and raising their self-esteem as readers.

The following are tips on helping pupils to be more positive about themselves as readers:

• Give pupils text material that is relatively easy for them to read, so that they are reading at a 'comfortable' level (95 per cent accuracy or better). This should be done at all age levels.

- Help struggling readers to improve their basic reading skills. For example, some teachers will spend 15 minutes each day before school teaching a pupil who has difficulty.
- Encourage children to read at home, but be sure to give them 'easy' books that they can succeed in.
- Encourage parents to be positive. They can say, 'I like it when you read to me'. They can be patient, giving their child up to ten seconds to work out a word before saying the word. They can correct just the important words, not all words. They should not let their child struggle with books that are too hard. They don't have to growl if their child doesn't know a word. They should do more interactive discussion-type reading. They should make reading a priority and not let it slip by.
- Give pupils positive feedback about their efforts. Smile at them when they are reading to you. Be positive (e.g. 'good girl'). Give rewards when children achieve certain milestones (e.g. can correctly read 100 words on a list). Give points toward a reward for consistent work (e.g. finished reading five pages from her book; paid lots of attention to the teacher).

## Appendix Reading Attitude Checklist

Name of pupil _____

### Instructions

Explain to the pupil that you are going to ask some questions about how they feel about reading, because you are interested in how they feel. Tell the pupil that this is not a test. Write down what the pupil says to you in the space between each question. Be sure to use "wait time" for those pupils who are shy about responding. Older children may wish to write their own answers for themselves.

**"How do you feel?" Reading Attitude Inventory (based on Campbell, 1978)**

1. How do you feel when someone reads you a story at home? Why is that?
2. How do you feel when your teacher reads a story to the class? Why is that?
3. How do you feel when it is your turn to read out loud to the teacher? Why is that?
4. How do you feel when you come to a new word while reading? Why is that?
5. How do you think your teacher feels when you read? Why is that?
6. How do you feel about writing a story for the teacher? Why is that?
7. How do you feel when you have to spell a new word that you don't know how to spell yet? Why is that?
8. How do you feel about getting a book for a present? Why is that?
9. How do you feel about going to school? Why is that?
10. How do you think you will feel about reading when you are (6, 7, 8, etc.) years old? Why is that?

**Profile of the Reader (based on Dymock, 1995)**

1. Would you rather watch television or read? Why is that?
2. Would you rather play with your friends or read? Why is that?
3. Would you rather clean up your room or read? Why is that?
4. How many days of the week do you read at home, when you are not at school? Why is that?
5. How long do you read for at home, after school, before you go to bed? Why is that?
6. How many children's books do you have at home (just your own books)? Why is that?
7. When do you do most of your reading at home? Why is that?
8. Do you like reading? Why is that?
9. Do you like writing stories? Why is that?
10. How much time do you spend watching TV? Why is that?

## References

Butkowsky, I.S., & Willows, D.M. (1980). Cognitive-motivational characteristics of children varying in reading ability: Evidence for learned helplessness in poor readers. *Journal of Educational Psychology,* 72, 408–422.

Campbell, P. (1978). Reading attitude inventory. In D. Lapp & J. Flood, *Teaching every child to read.* New York: Allyn & Bacon.

Chapman, J.W., & Tunmer, W.E. (1995). Development of young children's reading self-concepts: An examination of emerging subcomponents and their relationship with reading achievement. *Journal of Educational Psychology, 87,* 154–167.

Chapman, J. W., Tunmer, W. E., & Prochnow, J. E. (1998, April). *Reading Recovery in relation to language factors, reading self-perceptions, classroom behavior difficulties and literacy achievement: A longitudinal study.* Paper presented at the meeting of the American Educational Research Association, San Diego, CA.

Clay, M. M. (1993). *Reading Recovery. A guidebook for teachers in training.* Auckland: Heinemann.

Dweck, C. (1986). Motivational processes affecting learning. *American Psychologist, 41,* 1040–1048.

Dymock, S. J. (1993). Reading but not understanding. *Journal of Reading, 37,* 86–91.

Dymock, S.J. (1995). Title recognition test. In J. Wright & J. King (Eds.), *Best of Set: Assessment,* Item 7. Wellington: New Zealand Council for Educational Research.

Forell, E. R. (1985). The case for conservative reader placement. *The Reading Teacher, 38,* 857–862.

Henk, W.A., & Melnick, S.A. (1995). The reader self-perception scale (RSPS): A new tool for measuring how children feel about themselves as readers. *The Reading Teacher, 48,* 470–482.

Heyman, G.D., Dweck, C.S., & Cain, K.M. (1992). Young children's vulnerability to self-blame and helplessness: Relationship to beliefs about goodness. *Child Development, 63,* 401–415.

Jorgenson, G. W. (1977). Relationship of classroom behavior to the accuracy of the match between material difficulty and student ability. *Journal of Educational Psychology, 69,* 24–32.

Juel, C. (1988). Learning to read and write: A longitudinal study of 54 children from first through fourth grades. *Journal of Educational Psychology, 80*, 437–447.

McKenna, M.C., & Kear, D.J. (1990). Measuring attitude toward reading: A new tool for teachers. *The Reading Teacher, 43*, 626–639.

McKenna, M.C., Stratton, B., Grindler, M.C., & Jenkins, S.J. (1995). Differential effects of whole-language and traditional instruction on reading attitudes. *Journal of Reading Behavior, 27*, 19–44.

Nicholls, J. G. (1995). Big science, little teachers. Knowledge and motives concerning student motivation. In J. G. Nicholls & T. A. Thorkildsen (1995), *Reasons for learning: Expanding the conversation on student–teacher collaboration* (pp. 5–20). New York: Teachers College Press.

Nicholson, T. (1999). Literacy in the family and society. In G.B. Thompson & T. Nicholson (Eds.), *Learning to read: Beyond phonics and whole language* (pp. 1–22). New York: Teachers College Press.

Stanovich, K.E. (1986). Matthew effects in reading: Some consequences of individual differences in the acquisition of literacy. *Reading Research Quarterly, 21*, 360–406.

Thorkildsen, T. A. (1994).What is fair? Children's critiques of practices that influence motivation. *Journal of Educational Psychology, 86*, 475–486.

Wilson, M.G., Chapman, J.W., & Tunmer, W.E. (1995). Early reading difficulties and reading self-concept. *Journal of Cognitive Education, 4*, 33–45.

# 13

# READING IN THE SECONDARY SCHOOL

## Who Should Teach Reading?

In the Unites States, the reality for many years has been that high school subject teachers have resisted teaching 'reading' (Vacca, 1998). It is probably fair to say that this has also been the case in New Zealand. Subject teachers are trained to teach music or English, history or social studies, mathematics or science, but not reading. Yet reading is the hidden curriculum of high school. Reading is not only done in English; in mathematics, for example, there seems to be very little reading, yet there is a strong correlation between ability to read and mathematics achievement (Tseng, 1998). Asian students achieve very well in mathematics, especially if they attend schools in middle-class areas. Would these students achieve even higher scores if they were better at reading mathematics problems? The correlation between reading and mathematics is strong even for English-speaking students (Lim, 1998). This is because there is much more reading in mathematics than is commonly thought, especially the problem-solving sections of the mathematics curriculum.

## Is Reading a New Problem for High Schools?

In New Zealand, secondary schools used to be for the élite. The situation was similar in the United States. Only a minority of children attended school in New Zealand, at least until the Education Act of 1877 which made primary school compulsory (McLaren, 1974), and school was only for a few months each year. Christ College and Auckland Grammar were modelled on English public schools like Eton and Harrow. Students studied Latin and the classics. No science was taught in those early days. It was not taken seriously. Only English, maths, Latin and Greek were taught. The leaving age was not raised to 15 until 1945. Only one in 30 students at that time passed Matriculation, a prerequisite for university. My ex-Dean of Education, now retired, remembered that of the 35 students who started high school with him in Form 3 (year nine), he was the only one left in Form 6 (year 12). The history of high schools is worth remembering. For a long time, the top end of high school was élitist and exclusive. Even in 1970, the number of students in New Zealand high schools at 17 years of age was small, about 13 per cent (Thorndike, 1973).

In the 1990s, the situation is much different. In the United States, 75 per cent of 17-year-old youths are still at school; in New Zealand, about 65 per cent. Schools are no longer for the élite. There is a wider range of ability in schools today than was the case even 20 years ago (Calfee & Patrick, 1995; Ministry of Education, 1998).

**What Factors Cause Students to Stay at High School?**

Many New Zealand adolescents do not move forward to tertiary education, even though entry to university is very open. Why is this? And why are fewer adolescents still at school in New Zealand compared to the United States? There will be many factors that influence why young people will decide to stay at school or move on. It may be the size of the school, in that a large school may seem too impersonal. Smaller schools have fewer dropouts (Barker & Gump, 1964) and more equitable outcomes (Lee & Smith, 1997). It may be class size, in that students respond better to teaching if they are in small classes, especially in the first three years of school (Finn & Achilles, 1990). Teachers are less stressed if they teach in small classes, and are less likely to assign 'busy work', which may make school a lot more interesting for students (French, 1993).

Another possible explanation for the fewer numbers of our students going on to tertiary study is to do with teachers. Students achieve more with 'authoritative' teachers who have high goals and clear expectations of them (Rutter, 1983). Students will stay longer in schools and achieve more if the principal and staff have a strong belief that all their students will succeed. Finally, there may be factors outside the school that influence retention rates. An obvious factor is family income. It is expensive to stay on at school and to go to university.

There are many possible explanations for the success of some schools in holding students through the upper levels. Are the basic skills of reading and writing also part of the explanation for successful schools? Perhaps. Schools with a high success rate in national examinations have students who are above-average in reading. In contrast, failing schools have many below-average readers. Even successful schools will have some students who do not do well in reading and writing. On average, 20 per cent of students entering high school will be reading below what we would expect students to be able to read at that age. About half of these students (ten per cent) will be three years below average for their age in reading (Flockton & Crooks, 1997).

### Do High School Students Like Reading?

Here are some responses of Year 9 and 10 students in one high school to a questionnaire survey of feelings about reading. It was clear from the survey that many students did like reading, but some did not. Here is a selection of responses to the question 'Is reading important for you?' (see Table 13.1)

*Is low motivation a cause of poor reading?*

The causes of poor academic achievement can be difficult to identify. Students who are struggling with reading are likely to be unmotivated. Yet this lack of interest in reading may be a consequence of poor reading, and not the cause. Let's look at an example of this cause–effect problem. A study of the effects of part-time work on students' school achievement (Bachman & Schulenberg, 1993) found that high school students who worked more than five hours a week were more likely to smoke cigarettes, drink alcohol, use illegal drugs, argue with parents, get insufficient sleep and lack exercise. Their academic achievement was also poor. At first Bachman and Schulenberg thought all these things

**Table 13.1: Responses of Year 9 and 10 students to the question: "Is reading important for you?"**

| 1. Reading is fun |
| --- |
| "Yes, I don't know, but I just love to read." |
| "Yes, 'cos if I couldn't read I'd die of boredom." |
| "Yes it is, because I love reading. Reading is very important to me because it improves my reading skills." |
| "Yes. It makes me think. It is an escape from reality." |
| "Yes, exercises my imagination, fun." |
| **2. Reading is useful.** |
| "Yes it's a vital skill, very important. The more you read, the more you know." |
| "Yes, you can't spell if you don't read." |
| "Yes, because if you can't read you can't order at McDonald's or read anything else." |
| "If you don't read you can't get your driving licence." |

| 3. Reading is boring |
| --- |
| "Reading doesn't really appeal to me as fun it's very boring reading a big chapter book." |
| "No not really because I have much better things to do than read a book and while I have my head in a book I might miss something." |
| "No, because I hate reading." |
| "No because it's all sh**" |
| "No, because reading sucks." |

had been due to the part-time work itself, yet they eventually concluded that the part-time work was a result of poor achievement in school, not a cause. They found that students who were doing poorly at school sought an escape from school. This led them into more and more part-time work. The jobs they did also tended to have low value in terms of later careers. The students were doing mundane jobs such as cleaning offices, waiting on tables and filling grocery bags at supermarkets. The researchers concluded that these students would be better off if they were given extra instruction to lift their school achievement. Parents of these students needed to help by limiting opportunities to avoid schoolwork. They recommended that students who were 'vulnerable to the seductions of quick earnings and premature affluence' (p. 233) be given help by attacking their basic scholastic needs, providing a positive school climate of high expectations and ensuring that they received a thorough grounding in literacy skills.

### What Reading Problems Occur in Subject Learning?

*Vocabulary*

First, there were terminology problems. Perhaps teachers should review and reinforce all new vocabulary. Students need to be quizzed on new meanings and learn to spell new terms correctly. The teacher can break them down, talk about their origins and so on. For example, in science, discussing the water cycle involves lots of Greek and Latin terms. The word 'cycle' comes from the Greek word 'kuklos' meaning circle. Reading a diagram of the water cycle involves the student in reading words like evaporation, transpiration, condensation and precipitation.

To glue these words into students' minds, it is important to show the structure of words. Many content words consist of chunks of meaning. For example, the 'spir' in transpiration is from the Latin 'to breathe'. The chunk 'spir' is the core of other words like respiration and inspiration. The word inspire, for example, means 'breathe into' the mind. In science, transpiration means 'breathe across', which refers to the way water on the leaves of plants is lost into the air as vapour. The word evaporation means 'passing off vapour'. The word condensation means 'making more dense'.

In Science, a topic like the 'water cycle' uses complex terminology. The student needs do a lot of 'word work' (Calfee & Patrick, 1995) to understand the water cycle well. The teacher (with help from an etymological dictionary) can break special terms into chunks. Do students know that cycle means circle? Do they know what precipitation means? It comes from the Latin 'praeceps', which means to throw headlong. It's related to another word 'precipice', which students may understand.

### Text structure

Even if vocabulary is understood, another problem for students is understanding at the macro level. Students often can't 'see' the structure of what they are reading (Calfee & Patrick, 1995). It's useful to teach them to do this. Even a one-page handout can have a structure that is hard to 'see'. Students can be taught how to visualise the design of text material, and to use this design to reconstruct the details of what they are reading. They should be able to see the design of a text, just as an architect can visualise the design of a house. Let's take an example. A Year 9 student reads a novel called *Dracula*. Yet when it comes to examination time, many of the details are gone from memory. It would have been very useful if the student had some notes which showed the structure of the text.

For example, a story graph can show levels of action (high or low) on the vertical axis, while the sequence of what happened can be written along the horizontal axis. This can be drawn on a large sheet of paper. In *Dracula*, the high point is when Dracula is killed. After that, the level of action sinks as the story is concluded. Students can chart the key events in order and think about their relative importance in the flow of the story. Even a simple listing of the events in the plot can be useful. It makes the narrative content easier to remember.

Calfee and Patrick (1995) describe several different expository text structures. Expository texts are not stories. There are various kinds of expository structural designs. The three main types are sequence, description and argument. We have already talked about sequence-type structure, where information is presented in step-by-step fashion, such as making bread or the history of New Zealand. A 'sequence' text (like a continuum) shows something happening over time, such as the making of pizzas. The events follow a set order. The sequence can't be scrambled. In making pizzas, the yeast base has to be made first, then topping is put on the dough, then some seasoning and so on. In workshop technology, the process of soft soldering follows a sequence structure, from preparation of the joint through to application of the solder (see figure below).

**Figure 13.2**

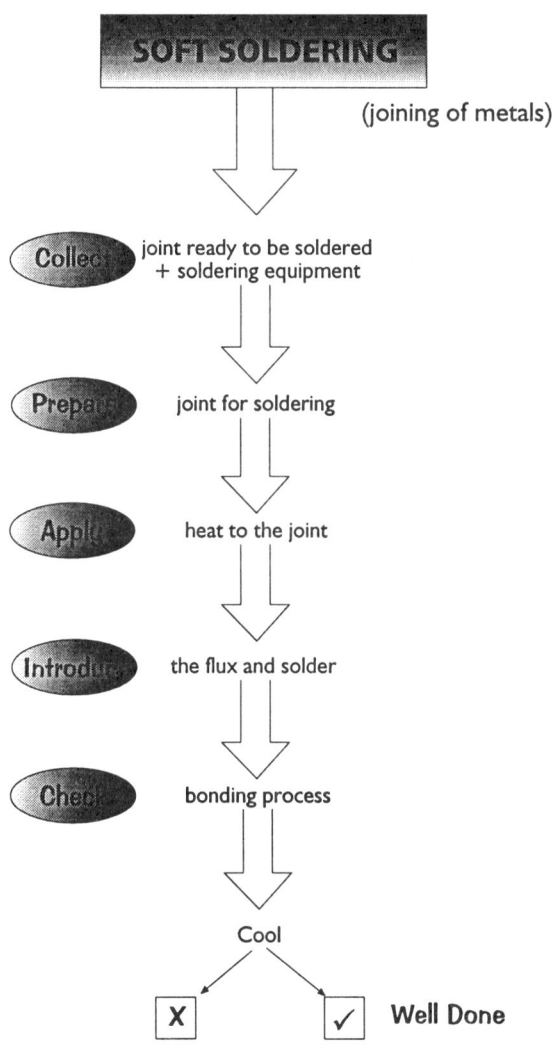

A 'description' text can have a list structure, where there is no set order. It may be a list of different kinds of drill centres for a lesson in Workshop Technology, or a list of different kinds of shortages that occurred in war-time for a social studies lesson. It doesn't matter what goes first in the list. Students can be challenged as to whether or not the text fits a list structure. Why isn't this a sequence? And so on.

Another 'description' structure is the 'weave' (or matrix). This is a grid structure. It is often called a weave structure in that it threads different ideas across one another. An easy example of a weave is a comparison of two countries, for example, Japan and New Zealand. In social studies, several countries can be compared on a number of dimensions such as population, area, language, culture, manufacturing, exports, and so on. In music, different types of music, such as jazz, rock, pop and rap, can be compared in terms of social context, time period, performers, songs and musical features (see below).

**Table 13.3: Comparison of different types of modern popular music**

| Types of Modern Music | Context | Times Period | Performer (Example) | Song (Example) | Musical Features |
|---|---|---|---|---|---|
| Jazz | New Orleans street music | 1920s –1930s | Louis Armstrong | Mack the Knife | Walking bass Swing rhythm Improvised melody |
| Rap | New York urban, black music | 1980s –1990s | Grandmaster Flash | "The message" | Cross-rhythmic talk (i.e. rapping) Strong back beat accompaniment |
| Rock | United Kingdom – youth culture post rock n roll | 1960s –1990s | Rolling Stones | "I can't get no satisfaction" | Simple, stylised, harmonic framework Strong melody Basic straight rock style drum patterns |
| Dance Pop | Global music industry | 1990s | Spice Girls | "Wanna be" | Fast dance beat Hook melody Pop-song format Highly stylised, club/dance orientation |

The 'argument' structure is persuasive text. A series of arguments are presented with supporting details. For example, the text might be on the topic 'Should the driving age be raised?' An 'argument' text has a point and counterpoint structure. An argument for raising the age might be that when you are older, you are better able to pay for maintenance of your car, insurance, etc. A counterpoint is that many young people use their parents' cars, so this is not a problem. The point–counterpoint structure can be diagrammed as just two columns, with the headings 'For' and 'Against'.

Text structure training helps students to be more disciplined in their reading. Some students lack good strategies for reading. For example, in Nicholson (1988), a social studies class was studying social change. The teacher gave the class a newspaper article called 'Why go North?'. The article started by saying that although there is a popular idea that people move to the North Island from the South Island because of the climate, that is actually not the reason. It gave various reasons why people move from the South Island to the North Island. All the reasons related to work opportunities. People came north for new jobs, for more advanced job training, and sometimes for better salaries. The article mentioned that moving north was expensive, and that people had to give up enjoyable hobbies such as mountaineering. Various people were mentioned in the article, such as a dentist who was employed by Auckland Hospital. The dentist felt that Dunedin was 'too dead', referring to lack of job opportunities; another person was working in Auckland as a stock-broker; and yet another was a customs officer, who was earning more money in Auckland than he had in Dunedin.

The teacher asked the class to read the article and write reasons to explain why people move from the South Island to the North Island. The student we interviewed had written 14 reasons, many of which were not the reasons stated in the article. He had sifted through the article, found key words, and made them fit into possible reasons for moving north. He had copied these key words out of the text. He mentioned 'more alive' as one reason (the text words were 'too dead', referring to lack of job opportunities). When asked why he wrote 'more alive' he said, 'Well, it said Dunedin and all those sort of places, it's pretty dead, but over in the North Island, you got skiing, you got roller-skating, you got more discos and that sort of stuff. It's more alive.' Yet none of these points was in the article. Another reason he gave was 'stock'. When asked what he meant, he said: 'And more stock handling. You know, getting more experience with stock.' He looked in the text for reasons to support this reason. He said, 'Where is it? Somewhere down here, that a guy became a stock agent. He reckoned you learned more about stock than you did in the South Island. Here you are, 'stock-broker'. Notice that the student had confused the meaning of the word 'stock', thinking it referred to animals, instead of the sharemarket. The 14 reasons were all plausible in his mind but it was clear that he lacked a disciplined way of attacking the structure of the text.

*Researcher:* Have you read the whole article?
*Student:* No, just picking out the bits, you know, that have to do with the question.

A text structure approach to this lesson, where this student worked with others to analyse the article, may have been more beneficial for him. A possible structure for the article is a matrix. In the vertical columns, you could put the names of the people interviewed for the article. In the horizontal columns you could list different categories such as person's occupation, reason for moving, advantages of moving, disadvantages of moving. This seems a more productive way of summarising the material. And would be less confusing. Students need a way of taking all the details and organising them into a smaller number of information chunks.

## Writing

Text structure strategies will be useful for essay writing. For example, in the 1996 School Certificate national examination for Māori (Ministry of Education, 1996), one question was to write an essay on the following topic: 'Imagine you are a seagull. You meet a kiwi. Before long you are having a conversation about your homes'. Obviously the student must be able to write in Māori. But what does the student write about? By using a weave structure, the student could draw a grid pattern, with seagull and kiwi in vertical columns and categories for comparison along the horizontal columns. For example, the home of the birds could be described in terms of 'location' (beach versus bush), features (straw and materials found on beach versus hole in ground), purpose of home (to be near fish, to be near worms), and so on. A weave structure would give the student a framework for writing an interesting essay in Māori.

## Poor Readers

Surviving in high school is difficult for poor readers. The transition into high school for a poor reader is huge in terms of reading demands and kinds of reading tasks. There is a flood of new subjects, terminology, and textbooks to study. On top of reading and writing difficulties, they may be required to take a full quota of content classes, such as Māori, English, maths, science and social studies. There are strong social reasons for doing this. Nevertheless, it is an uphill struggle.

Poor readers and spellers are sometimes able to apply for special assistance, such as someone to read (and write) for them in examinations. Yet poor decoding means that much of their textbook material will go unread. Even class notes will go unread. This means that it is difficult for them to study and revise the content of the subject. Thus, even with a reader-writer on examination day, it will still be difficult to pass examinations. This is why it is important to prepare poor readers well for class tests and examinations, with a clear list of things to study and some one-to-one verbal revision, where the teacher quizzes, coaches and explains. Without some explicit direction, poor readers often do not know what they have to study. The student has notebooks full of exercises that are copied in class, but it is hard to 'see' the structure of the curriculum. The teacher knows the curriculum, but do these low-achieving students? A page which sets out the curriculum of study could be placed at the front of their workbooks, and teachers could ensure that students check off each topic as it is completed.

Poor readers in secondary school need individual tutoring. Although these students desperately need tuition from specialist reading teachers, they may only have volunteer tutors available to them. If this is the case, it is very important that the tutors be properly trained. Juel (1996) found positive effects for literacy tutoring when the tutors were given weekly two-hour training sessions in how to tutor. The tutors were asked to do four hours of reading each week on their own and to keep a reading log.

The tutors used text material that had lots of repetitive, high-frequency vocabulary. The tutors also engaged in lots of letter–sound instruction.

## Conclusion

In high school, reading is not a specific subject as it is in the primary school, yet it is a crucial skill for success. Many reading skills can be developed as part of subject area instruction. Students can learn to decode technical terms, study the meanings of new vocabulary, and learn about the structures of content area texts. Giving students simple 'how to' guides for summarising content of text material and 'structures' to follow when writing essays is helpful. Probably the best thing that subject area teachers (e.g. maths, sciences) can do for poor readers is be an advocate for them so that they receive specialist literacy tuition and are not left to flounder. After-school tuition could also be provided. Some teachers may be willing to act as volunteer tutors after school. I have been an after-school volunteer tutor for some years. It is helpful for the pupils you tutor – and it is a nice thing to do.

## References

Bachman, J. G., & Schulenberg, J. (1993). How part-time work intensity relates to drug use, problem behavior, time use, and satisfaction among high school seniors: Are these consequences or merely correlates? *Developmental Psychology*, 29, 220–235.

Barker, R. G., & Gump, P. V. (1964). *Big school, small school*. Stanford, CA: Stanford University Press.

Calfee, R.C., & Patrick, C.L. (1995). *Teach our children well*. Stanford, CA: Stanford Alumni.

Dymock, S.J. (1999). Learning about text structure. In G.B. Thompson & T. Nicholson (Eds.), *Learning to read: Beyond phonics and whole language* (pp. 174–192). New York: Teachers College Press.

Finn, J. D., & Achilles, C. M. (1990). Answers and questions about class size: A statewide experiment. *Educational Research Journal*, 27, 557–577.

Finn, J. D., Achilles, C.M., Bain, H.P., Folger, J., Johnston, J.M., Lintz, M.N., & Word, E.R. (1990). Three years in a small class. *Teaching and Teacher Education*, 6, 127–136.

Flockton, L., & Crooks, T. (1997). *Reading and speaking assessment results*

*1996*. Wellington: Ministry of Education.

French, N. K. (1993). Elementary teacher stress and class size. *Journal of Research and Development in Education*, 26, 66–73.

Juel, C. (1996). What makes literacy tutoring effective? *Reading Research Quarterly*, 31, 268–289.

Lee, V.E., & Smith, J.B. (1997). High school size: Which works best and for whom? *Educational Evaluation and Policy Analysis*, *19*, 205–227.

Lim, B.S. (1998). Factors associated with Korean-American students' mathematics achievement. Unpublished doctoral dissertation, University of Washington.

McLaren, I. (1974). *Education in a small democracy: New Zealand*. London: Routledge and Kegan Paul.

Ministry of Education (1996). *School Certificate Examination, Te Reo Māori*. Wellington: Author.

Ministry of Education (1998, November). *Education Statistics News Sheet*, 8, No. 11.

Nicholson, T. (1988). *Reading and learning in the junior secondary school*. Wellington: Department of Education.

Nicholson, T. (1997). *Solving reading problems across the curriculum*. Wellington and Melbourne: Australian and New Zealand Councils for Educational Research.

Rutter, (1983). School effects on pupil progress: Research findings and policy implications. *Child Development*, 54, 1–29.

Thorndike, R.L. (1973). *Reading comprehension education in fifteen countries*. New York: John Wiley.

Tseng, S.M. (1998). Reading comprehension and motivation: A comparison of Taiwanese and English-speaking secondary school students. Unpublished master's thesis, The University of Auckland.

Vacca, R. T. (1998). Let's not marginalize adolescent literacy. *Journal of Adolescent and Adult Literacy*, 4, 604–609.

# CONCLUSIONS:

## PUTTING IT ALL TOGETHER

Let's take a short walk through the book. We started with the 'reading debate', which is a current topic in the news. Some say that the debate is a media plot, but we found that this wasn't so. We looked at the alphabetic nature of writing in English in order to show that some of the present controversy is to do with the unusual ways in which many English words are spelled. We looked at the history of reading in order to show that controversy is not new to the field of reading. The history of reading is a history of pendulum swings in our teaching and acrimonious debate. We talked about new discoveries in the field of reading, especially new research on phonemic awareness; that is, being aware that spoken words are made up of little sounds. Recent research on phonemic awareness has been of enormous help in understanding why so many children struggle with reading and spelling. We looked at the nuts and bolts of learning to read and write. Should we teach whole language or phonics? What is the best method? What is reading anyway? Can children learn to read before they start school? Why is it so hard for children to learn those 26 letters of the alphabet?

We discussed whether reading and spelling are similar. We decided that in some ways they are; in other ways they are different. We can't assume that a good reader will be a good speller. We looked at case studies of children who have progressed in reading, or fallen behind.

We looked at motivation to read. Why is it that every child starts school totally enthused about learning to read, yet just several months later some children will hate reading? And what about reading comprehension? It's the heart of reading, but what is it? How do you teach something as nebulous as 'comprehension'? Finally, we discussed reading in secondary schools. Many students struggle with the reading demands of high school. It's not much fun being 15 years of age and still unable to read a basic school textbook or novel, and still unable to write a coherent essay that is not riddled with spelling mistakes. We discuss some possible solutions to this problem. Let's now review the details.

## Pendulum Swings in Reading

Reading is an emotional touchstone for many people. Everyone, from all walks of life, will have a relative or know of someone who struggled with literacy. It may be a child attending an expensive private school; it may be a child from a home which is bursting with books; it may be a workmate at the local supermarket. Some very famous people have had difficulty with reading and spelling. Albert Einstein was a poor reader and speller as a child, yet went on to become the world's greatest physicist. General Freyberg was a great New Zealand military leader, yet his spelling was said to be erratic. So it is possible to rise above difficulties with reading and spelling and be a great success. Yet success does not come to everyone, and this is why there has always been public concern about learning to read and write.

We noted that 20–25 per cent of children find it difficult to learn to read and spell well. This is not just a New Zealand phenomenon; the problem exists in countries similar to our own such as England, Australia and the United States. We are all supposedly 'developed' countries, yet one in four of our children struggle to read. We also talked about what reading will be like in the new millennium. Will we still have to read? It seems clear that literacy will be more important than ever. The computer age will be helpful (e.g. computers will be able to do our writing for us), but there may still be a competitive advantage for skilled reading and writing. We talked about the politics of reading and decided there were two kinds of literacy. Literacy 1 is about the mechanics of literacy, how to read words like 'cat', and spell them as well. Literacy 2 is about the politics of reading. For example, when a child reads a story about a father who takes his child to the supermarket, is this 'social engineering' or is it just a simple story about going shopping? When a child in the 1950s in Peronist Argentina learned to read from a primer in which the initial pages had the words 'Evita me ama' (I love Evita), was this political? I'm not sure about the shopping story, but it seems unrealistic to expect that politics will never intrude into literacy. We concluded that pendulum swings in reading have been with us for many years. Reading debates have been about making reading happen for all children (not just some; not just most), while at the same time making reading both interesting and fun.

## The Story of the Alphabet

It's easy to take the English writing system for granted. Everything we read in English has those 26 letters of the alphabet. But what is not often known is that the alphabet is the end of a line of changes that started with picture writing, then went to syllable writing and finished as a system of letters that represented phonemes. In tracing the history of the alphabet, we started with Egyptian writing, i.e. hieroglyphic writing. We noted that hieroglyphic writing, although 5,000 years old, had become a syllable system. Pictures were used, but the pictures represented syllables. The Phoenicians, living in the Israel/Palestinian area, with a language similar to that of Hebrew, took the system the next step, using symbols to represent consonant sounds. They had a symbol called 'aleph' meaning ox, and a symbol called 'beth' meaning house. The word 'alphabet' is a combination of these two letter names, referring to their phonemic writing system. The Greeks took the Sumerian symbols, but since they had fewer consonants in their language they were able to recycle the remaining Phoenician letters to represent the Greek vowels as well. The Romans added some letters to represent sounds in their language. Thus, by the time the Romans invaded England, their writing system was very close to the one we use today. It was a phonemic alphabet.

But we also noted that the English writing system today is morpho-phonemic; that is, it represents both sound and meaning. The spellings of many words are phonemically irregular because they have the dual function of revealing the common meanings of some words. For example, debit and debt both contain the letter b, even though b in silent in debt. Our spellings are also complicated by history. We have borrowed words from many languages and have inherited their spelling patterns as well (e.g. the ch in chimney, an Anglo-Saxon word, is pronounced /ch/, but the ch in chic, a French word, is pronounced /sh/ and the /ch/ in school, a Greek word, is pronounced /k/). Another problem in English is that the most frequent words are irregularly spelled (e.g. was).

Yet it is important to know that our writing system has a history that went from pictures to sound. The historical trend in writing systems is to move to using letters or characters to represent sounds. English spelling is phonemic. Letters map onto sounds. And although we have borrowed words from at least 100 other languages, the spelling system is still basically phonemic. This is why learning letter–sound and sound–letter rules can still be argued to be extremely important for the beginner reader and speller.

## The Good Old Days

Many parents may not be aware that educators have been debating for centuries how best to teach reading. Parents may also not be aware of the ways in which children's primers and teaching methods have changed, especially in the last few decades. It is worth remembering that reading materials over the decades have been reflective of social mores and goals. Even 50 years ago society was less relaxed and parents were a bit more formal in their interactions with children. Mothers were the caregivers; fathers were the breadwinners. For many parents, that scenario has changed, which is why modern primers show fathers and mothers in different roles. In addition, ways of teaching reading have been the subject of intense debate.

In the 1970s there was a questioning of the cultural values of our teaching. The feeling was that many children were failing because of the culture of schools. There was a feeling that schools were not able to adapt to the increasing ethnic diversity and urbanisation within New Zealand, as more and more immigrants from Pacific Islands arrived and as Māori moved into the cities for work. Schools were said to be too middle-class, too puritan, too competitive, too authoritarian, and traditions were questioned – that teachers should correct children's errors, that children should be ranked, that classrooms should be competitive, that the teacher should be the font of all knowledge, that learning should be hard work. There was also a concern for reading failure. Researchers asked whether it might be possible to reduce failure to two per cent.

The 1970s was a time of ferment in reading methods. The psycholinguistic guessing game theory was making an impact on how reading was taught in schools. This approach questioned many of the assumptions of traditional schooling. In its place, the whole-language approach offered the alternative that children could teach themselves to read, that the teacher should facilitate and not be the font of knowledge, that children could correct their own mistakes, that learning should be cooperative, that assessment should be about what children can do rather than what they can't do. Whole language at that time seemed to be a solution. Academic experts claimed that it was more effective than traditional phonics. The mood of teachers was favourable to the child-centred principles of whole language. At that time, whole language was a solution. In the late 1990s, it is now seen by some as a problem. There is a perception that it is not working as effectively as it should. This often seems to be the pattern in education. Solutions today become problems tomorrow.

**Phonemic Awareness**

Phonemic awareness is 'hot'. Some educators see this research as a huge breakthrough in our understanding of how children learn to read and spell. Almost everyone agrees that phonemic awareness is important for learning to read and spell, though researchers are divided about how best to teach it. Some say it will happen as a result of reading (and writing) instruction; others say that it should be taught formally as an insurance, so that children have it when they start learning to read and spell at school. Phonemic awareness is a strong predictor of whether or not a child will learn to read. For example, it has been found that children's memory for nursery rhymes at three years of age is a good prognosis for their later reading success. Yet the picture is not quite as clear as it seems. A child may begin school with low levels of phonemic awareness and still learn to read. Why? One reason is that we are still learning how to assess phonemic awareness. Some children may have a little bit of phonemic awareness, which tests do not detect, and they are able to exploit these simple skills. Another reason is that many children respond to reading experiences provided in school and acquire phonemic awareness skills. For these children, phonemic awareness comes for free while they learn to read. The conclusion is that teaching phonemic awareness is like taking out an insurance policy. It can get a child off to a better start. Children who start school with high levels of phonemic awareness are likely to learn to read. But we must also acknowledge that children who start school without phonemic awareness can still become good readers. There are many children who lack phonemic awareness on school entry but are quick to pick it up. The real 'at risk' children are the ones who start school without phonemic awareness and who do not pick it up quickly. These are children who are still in the dark about sounds in words, even after several months of school. Without help, the prognosis for these children is not good.

**Learning the ABCs**

Knowing the letters of the alphabet has always been a good predictor of whether or not a child will learn to read. It is not as strong a predictor as phonemic awareness, in that nearly all children learn their letters in the first year of school, yet not all of them will acquire phonemic awareness. A child's knowing the alphabet when he or she starts school has obvious advantages. It means the child has less to learn, and so can devote his or her energies to learning about things like phonemes and how to sound out words. It is not easy to learn the alphabet. It takes many hours of study. This is why we have alphabet books, and television programmes like *Sesame Street*. Children's first reading books in school are printed mostly in lowercase letters (not all capitals), so it is suggested that children should learn both lowercase and uppercase letters, which means learning 52 letters, not just 26. It is also important for children to learn to write in lowercase and capital letters, since this will reinforce and consolidate their learning of letters for reading. Be sure to teach children to use the print style recommended for handwriting in schools in your area. New Zealand children learn to print letters in a slightly different way than do children in other countries. In Australia, for example, printing styles vary from state to state. Use lined paper? Yes, as long as the spaces between lines are generous. Encourage children to trace and copy letters to improve their handwriting? Yes, but be careful to supervise the child's efforts so that they copy correctly. To prevent boredom, let the child practice just the difficult letters. Naming and writing letters quickly is the goal, so that alphabet knowledge is effortless.

## Models of the Reading Process

There is no one theory of the reading process. There is a continuum of models. At one extreme is the bottom-up theory, that reading starts with letter identification and ends with meaning. At the other extreme is top-down theory, which argues that we start with meaning and end with letter identification. At various points on the continuum are theories that are similar to one or other of these theories, yet less extreme.

Top-down theory was very influential in the 1970s but it has come under considerable criticism since then. The idea that words can be recognised without having to process all their letters is hard to support. One top-down possibility is that words are recognised according to their shape, thus reducing the amount of visual processing needed. But this strategy has only a 60 per cent success rate. To rely on word shape would be very inefficient. Another possibility is that words have 'distinctive features' which could reduce the need to identify every letter. But this also seems unlikely. Even 'ransom notes' can be read easily, despite the fact that the letters in these notes are typed in unusual fonts and in different sizes, creating words that have no resemblance at all to their normal shape or look. A third possibility is that by reading for meaning, we are able to guess what words are. Some research in the 1960s supported this idea, but research since then has shown that guessing is a 'fickle friend'. Guessing is a strategy used much more by poor readers than good. Good readers can read words so effortlessly that it doesn't matter if they read words in context or in isolation.

The bottom-up theory has some good support in that most researchers nowadays agree that the reading process starts with word identification. First we identify words, then we immediately work out the meanings of those words. We process the vast majority of words in text and presumably we process the letters in which they are written.

There is no support for reading words according to their shape; we read letters, not shapes. The fact that readers are sensitive to misspellings in words suggests that the eyes do a fairly complete processing of letters in words.

There is still debate about whether or not we identify words by converting letters into phonemes or whether we simply match the written spellings with the visual spellings we have stored in memory. For many words, it seems likely that we use a 'direct route' from letters to meaning, but for many other words we probably use an 'indirect route' where we re-code letters into phonemes and then look up their meanings. When would we use the indirect route? Probably for words we either have not seen before or have seen very rarely. There are many words that occur rarely, so it may be that these words are often re-coded into sound before their meanings are accessed in memory. It may also be the case that both direct and indirect routes are used routinely in word identification, each route backing up the other. The use of both routes at once when processing words is an insurance policy, in case one route does not deliver. This possibility is advocated in connectionist theory.

### Reading Comprehension

Decoding is very important for reading comprehension. Comprehension difficulties are mostly associated with poor decoding skills. Thus, one avenue for improving comprehension is to increase children's word reading skills until they can read words effortlessly. Another avenue is to increase their understanding of word meaning, sentence meaning and text meaning. Word meaning knowledge, or vocabulary, is an important part of reading comprehension. Will teaching word meanings lead to better comprehension? You would expect so, but it turns out that good readers are adept at using context to work out meanings for themselves. So they may not benefit very much from vocabulary instruction. They teach themselves. Poor readers, however, do benefit from vocabulary instruction. They are not as efficient at learning word meanings on their own either through silent reading or through listening to stories read to them.

Will teaching about text structure help comprehension? It could be argued that teaching children to 'see' the structure of texts, the way an architect can 'see' the structure of a house, will improve reading comprehension. The research suggests that such teaching is helpful for *specific* texts. This is important. Pupils are often given 'required reading' (e.g. textbooks, handouts) which they are expected to understand.

How about teaching children relationships between questions and answers? Since reading comprehension is usually assessed by asking questions about the text, you would think that learning how best to answer questions would be useful. There is some research to show benefits for answering factual questions. Why only factual questions? The simple answer may be that it is easier for students to answer factual questions than inferential questions.

Can students improve their reading comprehension by reading? This is the rationale behind programmes such as 'sustained silent reading' (SSR) and 'drop everything and read' (DEAR). Yet research is inconclusive. Why should this be so? A possible reason is that pupils may not be getting the benefits that they could get if they were to read books aloud to someone. If the child reads to mum or dad, for example, they get immediate feedback if they make an error. They also get help with difficult words. Yet the child on his or her own does not get these benefits. Reading aloud to someone else (even to a computer) and getting feedback about your mistakes may have the double advantage of improving a child's decoding skills while also building vocabulary and general knowledge.

### Reading and Spelling

Reading and spelling overlap. Children who can read well also spell well. There are exceptions to the rule, such as children who are good readers but poor spellers, but even the exceptions turn out to have some problems with the decoding side of reading. Good readers who are poor spellers often exhibit gaps in phonological awareness, which may in turn mean that they have to rely on visual memory for the spellings of words, without having the back-up support that comes from knowing sound–letter correspondence rules. These rules are helpful in generating a 'temporary' spelling for a word (e.g. LFNT), which can then be modified.

Should children be able to spell words with 'invented' spellings or should they spell correctly? The advantage of invented spellings is that children are more likely to write longer and more creative stories. Also, it is usually possible to work out what they have written (e.g. wos for was). The disadvantage is that they may not attend very much to spelling correctness. In contrast, the advantage of teaching correct spellings is that children's writing is more readable, spellings are more accurate. Yet an emphasis on correct spelling may produce limited and uncreative writing, where the child only uses words they know how to spell. To gain the best of both worlds, it seems that children should get their ideas on paper with invented spellings, but follow this up by checking the spellings of words they are unsure about.

There is debate about how best to teach spelling. Some say that spelling is developmental. Children go through stages. It is argued that learning to spell correctly will occur naturally as children do more writing and reading of books, reading other children's writing, and so on. Others say that children can benefit more if they are given formal lessons and regular spelling tests. Which idea is correct? The developmental approach seems to be the approach most suitable for good spellers, whereas structured teaching and spelling tests are more useful for poor spellers. Why is this? The reason is that poor spellers do not write much (or read much). They restrict the words they use in writing to the words they know how to spell, so they do not get to learn new words. A teacher, however, can extend their spelling knowledge by getting them to practise other words that they do need for writing. In contrast to poor spellers, good spellers do a lot of writing and can extend themselves without the teacher's help. They love to construct their own personal spelling notebooks, and they can also pick up new spellings through the huge amounts of reading they engage in.

### The 'Best' Method

The search for the 'best' method of teaching reading is like the search for the holy grail. Perhaps it is a futile search. Yet many children do not learn to read, or only learn to read with difficulty. Thus, there is much interest in knowing whether one method is more successful than others. The search for the best method is still going on. In the 1990s, the search has narrowed down to phonics versus whole language. These methods are being hotly debated. Why is there no clear answer? One reason is that many of the studies that have been done in the past can be queried in one way or another. It is difficult to know whether gains that were made were due to the specific reading method used or to some other factor such as teacher enthusiasm or lack of enthusiasm, or the 'novelty' of a new method. If teachers are excited about what they teach, they get better results. At the same time, it may be unwise to be over-critical of research. When we look at the general pattern of results, simply counting the number of studies that are for and against whole language or phonics, the pattern seems to favour phonics. To the outside observer, there is certainly no evidence to suggest that phonics should be excluded or given a minor role in the reading programme.

If we put the enthusiasm factor to one side, it appears that whole-language methods work very well in the kindergarten area of schooling, where children are taught informally about books, how they work and so on. Once children start school, phonics instruction seems to get children off to a better start in reading words, especially if it is accompanied by teaching of phonemic awareness. Effects on comprehension are less noticeable in the first year, although there is some evidence that these effects manifest two or three years down the track. Whole language seems to produce more positive attitudes to reading initially, but these diminish quickly if children are not making adequate progress. It seems likely that a combination of whole language and phonics instruction will be more effective that one or the other method on its own.

## Reading Difficulties. Why?

Reading involves decoding the words on the page and working out what their meanings are in accordance with the role they play in sentences. In addition, we have to work out the overall summary meaning of complete texts. As we read, we soon forget the exact words and retain a more general meaning. Comprehending words and sentences is a complicated process but every beginning reader can do this. The ability to produce and comprehend language is part of our evolutionary inheritance. What the beginner cannot do is decode. This is putting it very simply, but for the vast majority of children this is really the situation they find themselves in. They enjoy it when you read a story to them. They understand it very well. They just can't read that same story themselves. This is the typical situation of the poor reader as well. They are not good at reading words. How can poor readers improve their word-reading skills? We have already discussed the value of teaching phonemic awareness and simple phonics skills. Teaching poor readers to recognise common phonograms in words is also useful. This will help to sound out words. But not all words are regular. In fact, many of the words they read have some parts spelled irregularly. Fifty per cent of the words children read (and write) are just 100 different words. They crop up very frequently in text. They include words like 'was' and 'come'. One way to help poor readers to read these words is to practise them. This can be done with flashcards. Another way is to use reading materials that have 'controlled' vocabulary, so that poor readers have many opportunities to see these words and practise reading them. This is the advantage of 'graded' readers over 'children's literature'; graded readers repeat words more often and difficulty levels are slowly and carefully increased so that children do not have to face new material at each level that is too difficult for them.

Poor readers also need to increase their language comprehension skills. As they become better decoders they will read more, and this in turn will improve their vocabulary, their ability to process complex sentence structures and general knowledge. But decoding skill is not acquired overnight, which is why other instruction will be useful, such as teaching of vocabulary and of ways to break text into manageable summary structures. Teaching students strategies for answering inferential questions may also be of value. Most of the questions that are asked in tests of comprehension are inferential. These are difficult to answer because the correct answer may require knowledge that is not stated in the text. Comprehension instruction can be effective, although often it is very specific in that it transfers just to the text material worked on. Yet this can still be very helpful to poor readers. The reason is that poor readers are less skilled than good readers at inferring meanings of words, at answering comprehension questions and at getting the main points of material they read. Direct teaching can help them learn the specific things in their textbooks that have to be learned.

We looked at interventions designed to assist low-achieving readers. The general findings are that interventions can have dramatic short-term effects on raising children's reading and spelling levels, but that these gains diminish after the intervention is completed. Children who have difficulties with reading and spelling are not helped by short-term interventions. Some researchers argue that many children need long-term help with reading, not just for several months but for several years. Reading difficulties can be compared in some ways to a chronic illness. Recovery is possible, but it should not be a 'quick fix'. Yet children are often on long waiting lists for reading help due to a lack of available resources.

### Feeling 'Cool' About Your Skills as a Reader

Many parents and teachers try to instil a love of reading in children by finding interesting books for them to read, by showing that they themselves are enthusiastic about reading, and by giving lots of positive feedback to children when they read. While these are very positive things to do, it seems that children are more likely to enjoy reading and read often if they are skilled at the reading process. It is easy to confuse the chicken with the egg. Which comes first? Even in classrooms that promote enjoyment and love of reading, children who have experienced failure in reading are not going to like reading. Children who have experienced years of reading failure are likely to feel bad about themselves as readers and are likely to misbehave in class as well. A discouraging feature of the research is that poor readers continue to dislike themselves as readers even after they have received remedial help. This may be because remedial interventions are usually not very effective in the long term. It seems that a strong focus on the improvement of reading skills is probably the most direct way in which teachers can improve children's attitudes to reading and children's perceptions of themselves as readers.

### Reading in the Secondary School

A hundred years ago, secondary schools were only for the élite. Remedial reading classes were for reading Latin and Greek, not for learning to read English. Many children did not go to secondary school. But those were also the days when academic qualifications were not as important as they are in today's society. Technology was less sophisticated.

Nowadays, even tasks such as setting an alarm clock or videotaping a television programme require instruction manuals that are hard to understand even if you have a university degree! As we enter the new millennium, everyone is expected to attend secondary school. Students in New Zealand sit their first national examinations after just a few years of secondary school. About two out of three students will complete five years of secondary school. The heavy emphasis on content learning in secondary school sets difficult demands on students. Technical vocabulary, complicated subject matter and formal writing of expository texts such as reports and essays are not handled well by many students. There is also a proportion of students who enter secondary school unable to read or write very well. Quite a few secondary school students think that reading 'sucks'. We discussed ways of teaching reading and writing for success.

## Conclusion

Time has made the English writing system more complicated, but it is still an alphabetic system, and it's important to know that. Despite the fact that many words are spelled in odd ways, the core of our writing is phonemic. This is why learning the letter–sound rules of English is very useful. Over time, as children become skilled readers and spellers, they seem able to recognise and spell words by both sight and sound. They remember the ways words are spelled, but they are also very effective at re-coding words into phonemes.

We have looked at ways in which reading methods have changed over the years as teachers have made 'improvements' in their teaching of reading. The traditional approach has been phonics. The advantage of the approach is that it teaches children rules for sounding out words on their own, without help from someone else. A criticism of the approach is that it can degenerate into drill and practice without much actual reading. Teaching reading with the whole-language approach has been offered in recent times as a better alternative than just phonics. The advantage of the approach is that children 'read' books from the first day of school. A criticism of the approach is that it can lack structure and sometimes leaves children in the dark about how to decode words.

Learning to read and spell is by no means straightforward. Children have to learn some counterintuitive things. Their unconscious knowledge of language has to become conscious. They have to become aware that their speech stream is a continuous flow of sound and that we are able mentally (and unconsciously) to analyse and dissect that stream of speech into phonemes, words and sentences. Children must learn that we talk in sentences, that the sentences are made of words, and the words are made of phonemes. With this ability to think about the building blocks of spoken words, children can apply their knowledge to the task of learning how speech sounds are represented by letters. Written language is speech made visible. This is the secret of writing that children have to discover. Once they realise that writing represents speech, they have to become code-breakers so they can decipher the writing system. To break the code, they have to become skilled at recognising the 26 abstract squiggles called the alphabet. They then laboriously have to learn hundreds of rules for relating letters to sounds. Some of the rules will be taught to them, but they will learn many on their own through the process of decoding words while reading.

Children not only have to learn to read words effortlessly, they have to understand what they read. They have to figure out the meanings of new words and ideas, and learn efficient ways of reporting on what they have read through discussion, writing reports, essays and so on. We've looked at how it is that many children learn to read. Yet a sizeable minority of children struggle. We've looked at possible reasons and possible solutions for this.

Our understanding of reading has progressed greatly in the last several decades. There are still many questions and many issues to resolve. Yet what makes this area of study so fascinating is the thought that new discoveries and insights have the potential to help all children become better readers and writers. We are making real progress in our theoretical and practical understanding. Translating research into practice is never simple. Current debates about reading reflect the tension between old and new. If I have learned one thing from the past, it is that debate is important. There will always be change. We should never let new theories and methods take over our hearts and minds without proper research and scrutiny. Many children still struggle with reading and writing and can benefit greatly from new findings, but we must also make sure we give these children instruction that we are confident will work.

## A Final Word

Reading can be a tough and frustrating area of research and practice. Many children just don't get it. It's heartbreaking to watch them labour to read and spell. We can help more children to succeed as readers.

The recent debates among researchers and in the media about how best to teach reading have sometimes been acrimonious. Those who have advocated more phonics have sometimes been reviled as 'phonicators' who chain children to worksheets and mindless drills and refuse to let them read a book. Those who have advocated whole language have been seen as destructive and undemocratic because they have denied children the right to learn phonics. When whole-language educators say that they *do* teach phonics, then phonics teachers reply that it's 'phony' phonics. It's not very pleasant to be at a conference where some people will walk away from you because you mention the word 'phonics', while others walk away because you mention 'whole language'.

But hopefully those days are in the past. The pendulum has to stop swinging. It's not a matter of whole language going away. Its best characteristics, especially the emphasis on literature, will stay with us. Nearly everyone acknowledges that reading for meaning and using context to help with reading new words are useful. But phonics must live on as well. For too long it has been an outcast from some classrooms, even though teaching method research shows that it compares very well with whole language, if not better. Yes, phonics can be a ghastly diet of dull, dry drill but this is not good teaching practice and good teachers of phonics are not like that. They want children to read 'real' books, just as much as do whole-language teachers. Also, whole language can be taught badly. Reading for meaning and relying on context clues, can become excuses for sloppy teaching. Some children will sink in a whole-language classroom if they are not given enough explicit instruction to acquire letter–sound correspondences.

It is clear that teaching children to rely on contextual 'guessing' as the main strategy for reading words is not the right way to teach reading. Children need to learn to read words effortlessly, and to do this they need to be able to identify words without relying on context. If children can learn to be good decoders with whole language, then we should congratulate their teachers; likewise if teachers can achieve this goal with phonics. It seems absurd to subscribe to an extreme form of phonics where children never read anything except 'the fat cat sat on the mat'. Likewise, it is absurd to believe in an extreme form of whole language where children are never taught phonics, never told simple but useful letter–sound rules like <u>ch</u> says 'ch' in nine out of every ten words we read, never taught that words can be sounded out.

Is the reading debate over? I hope not. Some say that debate is unhelpful. But many would argue that debate is healthy. What is unhelpful is the effort to silence debate and to exclude different opinions. The reading debates around the world have not been a media plot or a right-wing conspiracy, as some would have it. The debates have happened because some researchers have challenged the dominant view, and brought new insights to the attention of the public. Just saying 'we teach phonics' or 'we teach whole language' or 'we teach balanced instruction' is not enough. We should be suspicious of new magical products, these silver bullets that are said to guarantee that children will learn to read. There are lots of people who say they have the solution, but have no research to support them. I'm sure that nearly every child can read and write for success. If it's not happening to your child, or to the children in your class, then fight to make it happen.

# POSSIBLE ASSIGNMENT
# QUESTIONS

1. Why have reading debates persisted over the decades? What are the issues? What is the present situation?

2. Describe the history of the alphabetic writing system. What complexities characterise the English writing system? What does history reveal about the basic nature of English spelling?

3. Why have reading methods changed over the centuries? Review the research.

4. What does research say about the best way of teaching children to read?

5. Phonics and whole-language methods of teaching reading often conflict. Write an essay that

    (a) explains the main features of these two reading methods and
    (b) reviews research on the relative effectiveness of each method.

6. Learning the 26 letters of the alphabet at first glance appears a simple enough task for children. Write an essay that

331

    (a) explains why this is *not* so and

    (b) reviews research studies that have tried to make the task of learning the alphabet easier.

7. Is it true that children who start school with high levels of phonemic awareness have a better chance of learning to read than children who have low levels of phonemic awareness?

8. 'Reading comprehension is only incidentally textual'. What are the arguments for and against this idea?

9. Write an essay that reviews research on the relationship between reading skills and self-esteem.

10. Write an essay that discusses research on the relationship between reading and spelling.

11. Is it possible to design reading interventions that help poor readers over the long term? Describe research on the effectiveness of interventions such as Reading Recovery.

12. Regarding reading in the secondary school, what are the issues?

# QUIZ QUESTIONS FOR TUTORIALS

**Quiz – Pendulum swings**

1. What does the evidence say about trends in reading achievement over the last 30 years?
2. Why is there a public perception that standards of reading achievement are not as high as they used to be?
3. Is public concern driven by the media and politicians, or vice versa?
4. Is it possible that reading will become even more important in future years than it is already? Why should this be?
5. 'Keep politics out of the reading classroom.' How realistic is this? Can politics be a positive force in terms of gaining a better deal for children?
6. What is the difference between Literacy 1 and Literacy 2?
7. What is the tension in reading instruction that has created pendulum swings across many previous decades, and even today? Is a solution possible?
8. What are the main points of this chapter?
9. Has the reading debate been helpful or unhelpful?
10. Where will the pendulum be in Year 2030?

## Quiz – Historical perspectives

*A. Writing systems in general*

1. What is a writing system exactly?
2. What were the pluses and minuses of writing with pictures?
3. What was the earliest form of alphabetic writing?
4. Why is alphabetic writing attributed to the Greeks?
5. How did the Romans change the alphabet?
6. What are the pluses and minuses of an alphabetic way of writing?

*B. A brief history of reading instruction*

1. Can you describe how reading was taught in Colonial Times in the United States?
2. In New Zealand, how was reading taught in Colonial times?
3. Can you describe the public protest of the 1950s in the United States against the meaning method?
4. Why did a combination of 'look and say' and phonics become popular in the 1920s?
5. How did the mix of phonics and 'look and say' change in the 1960s?
6. Why did the whole-language approach become influential in the 1970s and 1980s?

## Quiz – Whole language and phonics

1. How were views of teaching reading changing in the 1970s in ways that supported whole language?
2. What are the features of the whole language philosophy?
3. What is a whole language approach to writing?
4. How does whole language see itself as different from phonics?
5. What are some basic whole language reading strategies?
6. What is the rationale for teaching phonics?
7. What is the teaching curriculum in phonics? How does it start?
8. Clymer (1963) checked the reliability of phonics rules. But was he too strict on phonics?
9. Will children read differently because of phonics or whole language?
10. Fill in this table, giving the pros and cons of whole language and phonics:

| Whole Language | Phonics |
|---|---|
| *Advantages* | *Advantages* |
| *Disadvantages* | *Disadvantages* |

## Quiz – The search for the best method

1. What makes researchers search for a 'best' method?
2. What were the conclusions of the Cooperative First Grade Studies Project? What problems were there in understanding the results? What positive findings were there in favour of phonics?
3. What criticisms have been made of Chall's research on 'The great debate'?
4. What were the conclusions of Stahl and Miller's review of whole language?
5. Which recent studies conclude in favour of whole language?
6. Which recent studies conclude in favour of phonics?
7. What does the overall pattern of research findings suggest about the 'best method'?
8. What does New Zealand and Scottish research have to say on the issue of the 'best' method?
9. Can you identify areas of possible agreement among researchers about how best to teach reading?
10. What are the main points of this chapter?

**Quiz – How does the skilled reader read?**

1. Is it a good idea to equate a theoretical view of the reading process with a particular way of teaching reading?
2. What evidence supports a top-down view of reading words, i.e., using distinctive features and prediction to reduce uncertainty?
3. What is the bottom-up view of reading words? How does the reader go from print to meaning?
4. What is meant by 'direct', 'indirect' and 'dual' routes in processing words?
5. What support is there for an indirect, phonological route?
6. What support is there for a direct, visual route?
7. How much support is there for a 'dual route' theory?
8. It may be that both routes cooperate and help each other in recognising words. How might this cooperation occur?
9. Imagine you work at a school where the principal believes that reading is a 'top-down' process, but that several parents of children in your class want their children to be taught phonics. What research about models of reading can you muster to convince these different interest groups that each teaching method has something to offer.
10. What are the main points of this chapter?

**Quiz – Emergent Literacy**

1. How many letters of the alphabet is a child likely to know at school entry?
2. Can knowing the alphabet names lead to some knowledge of their sounds?
3. Are there differences in the literacy environments of children's homes?
4. It turns out that children who learn to read often have books at home. Does this mean that children who do not have books will become better readers by giving them books?
5. What is 'emergent literacy'? Is it like learning to talk?
6. Should parents read to their children? What do children gain?
7. Why are some children able to read before starting school?
8. When is the best time to teach a child to read?
9. Do early readers maintain their gains long term?
10. Are there cultural differences in learning to read?

## Quiz – Phonemic awareness

1. What is phonemic awareness?
2. How does it differ from phonological awareness? And phonics?
3. What are the different levels of phonemic awareness and how are they ranked in terms of difficulty?
4. What are onsets and rimes?
5. Why might syllable segmentation tasks be better predictors of future reading than more sophisticated tasks such as deletion or reversal?
6. Does phonemic awareness predict reading and spelling success?
7. Where should assessment of phonemic awareness start? When does it dawn?
8. What is the history of research on phonemic awareness?
9. Is there evidence that learning about onsets and rimes may be an instructional bridge to phonemic awareness?
10. What level of research support is there for teaching phonemic awareness?

## Quiz – First steps in learning to read

1. How do children first start reading 'words'?
2. When a preschooler calls out 'MCDONALDS' as you drive past one of their food outlets, to what extent is the child reading the print on the sign?
3. Can early reading strategies (i.e. cue reading) affect reading progress in a negative way?
4. Is there support for learning to read by listening to stories?
5. What do children learn by being read to?
6. Why is it that some children are able to become aware of the alphabetic principle before others?
7. What is meta-linguistic awareness? How is it relevant to reading and spelling?
8. How do we know that some children do not know what a 'word' is?
9. You show a child two printed words, 'train' and 'dandelion'. You say to the child, 'One of these printed words is train and one is dandelion. Which one is train?
   (a) How likely are preschoolers to pass this test?
   (b) Does it matter?
   (c) Why?

10. Why is it hard to learn the alphabet?
11. Summarise the case histories of Jenny, Leon and Marcel and find two or three common characteristics that explain why they succeeded in reading.
12. Summarise the case histories of Javier, Anna and Grace and pull out two or three reasons why they did not progress in reading.

**Quiz – Reading comprehension**

1. What is the difference between the text driven and reader driven views of reading comprehension?
2. How does reading comprehension happen? Explain the process.
3. Can reading comprehension be taught?
4. What is text structure instruction? Does it help?
5. What is question-answering instruction? How useful is it?
6. Can vocabulary be taught? What is the research on this?
7. List three successful ideas for teaching vocabulary.
8. Is sustained silent reading a useful technique?
9. What role does quick/automatic recognition of words play in comprehension?
10. If you were asked for three good ideas to improve reading comprehension, what would you recommend? Why?

**Quiz – Reading and motivation**

1. What is reading self-efficacy?
2. If children enjoy reading, is this enough to learn to read?
3. When do children start to feel bad about themselves as readers?
4. Can a child like reading yet have low reading self-efficacy?
5. Does remedial reading tuition improve children's reading self-efficacy and classroom behaviour?
6. Is there a correlation between the reading materials given to children and their classroom behaviour? Why?
7. Are there individual differences in children's reactions to the experience of failure?
8. Do children enjoy reading more in a 'meaning emphasis' approach such as whole language?
9. What things can be done to help children feel good about themselves as readers?

10. What features of reading instruction have positive effects on motivation to read?

## Quiz – Reading and spelling

1. What is spelling?
2. Is there a relationship between reading and spelling?
3. What did Ehri and others find when they taught children to spell?
4. What are the main features of invented spelling?
5. What have researchers found out about the relative effectiveness of modern and traditional spelling methods?
6. What strategies have been found to be effective for improving the quality of spelling?
7. What New Zealand research is there on the teaching of spelling?
8. How do children learn to spell?
9. How do children acquire knowledge of how to spell irregular words?
10. What are the main points of this chapter?

## Quiz – Reading difficulties

1. What is the 'simple view' of reading disabilities?
2. How does dual route theory help to explain disabilities?
3. Skilled readers are able to split long words into syllables. Poor readers have difficulty with long words. How can poor readers learn to split syllables?
4. Teaching blends, digraphs, and phonograms can improve reading ability. Why?
5. Context can assist the word reading of unskilled readers but it should not be relied on, especially as a long-term strategy. Why not?
6. Comprehension will be impeded if the reader is unable to identify words automatically. Why is that?
7. Phonological processing of words in text is very important for skilful reading. Why?
8. Teaching spelling to struggling readers contributes to their ability to read as well. Do you agree? Why?
9. How effective are reading interventions (e.g. Reading Recovery)?
10. What are the main points of this chapter?

## Quiz – Reading in the secondary school

1. Historically speaking, is reading a new problem in secondary schools?
2. How relevant is reading skill to general school achievement, especially in subjects like maths where students deal mostly with numbers?
3. Why do students drop out of high school? Why do they stay?
4. Is low motivation a cause of poor reading?
5. What kinds of problems face students when they read their textbooks, especially in science, maths and social studies?
6. How is text structure instruction useful for dealing with textbook material?
7. Is text structure instruction helpful for writing reports and essays?
8. Do high school students sometimes lack good strategies for reading?
9. Can text structure strategies assist in writing essays? How?
10. What does research say about helping poor readers to succeed in high school?

## Quiz – Putting it all together

1. Why is it useful to know that the 'reading debate' is an old debate? Why has the debate continued? Does it matter?
2. What is it that is different about whole language and phonics?
3. Is there a 'best' way0 to teach reading?
4. What are the key characteristics of a skilled reader? What does this tell us about what we want to achieve when we teach reading?
5. What are the best predictors of a child's likelihood of reading and spelling success?
6. Is spelling better taught or 'caught'?
7. Can you teach reading comprehension? If so, how?
8. How can we explain the different kinds of reading difficulties that occur?
9. Why is reading in secondary school difficult to get on the school's agenda?
10. The debate about teaching with a code- or meaning-emphasis is neither new nor local. It is worldwide and is age-old. Would it help to calm down the 'reading wars' if more parents (and teachers) were aware of this? Should we expect reading methods to be debated, and to change and improve, just as we expect medical research to

improve our health? Or does debate have too many negative effects, such as parent concern and pressure on teachers to justify to parents what they are doing?

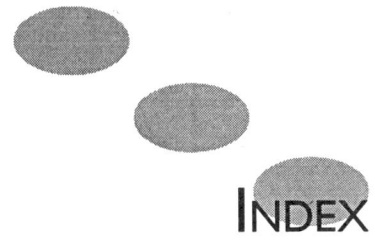

# INDEX

ABC Method, 45–51
alphbet, 40–43, 165–166, 188–191, 318
Ashton-Warner, Sylvia, 67–68
assignment questions, 331–332
automaticity, 254

babies learn to read?, 168–169
books in homes, 169–170
best reading method, 127–138, 322
bottom-up theory, 149–152, 319

California reading debate, 18
Case Studies;
    early readers, 206–208
    children who succeeded, 209–211
    children who fell behind, 211–213
    Reading Recovery, 269–270
child-directed learning, 85
Chinese writing, 39–40
clan size, 300
classroom behaviour and reading, 287

comprehension, 11, 237–256,
    theory, 237–238
    instruction, 240–253
connectionist theory, 152–154
consonants
    blends, 111, 114
    digraphs, 111, 120
constructionism, 88–90, 104
context and word recognition, 66–67,
    72, 144–148, 152–154
cue and cipher strategies, 178–181, 227
cultural factors, 171–172

decoding and reading comprehension,
    254–255, 260–262
dialect readers, 68
dialogic reading, 161, 183–184
*Dick and Jane*, 59
direct route hypothesis, 150, 153, 265
distinctive feature theory, 145–146
dual route hypothesis, 266

early readers, 163–165
long-term effects, 167–168
case studies, 206–208
emergent literacy, 10, 159–172
defined, 159

First Grade Studies, 128–129
first steps in learning to read, 10, 177–192
flashcards, 164
Freire, Paulo, 27

gender sterotypes, 61–63
good old days, 316
Greek alphabet, 41
guesing, 146–148
handwriting, 191–192
hieroglyphics, 36–37
history
of the alphabet, 33–43
of children's primers, 43–47
of reading, 43–74

IEA surveys, 16
indirect route hypothesis, 151, 153, 265
interventions, 268–274
invented spellings, 91–92, 102, 135, 225–233, 321

*Janet and John*, 58–62
Japanese writing, 40

knowledge sources theory, 97–100

language comprehension, 239, 260–262
language experience approach, 67–68
learned helplessness, 288–291
letter names and sounds, 189
Letters to the Author, 22–24
Literacy 1 and 2, 28
Literacy Task Force, 17
literacy hour, 20
look and see method, 51–58

Maori primers, 47–48, 67, 170–172, 316
Mayan writing, 37
media debate, 7
metalinguistic awareness, 184–185
syntactic awareness, 185
pragmatic awareness, 185
word awareness, 186
phonological awareness, 187
methods of instruction, 9, 81–122
Millenium, reading in the new, 24
models of reading, 9, 143–155, 260–264, 319–320
motivation and reading, 11, 281–292, 301–303, 325

NEMP survey, 16
New Zealand reading approach, 83–88
and whole language, 92–93
and other approaches, 103–104

parallel transmission of phonemes, 36
parent concern, 7
parents and reading, 23, 161–165
part-time work and reading, 301–303
pendulum swings, 9, 15–29, 314

phonemic awareness, 197–206
and reading, 10
defined, 36, 197
and connectionist theory, 153–154, 187
necessary, 184
history, 200–201
teaching, 201–205
as a prediction, 202, 317
phonetics, 198
phonics, 9, 81–104, 198, 205
history, 51–58
defined, 95
problems, 95–96, 328
instruction, 104–122
resource, 133–138
phonograms, 108–109
phonological awareness, 154–155, 187, 199–200
phonology, 36
pictography, 38
picture clues, 181
politics and reading, 26
precocious readers,163–165
prediction theory, 146–148
Primers
history, 9, 43–74
problems in reading, 11
psycholinguistic guessing game theory, 66–67, 72, 144–148
public concern, 20–22
putting it all together, 12, 313–329

Quiz questions, 333–340

reading
defined, 9, 143–155

Reading Attitude checklist, 294–295
reading books to children, 183–184, 214–215
reading comprehension, 11, 237–256, 320
theory, 237–238
instruction, 240–253
reading debate, 15
history, 43–74
reading disabilities
hyperlexia, 262
dyslexia, 263
'garden variety', 263
summary, 323–324
reading instruction
history, 43–74
Reading Process, 143–155, 319
Reading Readiness, 166–167
Reading Recovery, 268–273, 286–287
Ready to Read, 63–74
reciprocal reading, 241–242
Resource Teachers of Reading, 273–274
Roman alphabet, 42
running records, 90, 97

secondary school, 12, 299–310
and poor readers, 309
summary, 325
self-efficiency and reading, 285–286
self-esteem and reading, 284–286
sign and label pre-reader, 178–180, 184
'simple view' of reading, 260–264
social explanation, 8
speech, 33–34, 160, 239, 260–262
spelling, 10, 321
traditional, 222–224
defined, 224, 227

acquisition, 225–226
invented, 225, 228–233
orthographic patterns, 226
and reading 226–227
and graphs – phonemic awareness, 231
correct spelling, 231–232
English spelling, 255
standards in reading, 150–20
storybook reading, 162
sustained silent reading, 252–253
syllably writing systems, 38
syllables
teaching, 119, 266
defined, 197–198

text structure, 242–248, 304–308
and writing, 308
theories of reading, 9, 143–155, 260–264
top-down theory, 144–149, 319

vocabulary acquisition, 183–184, 250–252, 303–304

vowels
long and short, 107, 113
digraphs, 113–115

whole language
introduction to, 9, 68–74
debate, 81–104
research, 130–133, 135–138
and reading attitudes, 291–292
summary, 328
word recognition theory
indirect route, 151, 153, 265
direct route, 150, 153, 265
dual route, 266
writing and ...
history of, 9, 33–43, 315
defined, 35
invented spelling, 91–92, 102, 225–233, 321
whole language, 91–92
spelling, 221
text structure, 308

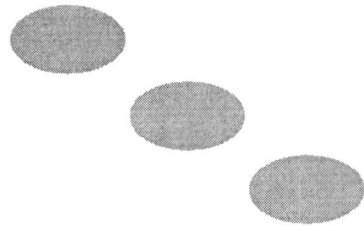

# THE AUTHOR

Tom Nicholson is well known and highly regarded in the field of reading. This is his twelfth book. He is also an accomplished and sought-after speaker in this controversial field, and is known for speaking out against the mainstream where necessary.

Tom Nicholson is an Associate Professor in the School of Education at The University of Auckland, Auckland, New Zealand.

Email: t.nicholson@auckland.ac.nz
Internet: http://www.arts.auckland.ac.nz/edu/school/nicholson.html

## Contributing author

Doris Ferry, a retired primary school teacher and an experienced phonics tutor. She lives on the Kapiti Coast, near Wellington.